Joe Pulizzi and Newt Barrett take one of the core concepts of new marketing—that providing consumers with valuable content trumps bombarding them with irrelevant advertising—and give brands a treasure trove of tips, tricks, best practices, and actionable approaches for using original online and offline content as a weapon in the battle for bottom-line results. Get Content Get Customers *provides a play-by-play for any marketer who is serious about breaking away from the pack, upsetting the status quo, and moving beyond interruption marketing by offering compelling content that delivers real value for consumers and real revenue for their companies.*

—Greg Verdino
Chief Strategy Officer, Crayon, LLC
and marketing blogger at www.gregverdino.com

Get Content Get Customers *highlights the role content plays in making your customers tick, click, and stick. An eye-opening book that takes you through a step-by-step strategy to enhance your content and to connect to your customers through words, pictures, sound, and video. If creating great content that serves your customer and your customer's customer is important, this book is for you.*

—Samir Husni, aka "Mr. Magazine"
Chair of the Journalism Department
University of Mississippi

When it comes to online marketing, you've got to reach people with what is desired and valued (content) instead of what is despised and ignored (advertising). Online, great content is effective advertising, and smart marketers are the new media. The trick to content marketing is getting your message across while keeping people engaged, and you're about to discover exactly how to do that with this book.

—Brian Clark
Copyblogger.com

As we rapidly enter the Post-Advertising Age, marketers are scrambling to find new ways to engage their brands with customers, amid the growing realization that the old ways are dead. If intrusion is dead and consumers are in control, Get Content Get Customers *brilliantly manages the feat of combining the theory of engaging customers through content marketing with alarmingly simple and practical approaches to doing it. All of this is clearly and intelligently illustrated through many different case studies. For marketers who understand that narrative marketing is the only marketing left but are struggling to understand how to do it,* Get Content Get Customers *finally offers the solution.*

—Simon Kelly
Chief Operating Officer
Story Worldwide

GET CONTENT GET CUSTOMERS

Turn Prospects into Buyers
with Content Marketing

Joe Pulizzi
Newt Barrett

Mc
Graw
Hill

New York   Chicago   San Francisco   Lisbon   London
Madrid   Mexico City   Milan   New Delhi   San Juan
Seoul   Singapore   Sydney   Toronto

1 2 3 4 5 6 7 8 9 0   FGR/FGR   0 1 0 9

ISBN 978-0-07-183173-4

MHID: 0-07-162574-7

This publication is designed to provide accurate and authoritative information in regard to the subject matter covered. It is sold with the understanding that the publisher is not engaged in rendering legal, accounting, or other professional service. If legal advice or other expert assistance is required, the services of a competent professional person should be sought.

—From a declaration of principles jointly adopted by a committee of the American Bar Association and a committee of publishers.

McGraw-Hill books are available at special quantity discounts to use as premiums and sales promotions, or for use in corporate training programs. To contact a representative please visit the Contact Us pages at www.mhprofessional.com.

Library of Congress Cataloging-in-Publication Data

Pulizzi, Joe.
    Get content get customers : turn prospects into buyers with content marketing / by Joe Pulizzi and Newt Barrett.—1st ed.
        p. cm.
    Includes index.
    ISBN 0-07-162574-7 (alk. paper)
    1. Target marketing. 2. Customer services. I. Barrett, Newt. II. Title.
HF5415.127.P85 2009
658.8—dc22

                                                                        2008052426

For Pam and Maxine,

and to what is truly relevant

and meaningful in life

Contents

Foreword, by Paul Gillin   xiii

Introduction   xvii

PART ONE

Coping with the Content Marketing Revolution

CHAPTER 1   The Shift to Content Marketing   3

CHAPTER 2   Six Reasons Businesses Are Making the
Change to Content Marketing   9

PART TWO

How to Put Content Marketing to Work

CHAPTER 3   How to Develop a Content Marketing
Mindset—and a Process to Match—within
Your Organization   23

CHAPTER 4   How to Select the Content Types That Best
Match Your Strategy   31

CHAPTER 5   Making Great Content Happen   49

CHAPTER 6   Putting the "Marketing" in Content
Marketing   61

PART THREE

Learning from Smart Marketers—
Best Practice Success Stories

CHAPTER 7   Best Practice Success Stories Overview   77

CHAPTER 8   Yes, Content Marketing Can Make
Welding Cool   79

CHAPTER 9   Creative Content Marketing Enables a
David to Compete Successfully against
Goliaths   89

CHAPTER 10   Finally, a PR Agency That Understands
both Boomers and Blogging!   97

CHAPTER 11   How to Create a World-Class Web Site for
a Superb Nonprofit—without Breaking
the Bank   107

CHAPTER 12   Solopreneur Sagas—Even Microbusinesses
Make Content Marketing Pay Off   119

CHAPTER 13   Content Marketing Pays Off on the Bottom
Line in Australia   133

CHAPTER 14   You Can Trust Northern Trust to Deploy a
Great Content Marketing Strategy   141

CHAPTER 15   Leveraging Content Marketing to Strengthen
Member and Community Relationships   151

CHAPTER 16   At Best Buy, It's All about Strengthening
Customer Relationships   165

CHAPTER 17   Using Content Marketing to Accelerate the
Acceptance of a Concept and a Product   173

CHAPTER 18   Preserving the Value of Content   183

CHAPTER 19   ThomasNet—A Content Marketer's
Content Marketer   191

CHAPTER 20   E-mail Software Provider Teaches
Customers to Market Effectively   201

CHAPTER 21   U.K. Law Firm Uses Content Marketing
to Build Powerful New Brand   211

CHAPTER 22   Rockwell Automation Uses Content
Marketing to Be Global, Local, and
Cost-Effective   221

PART FOUR

Putting the Lessons into Action

CHAPTER 23 Top 10 Content Marketing Lessons Learned
from Successful Practitioners   233

CHAPTER 24 An In-Depth Case Study—Developing a
Content Marketing Strategy from Start
to Finish   235

CHAPTER 25 Marketing Survival   245

Notes   247
Acknowledgments   249
Index   253

Foreword

If you're a marketer reading this book, you know that your world is changing. The seeds of those changes were actually planted nearly a decade ago. In 1999, Google arrived on the scene and set in motion a sequence of events that would transform markets and even culture around the world.

By introducing technology that delivered information that its architects considered to be truly useful, Google began to change the language of business. Today, Google provides three-quarters of a billion search results a day and acts as the Internet's universal home page. That's a reality that successful marketers must embrace.

Marketing is moving online at a breakneck pace. Several research firms now forecast that the Internet will become the world's dominant advertising medium by 2012, or a mere 18 years after Yahoo! was founded. And if you believe that today's business users are online-savvy, you ain't seen nothing yet. The next generation of consumers and business professionals, now percolating in colleges and high schools, spends 60 percent less time than their parents watching TV and 600 percent more time online, according to the Arthur W. Page Society.

At the same time, people are tuning out conventional marketing at a dizzying pace. Today, your carefully crafted messages bounce off a wall of digital video recorders, pop-up blockers, spam filters, and digital music players.

In the new reality, customers choose which messages to listen to and which marketers to let in the door. The days of what Seth Godin calls "interruption marketing" are over. The future is in "invitation marketing."

Customers have powerful new ways to reach out to one another. The population of the blogosphere skyrocketed from 1 million to 60 million between January 2004 and December 2005. Then social networks exploded onto the scene, giving people the means to form groups easily. In these groups, they could share experiences and rate the organizations they did business with. Emory University surveyed its incoming freshmen in 2007 and found that 97 percent of them had Facebook accounts. For the first time in history, people are engaging in a global discussion with others just like them—people they trust.

No longer can weak product be covered up by expensive advertising. Today, 7 out of 10 customers consult online peer reviews before making a major purchase. Buyers are engaging in discussions among themselves, and marketers are rarely invited. Years of shoving messages down the throats of customers who were helpless to talk back have denied them a seat at the table. They have to find a new way to get invited to the party.

That way is through content marketing, a concept that some people regard as New Age, but that is really as old as the village bazaar. Content marketing is about relationships and trust. It's about suppliers and customers forming bonds that spring from mutual dependencies and shared interests. It's about businesses really listening to their customers and endeavoring to deliver the goods and services that those customers need. It's about customers returning the favor by offering advice.

Many marketers are paralyzed by these developments. Business school taught them to analyze CPMs and response rates, not to engage in discussion. They learned marketing-by-Excel, not marketing-by-excellence. Some hope that content marketing is a fad, that we'll soon return to the good old days when conversations consisted of only one person talking. These people will soon be unemployed.

It's a Good Thing

Content marketing is actually the best thing to happen to the marketing profession in decades. That's because the barriers that for years have made marketers subservient to the media have fallen. No longer is it necessary to buy ads or to grovel before editors to get your message out. Today, marketers can *be* the media.

Search engines don't discriminate by source; they care only about the relevance of the content. To Google, you are every bit as credible a source as the *New York Times* when your content is crafted appropriately. You just need to think differently about what you do.

This book is about marketing with content, which makes it an essential strategy manual for any company that hopes to compete in the new online world. Content marketing isn't about marketing in the old way. It isn't about intercepting and bothering prospective customers while they're doing something else. It isn't about intrusion at all. Content marketing is about getting customers to invite you to interact with them. It's about creating relationships that transcend transactions.

The few companies that are doing this right have seen remarkable dividends. Go to Willitblend.com for an example of a company that has used offbeat and entertaining viral video to convince customers of its products' superiority and drive sales up 400 percent in one year. Check out ClutterControlFreak.com or RoadWarriorTips.com to see how businesses can engage with customers by offering helpful free advice. These companies have a clue. And you know what? They're having fun, too.

You don't need expensive campaigns or custom-built Web sites to reach customers. The secret of content marketing is to put yourself in the customer's shoes and look for opportunities to simplify and improve her life. It's about using the same words in your marketing materials that customers use in their search queries. The more in tune you are with the customer, the easier this process becomes.

Most of all, content marketing is about engagement. That's the dynamic by which companies find shared ground with their customers to solve problems. When you come right down to it, that's what successful companies do.

This book is your guide to content marketing. The authors have years of experience helping companies establish and grow conversations with their customers. The case histories they present should inspire you. The arguments they present should challenge your thinking. The guidelines they propose should change the way you work.

We live in a world in which the old standards of competitive advantage no longer apply. Today, your best ideas are knocked off by your competitors and manufactured offshore at half the cost within six months. In this global and rapidly changing business environment, the only sources of competitive advantage are continuous innovation and outstanding customer service. The world's most admired companies—Southwest Airlines, Dell Computer, Nordstrom, Progressive Insurance, Disney, Starbucks and, yes, Google—build multiple two-way channels between themselves and their constituents. They listen till it hurts. They see their success as being wholly dependent on the success of their entire ecosystem of partners, suppliers, and customers. To these companies, conversations aren't artificial or unnatural. They're just good business.

—Paul Gillin
Author, *Secrets of Social Media Marketing:*
How to Use Online Conversations and
Customer Communities to Turbo-Charge Your Business
and *The New Influencers: A Marketer's Guide*
to the New Social Media

Introduction

Your job as a marketing professional is to get more customers to buy from you. It's that simple. This was true 50 years ago, and it is still true today.

But you cannot get more customers to buy from you by relying on the traditional marketing approaches that worked 50 or even 10 years ago. Why? The Internet has transformed buyer behavior. Customers have access to vast amounts of online information from a broad range of sources. They can find almost anything they want or need in order to make an intelligent buying decision. They want plenty of information from you as well, but they want it on their terms. They expect to gather the information they need without being interrupted by unwanted marketing messages.

Because this behavioral transformation is so new and so dramatic, most marketers are finding it challenging to adapt. Yet there is a way to shape this transformation to your advantage. That's what content marketing is all about, and that's why the content marketing revolution is on its way.

Content marketing is the art of understanding exactly what your customers need to know and delivering it to them in a relevant and compelling way.

This new way to connect with your customers extends way beyond the offering of product information and into the realm of best practices, case studies, success stories, thought leadership, and more. Once you have delivered relevant content, you become a trusted resource. Content marketing enables companies to build a level of trust among their customers that makes it easy for those customers to buy. This is easy to say but hard to do, because it almost certainly means changing the way you think and act about marketing.

How Did We Get Here and Where Are We Going?

Ten years ago, the Internet was well into its commercial phase, with companies of every size establishing some kind of Internet presence. Even so, the Internet was more of a marketing footnote than a marketing mainstay. Most buying decisions were still made the way they had been made since the 1950s. Print, radio, billboards, TV, and direct mail were the primary marketing vehicles chosen. They were chosen because they worked. Publishing and media companies provided most of the content. Because consumer and trade media owned the toll roads, brands were forced to use these outlets as middlemen in order to communicate with their customers and prospects. Publishing and media companies were healthy and profitable, and all seemed right with the world.

That is, until the Internet loomed large on the business horizon. Today, buyers and sellers can communicate with one another directly, without the assistance of traditional media outlets. Mass marketing is dying, and personal communication with customers is here to stay.

A perfect scenario, right? Well, not really, at least not yet. While media companies are suffering financially and even cutting back on their long-standing tradition of content creation, most businesses are still unsure of how to communicate with their customers now that the giant walls have come crashing down.

The Start of Something Great

While many organizations and some of the largest and most popular brands in the world are continuing to bang their heads against the wall of mass marketing, smart organizations have begun to do things quite differently.

These smart companies know that they need to be something more than just vendors, so they've learned how to become significant content providers for their current and future customers. They've realized that they can be publishers and can fill the void left by the faltering media. They've taught themselves to answer the call of this "new" Internet-age buyer. Slowly but surely, more companies are picking up on this idea that they can not only create products and services for their customers, but also provide the information that will help their customers prosper and succeed.

Today, we're in the middle of marketing warfare. What began as a minor revolt against traditional marketing strategies has now become a full-fledged content marketing revolution. An irreversible shift has begun—away from media company–driven content and toward content created specifically for customers.

Marketing organizations are now realizing that they can create content whose quality is equal to or better than what many media companies are producing. Moreover, they are seeing that they can deliver tangible benefits to prospects and customers by offering relevant content that helps provide solutions to some of the toughest problems their prospective buyers are facing. This type of content marketing benefits the customers, of course. Customers love it. Who wouldn't? But what we are also finding is that content marketing drives revenues and may ultimately be the most important and effective marketing strategy available to successful marketing professionals.

Why Is This So Important?

All the rules have changed. You need to relearn the marketing game with a brand-new marketing mindset. Those who can adapt will flourish. Those who don't . . . well, think of dinosaurs.

Old-fashioned marketing is less and less effective with the new breed of buyer.

Unfortunately, most marketers have been trained to approach prospects with bold headlines, flashy graphics, and minimal text. We think of that as *billboard-style* marketing, or, in the more popular term coined by marketing guru Seth Godin, *interruption* marketing. Interruption marketing is still very prevalent in TV, radio, and print platforms.

In the days of mass marketing, interruption marketing worked very well. Your job was to hype your product while your prospect was engaging with a piece of wanted content or information. In an era where three TV networks, top-40 radio, and authoritative trade magazines were monopoly information providers, interruption marketing worked more often than not. Today, things are completely different. In a world of infinite informational choices, buyers will stop only for what's truly relevant and ignore the rest.

We live in a world in which both consumers and business buyers want to make up their own minds about what they need. They search out and find the information they need to do their jobs better or make their lives easier.

By the time customers are ready to talk to you—the seller—they are armed with information about your company, people, and products. This is true whether they are planning to buy a Mazda or machine tools. It may not sound like it, but this presents a substantial opportunity for you and your company—an opportunity to educate potential buyers about your industry, possible solution choices, best practices, and the right questions to ask. Do this before the potential buyers even call you or walk through your front door.

By doing this, you have already begun a relationship that will make it easier for people to buy. That's what content marketing is all about. In essence, the customer has initiated a conversation with you before you even know he is interested in your products and services. Simply amazing!

By delivering content that is vital and relevant to your target market, you will begin to take on an important role in your customers' lives. This applies to your online, print, and in-person communications. And this is the same role that newspapers, magazines, TV, radio, conferences, workshops, and Web sites have played in the past. Now it's time for your organization to play that role.

This may sound like a pretty tall order. But we've gathered the essential knowledge, examples, processes, and how-tos that you'll need in order to go from traditional marketing to content marketing, from interrupting to relevance. We've combined our decades of experience with that of the smartest content marketing practitioners on the planet to help you make this happen.

How to Put This Book to Work

We've written this book to simplify the process of developing and deploying a successful content marketing strategy. This is not a book about arcane marketing theories. It's a practical book about how to cope with the new buyer realities. We provide you with an understanding of why content marketing is the optimum approach to coping with the fundamental changes in the way your customers are buying. Perhaps most importantly, we show you exactly how to make the necessary changes with plenty of best practice success stories.

Here's what you'll learn:

- Why fundamental changes in the marketing universe demand that we become content marketing practitioners
- How to cope with the fundamental changes in buyer behavior by engaging in a dialogue with your prospects and customers that will make them want to buy from you
- How content marketing, executed properly, can accelerate the growth of your customer base, grow your revenues, and improve your bottom line
- How to really understand your customers, their concerns, and the best way to communicate with them by asking the right questions
- How and when to use the most important types of content to connect with your customers in print and online

- Best practices from organizations that are executing content marketing successfully
- How to develop a set of processes that will enable you to create, de ploy, and replicate effective content marketing strategies throughout your organization
- How to take advantage of a rich set of resources, including checklists, online links, and a list of experts in various elements of content marketing

You don't have to read this book from cover to cover. You may already understand the importance of content marketing and just want information on how to make it work. Feel free to dive into sections that are particularly relevant to your company.

You are in the middle of a content revolution, a revolution like none we've ever seen before. It is simply the greatest opportunity businesses have ever had to communicate directly with their customers. So, by all means, mark up the book, turn down pages, and write notes everywhere. Do whatever you have to do to put this book to work right now.

PART ONE

Coping with the Content Marketing Revolution

CHAPTER 1

The Shift to Content Marketing

We're not in the business of keeping the media companies alive . . .
we're in the business of connecting with consumers.

—TREVOR EDWARDS
CORPORATE VICE PRESIDENT FOR GLOBAL BRAND
AND CATEGORY MANAGEMENT, NIKE, INC.[1]

Nike and other huge companies such as Procter & Gamble, Johnson & Johnson, and General Motors are all moving away from the basic advertising and sponsorship strategies that helped make their brands as well known as they are today.

That's a frightening proposition for both major media organizations and established brands. It's hard to fathom that the once-coveted marketing strategies that vaulted the best of brands to the top are becoming obsolete. Once you get over the initial shock that the world we live in has changed, you realize that this is perhaps the greatest marketing opportunity we have ever seen for brands in both the business-to-business and the business-to-consumer markets.

We are seeing nothing less than a marketing tsunami that is affecting businesses of every size, regardless of what they're selling. Prospects are simply not responding to the kinds of marketing that have worked for decades. So most marketing organizations are asking, "What now?"

Beginning to Tell the Story

"We want to find a way to enhance the experience and services, rather than look for a way to interrupt people from getting to where they want to go," says Stefan Olander, global director for brand connections at Nike. "How can we provide a service where the customer says, 'Wow, you really made this easier for me!'?"

Olander's comment reflects buyers' increasing dislike of interruption marketing—those incessant advertising messages that stream and scream at people in print, on the radio, on TV, and even on the Internet—or, essentially, anything that tries to take their attention away from the content they really want to engage with.

Big brands from around the world have realized that they need to market to their customers in a different way. The proof is in the dollars. The *New York Times* notes, "The 25 companies that spent the most on advertising over the last five years cut their spending last year in traditional media by about $767 million, according to *Advertising Age* and *TNS Media Intelligence*." During the first six months of 2007, those same companies decreased their media spending an additional 3 percent, or $446 million, to $14.53 billion, according to *TNS Media Intelligence*.

But those marketing dollars haven't disappeared. They are moving in different directions, many of which are content marketing initiatives, in which money is being spent on custom magazines, newsletters, Webcasts, content for Web sites, blogging, social content efforts, and other such activities. In fact, *ContentWise* (formerly *Publications Management*), a research-based newsletter covering the content marketing industry, found that more than 25 percent of corporate marketing budgets is now being dedicated to some type of content marketing activity. And this number is growing. A recent IBM Global Solutions survey found that advertising executives plan to shift approximately 20 percent of marketing funds from impression-based advertising to impact-based advertising over the next three years.

Blendtec, a manufacturer of (you guessed it) blenders, has had tens of millions view its "Will It Blend?" video series over the last few years. The thirty-second to two-minute videos show Blendtec founder Tom Dickson attempting to "blend" various items, including golf balls, a toilet plunger, and even an iPhone. According to Blendtec executive George Wright, retail sales have increased by more than 500 percent, which he attributes almost solely to the video series. Talk about return on investment! With less than $1,000 and a YouTube account, Blendtec is now perceived as the undisputable blending king. Smart marketers like Nike and Blendtec are beginning to understand that they need to be telling their own story. They are learning to create their own valuable and relevant content to enable their customers to join the conversation. They are also learning that it's hard to create meaningful relationships with customers through 30-second TV ads or radio jingles.

Nike's global sales have climbed from $10 billion to more than $16 billion in the last four years. And executives say that the company's new focus on telling a relevant content story is a major contributor to that trend. In other words, content marketing has had a lot to do with growing global sales by 60 percent in a four-year period. Nike, through microsites such as its customer experience site Nike+, is not just talking at buyers anymore, but rather conversing with them.

You don't have to have Nike's powerful brand, huge budget, and global reach, or even Blendtec's creativity, to embrace a content marketing strategy that will grow your customer base and drive increased revenues. In fact, start-ups, small and medium-size companies, associations, and nonprofit groups are all benefiting from rethinking how they market their products and services. Just as Nike and Blendtec have experienced significant growth in tandem with the development of a content marketing strategy, so, too, can you deliver top-line and bottom-line results for your company.

How Many Names Can One Industry Have?

As you become a content marketer, it's important for you to realize where this industry came from. Many marketing professionals and publishers recognize the term *custom publishing*, which in the last few years has become the most popular term for the industry. John Deere is often credited with producing the first actual custom publication/content marketing device when it launched its newsletter, *The Furrow*, in the late 1800s. Yet, even though this industry is more than a century old, most marketers recognize it as young. While we will adapt to any term that promotes business content initiatives, our research indicates that *custom publishing* is an often misunderstood term. Most marketers and publishers perceive custom publishing as referring mostly to custom magazines, newsletters, and other customized print initiatives, thus downplaying the huge increase in online branded content. Actually, in a small research project we conducted with approximately 100 marketers and publishers in May 2007, most respondents chose to use the terms *content marketing* and *custom media* for the delivery of valuable, targeted business content.

Who knows which phrase will stick with people? Frankly, it doesn't matter. We chose *content marketing* because it seems to be the term that's most understandable to marketing professionals. It's the blend of both content and the marketing of that content that enables customer behavior. But just in case, we've provided a list of relevant terms that are often interchanged with content marketing. You probably know a few more:

- Content marketing
- Custom publishing
- Custom media
- Corporate content
- Corporate media
- Custom content
- Branded content
- Branded editorial
- Branded editorial content
- Branded storytelling
- Information marketing
- Advertorial
- Private media
- Customer publishing
- Customer media
- Contract publishing
- Corporate publishing
- Corporate journalism
- Member media
- Info-content

Regardless of which name you associate with it, content marketing is here to stay and may very well be the biggest opportunity your organization has to communicate with your customers as never before. That means that you need to take very specific and strategic steps, not only within your marketing, but within your culture, to take advantage of this opportunity.

CHAPTER 2

Six Reasons Businesses Are Making the Change to Content Marketing

The shift to content marketing didn't just happen. It's been naturally progressing for years, ultimately reaching a "perfect storm" environment that sets the stage for this new kind of marketing. Here are six fundamental reasons why organizations are shifting, or must shift, their marketing efforts from interruption marketing to content marketing.

1. Change in Buyer Attitudes toward Traditional Media and the Credibility of Content

Today's Internet-savvy consumers look everywhere for essential content that will enable them to make smart buying decisions. In the last few years, buyers' behavior has changed dramatically. Your customers are now increasingly knowledgeable about what they want to buy. They aren't surfing aimlessly, hoping to be influenced by marketing messages that arrive from out of the blue. And they aren't sitting around waiting to hear from you. They have no time to waste, and they deeply resent unwanted advertising messages. In short, buyers don't want to be sold. They want to make up their minds based on their own information gathering. Therefore, buyers need content that makes them smarter and more knowledgeable. Businesses that provide that content will win.

Moreover, as long as they get their answers, today's buyers don't care where the content comes from. They are open to learning from and acting on high-quality content, whether it comes from media veterans such as Condé Nast, NBC, CNN, or NPR—or from a custom publication, a newsletter, a company Web site, a favorite blog, or an RSS feed. That's bad news for traditional media.

David Levin, CEO of United Business Media, which owned the formerly named CMP Media in the United States, recently stated that "magazines as a vehicle for on-time delivery of news are clearly dead."[1]

This seems obvious, since the just-in-time news outlets are growing on a daily basis, but what is not as obvious is the increasing number of news and informational resources that are coming from businesses, not from traditional media companies. According to Alexa.com,[2] 6 of the top 10 most trafficked Web sites are either social media or branded-content sites such as YouTube. It is on many of these sites that businesses are marketing and creating their own content.

Search engines such as Google have democratized content to such an extent that anyone who has a little good content and a bit of search engine savvy can get his content on the first page. Buyers want information fast, and search engines help them get it. All of this means that you have the opportunity to replace formerly vital media choices with your own high-quality content. You can be timely, considered, and reasoned. Your company can become the new thought leader among your many prospects who are completely open to great content from new sources.

2. Traditional Media Sources Can't Be Counted on to Assist You in Reaching Your Customers

In the past, publishing companies drew their strength from their unique ability to deliver target demographics for a myriad of definable markets. They invested millions of dollars in developing high-quality circulation that closely matched advertisers' marketing targets. They were able to tell advertisers exactly who read the publication, what kind of company these people worked in, what types of products they bought, and how much money they spent each year on those products.

Just one look at what's happening in the newspaper industry tells the tale for the fate of traditional media. Daily newspaper readership has plummeted between 1970 and 2006, according to the Newspaper Association of America (see Figure 2.1).

Age Group	18–24	25–34	35–54	55+
Readership Decline	–50%	–55%	–39%	–15%

Figure 2.1

As of 2006, only 35 percent of 18- to 34-year-olds were daily newspaper readers. November 2007 saw reports of continued drops in circulation averaging 2.5 percent for the top 538 U.S. dailies, as reported by the *New York Times*. Some of the biggest suffered even worse declines:

- The *New York Times* daily circulation fell 4.51 percent to 1,037,828, and Sunday circulation plunged 7.59 percent to 1,500,394.
- The *Washington Post* daily circulation was down 3.2 percent to 635,087, and Sunday circulation was down 3.9 percent to 894,428.
- The *Boston Globe* daily circulation tumbled 6.6 percent to 360,695, and Sunday circulation fell by about the same amount, 6.5 percent, to 548,906.

According to IBM and the University of Bonn, 71 percent of consumers use their PC for more than two hours per day during their personal time, as opposed to 48 percent spending that much time watching TV. The trends continue to show that traditional vehicles are getting less share of voice, which means that they will be less helpful in getting your message in front of your customers (regardless of customer behavior changes).

Do Marketers Know More about Buyers than Media Companies Do?

While magazines, newspapers, and TV offer less and less reach to buyers, disenchanted advertisers have built substantial databases of customers and prospects.

Smart companies of every size are using database technology to capture very detailed information about their customers and prospects, including all-important e-mail addresses. In fact, many companies today have much better buyer information in their customer relationship management (CRM) systems than do the publications trying to sell them advertising.

In fact, a former trade magazine chief editor confided that a prospective advertiser had four times as many qualified prospects in its customer database as the publication had in its circulation records. This four-to-one advantage left little incentive for the prospect to spend advertising dollars with this publication.

Within your market niche, you may well have access to more and better buyer data than your traditional media partners have. You should consider targeting your database with focused content marketing efforts. That makes for a cost-effective way to reach and interact with your very best prospects. Eliminate wasted distribution. Create precise content marketing campaigns for well-defined sets of buyers.

3. Shrinking Media Company Budgets Reduce Content Quality

Corporations often have bigger budgets and more resources to find and pay for the best research and content in the markets they serve. Unfortunately, too many media companies have been cutting both research and editorial budgets. Layoffs, pay cuts or freezes, and mass reorganizations are now commonplace within the traditional media environment. The worldwide recession has only made this a more frequent occurrence.

Media companies in both business-to-business and business-to-consumer markets are facing a downward spiral in which reduced advertising revenues lead to cutbacks in editorial staff and editorial pages, and in the circulation size of their magazines and newspapers.

Folio, a company that reports on the magazine and media industry, showed these headlines in its November 2008 e-newsletter:

- Forbes Restructures, Cuts 43
- B-to-B Publishers Seeing 2009 Advertising Contracts "Disappear"
- Hanley Wood Cuts 20
- Layoffs at Texas Regional D Magazine
- Scholastic Begins Hiring Freeze; 110 Accept Retirement Package
- Time Inc. Restructuring to Cost $100M
- More Layoffs: Hearst Makes Companywide Cuts

The decline in newspaper circulation, ad revenues, and staffing size is well documented. Among the many reasons for these multiple, interrelated declines is the fact that young people have deserted newspapers for multiple venues on the Internet. Studies show that the average age of a newspaper reader today is 60, which is not the ideal demographic for most organizations.

In a 2005 post on the Newsosaur.com blog, Allan Mutter opined: "The decline in circulation, while no cause to rejoice if you love newspapers, could be a sign that publishers increasingly understand the need to scale circulation down to a core level of committed, valuable readers." He also warned that "shrinking circulation isn't necessarily a bad thing—as long as it stops *real* soon." Unfortunately, over the last two years, circulation has continued to decline. In October 2007, Mutter said: "But the good news for publishers—that no one is demanding their liquidation any more—is also bad news, because it means they will be stuck tending to the massive and so-far insoluble problem of cauterizing the sales losses that have eroded profits at a quickening pace for the better part of two years." As bad as it is for the giants—the *New York Times*, the *Los Angeles Times*, the *Christian Science Monitor* (now gone in print), and the *Washington Post*—things are even grimmer for local newspapers such as the venerable *Akron Beacon Journal*, whose business section is gone on weekdays but survives on Saturdays and Sundays.

"We were one of the last papers to put the majority of stocks online. That's where the users are," said Bruce Winges, vice president and editor of the *Akron Beacon Journal*. "If I had my druthers, of course I would want a stand alone business section. I don't think the quantity or the quality of our business reporting has gone down, but the perception of the reader is that they have lost something."[3]

Continued Cutbacks Reveal Significant Opportunity

We could go on at length about the decline in traditional media outlets, but the real story here is the significant opportunity for nontraditional content creators to fill the void. Traditional media are suffering because the business models have changed, not because there is less information needed in the world. Actually, buyers need more information than ever. If Time Inc., the *New York Times*, or your industry trade magazine is not going to provide it, who will?

Businesses are beginning to understand that today's marketing is a whole lot like publishing. The quality of many corporate publications and content Web sites today is excellent and ever-improving. If the trend continues at this rate, the quality of these vehicles will eventually surpass that of independently produced publications at some point in the future.

You have every opportunity to become a trusted content provider, even if you are a small company in a niche market. As media quality declines, look for the content gaps. Has your local business section disappeared? Perhaps, as a bank or insurance company, you could step in with relevant content. Have your favorite trade publications disappeared or declined in quality? Fill the void with solution-oriented content that your buyers still need. Buyers need content. Be the new provider.

4. Selling to Your Customers Is Becoming More Challenging

The more informed the consumers or buyers are, the more difficult it is to sell them. Smart marketers know this and are creating strong brand relationships by providing good, authoritative, even leader-ship-type content.

Great advertising still works. Think about the Aflac duck, the GEICO cavemen, or the legendary Absolut vodka print campaign. These are all memorable and effective strategies and, most impor-tantly, they have led to increased sales. The genius of the Aflac duck campaign, for example, is that it is amusing and memorable, and still makes a very detailed case for why you would be smart to pur-chase Aflac insurance. Even in a very challenging financial environ-ment, Aflac continues to be a stable brand.

Increasingly, however, the old-fashioned strategies are taking a backseat to content marketing in which companies engage in an interactive dialogue with prospects.

Paul Gillin, who wrote the foreword for this book, points out in his book *The New Influencers: A Marketer's Guide to the New Social Media*:

> *Traditional marketing and traditional media will always have a role to play in commerce. They will morph and can adapt to changing demographic trends. But it is clear that growth will be centered around conversation-based tactics. The next generation of customers will want to interact with businesses in very different ways. The new influencers are here to stay. Your challenge, and your opportunity, is in learning how to influence them and becoming an influencer yourself.*

As Gillin suggests, content marketing is all about engaging in a con-versation with your customers and prospects. You can make this hap-pen just as media companies have done for decades. For years, the best business-to-business and business-to-consumer publications delivered must-read content for the buyers that marketers wanted to reach. These buyers, in turn, became loyal followers of the publications and responded actively to both editorial and advertising messages.

Although many media companies can't deliver on reader needs because of the evolution of these business models, readers and cus-tomers are still hungry for content that offers solutions to their problems and that helps them lead more successful, productive, and enjoyable lives. However, they are also inundated by thousands of marketing messages every day—and they ignore almost all of these messages. To get through, you need to communicate differently.

You have the opportunity to transform the way in which you market by providing relevant content that positions your company as a trusted source. You begin as a source of information and continue as a source of products and services. It's neither necessary nor desirable for you to attempt to sell prospects who don't want to be sold. Instead, your thought leadership in print and online should position your company as the obvious source of solutions. As you become more customer-centric, you will develop an increasingly loyal and lucrative base of repeat customers, as Nike and Blendtec have.

5. Because Technology Is Both Cheap and Easy to Use, Even Small Companies Can Deliver Great Content Solutions to a Targeted Customer Base

Fortune 500 companies have long had the technological resources and investment capital required to build sophisticated content marketing solutions—and to manage huge amounts of demographic data relating to their prospects and customer bases. Many of these firms, such as Best Buy, Microsoft, and Amazon.com, probably know more about us than some of our relatives do. They also do a terrific job of delivering relevant and compelling content to different segments of their prospect bases.

Smaller companies, however, have had to rely on media companies to deliver their message to their targeted buyers. This has certainly been true with print publications and, until fairly recently, online as well. Affordable technology is now changing all of the rules.

Just a few years ago, it would have been laughable to imagine that a very small organization could create and maintain a Web site that could be updated daily—and that would allow visitors to interact and even buy products and services. Today, this is not only possible but pervasive. In fact, a 10-person company may be able to outmarket a 10,000-person company in a carefully chosen niche.

There are three core components underlying the shift in the technological balance of power away from media giants and toward companies of all sizes:

- The ability to create sophisticated online publications such as Web sites, digital magazines, and e-newsletters
- The ability to manage huge amounts of data relating to current and future customers
- The ability to do both of these simply and inexpensively

A sophisticated Web site cost $500,000 in 2004, but only $13,000 in 2007. Apple Inc. alumnus and serial entrepreneur Guy Kawasaki recently proved it. In an August 2007 interview for NPR's *Tech Nation*, he described how unbelievable changes in the price and usability of online technology had enabled him to launch a social media Web site for less than $13,000. Just a few years before, according to Kawasaki, it would've taken $500,000, months of work, and a big team to get the site up and running. Although the Web site, Truemors.com, may still be an unproven attempt at social media, it shows what any small business can accomplish. For example, the underlying content management capability would have cost six figures until very recently. Truemors.com is powered by the free blogging application WordPress.

Low-cost, easy-to-use Web technology now enables medium-sized manufacturers, small companies, or one-person service firms to build online content solutions that are more sophisticated than what most media companies were putting online just a few years ago. In fact, with focus, creativity, and a little outside help, these smaller organizations may be able to do a better job of providing targeted content to their best customers than some of their billion-dollar competitors.

Bye-Bye, Middleman!

In the past, all but the biggest corporations had little power to target anyone. Sophisticated CRM software was expensive and hard to manage. Businesses relied on media companies because of their sophisticated circulation databases, which included lots of demographic information, enabling more precise targeting.

This meant that you could advertise in a magazine or you could choose a direct-marketing campaign to an important subset of buyers. In the early days of the Internet, media companies were also doing the best job of capturing e-mail addresses, which have become an essential part of any corporate customer database. So businesses would even rent expensive e-mail lists from magazines whose readers matched up with their target audience.

Today, corporations and associations have created powerful databases that in some cases are better than those of audited trade publications and Web sites. Because the software technology required to manage a customer database is now affordable for any size organization (Highrise is less than $300 per year for a 5,000-count database), even small companies have less need for the services of trade and consumer publishers.

Moreover, there are plenty of online distribution partners, such as Digg, del.icio.us, and StumbleUpon, that enable you to reach well beyond your current database to prospects who are looking for solutions to their problems. Unlike most media companies, these new Internet buddies work for free. The result: affordable and easy-to-use technologies are enabling a broad range of companies to disintermediate trade publications and their media parents because they can now communicate directly with their customers and prospects. In doing so, companies are both reducing their costs and increasing their precision. Very importantly, effective and efficient distribution powers the very best content marketing strategies. After all, there's not much point in creating great content if you can't deliver it. Now you can do both.

6. High-Quality Editorial, from a Business?

The key to successful media programs for corporations is great content. Not just any content; great content. Buyers know the difference between great content and a blatant sales pitch that has no inherent value. Corporations can and do address this issue by estab-lishing editorial standards that in many cases exceed those of some traditional publishing companies. For example, *Best* magazine, from Best Buy, targets the company's very best buyers with high-quality content, rich in both information and design. Best Buy does not compromise quality with this publication because its goal is to strengthen its relationships with those customers who invest the most time and money with the company year after year.

Media companies, however, are often headed in the opposite direc-tion. These companies serve two masters: their readers and their advertisers. Sadly, as their ad revenues crater, they are caving in more and more to advertisers' demands that they compromise content, which shortchanges their readers. That weakens the editorial prod-uct, which ultimately results in lower reader engagement, lower reader response, and an ongoing downward spiral of ad revenues.

Of course, not every media company and not every publication has to make these compromises. But our own experience—and that of many former colleagues—makes it clear that this is an ongoing and almost certainly accelerating trend.

In a parallel trend, some of the best editorial talent has been forced out of media organizations to save money. In addition, hun-dreds of great editors are leaving voluntarily because they cannot do good work within the content constraints of the struggling media companies. Many of the very best are moving to corporations, where they are given the resources to create great content without severe budget limitations. Because smart companies understand that high-quality content is a key marketing driver, they are paradoxically less inclined to compromise in the way that formerly pure media orga-nizations are now doing. Writing for Microsoft, Cisco, or Parker Hannifin actually looks good on a résumé these days. Not only can corporations afford to create high-quality content, but they are also attracting high-quality journalists.

Great content underlies great content marketing. Your buyers want and need great content. They used to receive it from media companies. Today, they can and should be receiving it from your organization. Even if you do not have internal editorial talent, plenty of brilliant journalists, editors, and publishers will be happy to put their talents to work on behalf of your company. Find your content niche, one that the media companies have forgotten or deserted, and become the trusted content resource that will attract and retain customers and prospects.

PART TWO

How to Put Content Marketing to Work

How to Develop a Content Marketing Mindset—and a Process to Match—within Your Organization

The goal of this chapter is to help you develop a level of expertise in content marketing that will enable you to become an effective change agent within your organization. Specifically, you will need to develop a content marketing mindset, first for yourself and then for your organization. This will almost certainly require a major rethinking of your current marketing approach. It may not be easy, but it's essential.

By now you understand the irreversible trends that are changing the face of marketing. You also understand why it's possible for organizations like yours to think and act like publishers so that you can provide valuable content that makes you a trusted source for your current and future customers.

That's the all-important beginning of developing a content marketing mindset. But, because content marketing is a relatively new concept as it pertains to all media, it will not come naturally to you and your organization. Moreover, there is a skill set that media companies have developed over centuries that is probably brand-new to your organization. As you begin to think like a publisher, you will also need to learn how to create the kind of high-quality content that emanates from great publishers and great corporations.

Developing and executing content marketing initiatives that work take time, effort, and expertise. It's extremely difficult to extract content from organizations that have no experience with content marketing.

Why the Reluctance to Move Away from Traditional Marketing Strategies?

Today, most companies are still using traditional marketing approaches that they may have been using since the middle of the twentieth century. There are several reasons for this:

- Most companies are set up to sell products, not to provide relevant and valuable information to customers and prospects.
- Most companies have well-worn marketing paths that are easy to follow. Going off the beaten path into uncharted territory is intimidating.
- Most companies have strong relationships with media partners that may go back decades. It's not easy to break those relationships by pursuing a brand-new content marketing strategy.
- Many companies aren't measuring their marketing, so they aren't even sure what is and what is not effective.
- Many companies lack both the right people and the right processes to implement a new kind of marketing.
- Many businesses are reluctant to abandon traditional marketing tactics for what they may believe to be unproven content marketing practices.
- Most companies lack content marketing role models from which they can learn best practices.

Or maybe you work in the kind of organization where no one even realizes that traditional marketing is no longer working. Perhaps no alarm bells have gone off yet.

In Chapter 21, you will learn more about the innovative print and online content marketing efforts of British law firm Pinsent Masons.

Despite its success with content marketing, it used to be a strictly traditional marketer.

In 2000, Pinsent Masons was still cranking out traditional brochures by the thousands. They were easy to produce, but they contained the same boring, company-centric, feature-laden content that is found in most traditional marketing materials. For the most part, business executives who receive marketing materials like these toss them out soon after receiving them.

The business development folks at the firm finally realized that they were spending money on something that no longer worked—if it had ever worked. So as part of an overall content marketing strategy, the firm launched a magazine that was designed to be read and valued by its target client base.

Making this change required the same kind of shift in mindset that will be required of all marketers from now on. It also required an investment in people, time, and processes. As you will read, Pinsent Masons has achieved dramatic positive benefits from the shift away from traditional marketing toward a multifaceted content marketing strategy.

Think Like a Publisher

As we have discussed, you must think like a publisher by delivering relevant content that will have intrinsic value to your targeted customers. Bad, boring brochures are only part of the problem with traditional marketing. Fundamental changes in buyers' behavior mean that advertising and marketing approaches that used to work are now ineffective.

The Yellow Pages is a classic example. Historically, whether you were selling consumer products or business products, you needed to be in the Yellow Pages. For a very high percentage of marketers, this is no longer true. Why? Because fewer and fewer prospective buyers rely on the print Yellow Pages to find products and services. Instead, they are going first to the Internet to seek out both product and company information. On the Web, the Yellow Pages must compete for attention just like everyone else—especially when buyers' first instincts involve search engines.

This fundamental change in buyers' behavior means that your most important investment will be a Web site and/or a blog that offers content that will put you at the top of the list of possible vendors. But this requires a completely different mindset from that required to run effective Yellow Pages advertising.

In a December 20, 2007, *Wall Street Journal* blog about whether advertising in the Yellow Pages still works for small businesses, the writer quoted a recent study that said: "About one in five (21%) of respondents cited it as the source that produces the most calls from potential customers. Word-of-mouth is a close second, cited by 19% of respondents, and company websites are next, cited by 12%."

Here's what is really interesting about these statistics: although the Yellow Pages came out number one, it was only slightly ahead of word of mouth—and company Web sites came in at a strong number three, not that far behind the Yellow Pages. When you consider that the respondents were all businesses with 25 or fewer employees, this statistic is even more meaningful. Many small businesses don't even have Web sites. That makes this third-place finish astonishing.

Imagine what would happen if these same small businesses were devoting their Yellow Pages advertising dollars to creating great Web sites! Imagine, too, that they were driving traffic to those Web sites through the use of excellent content and intelligent search engine marketing! You can be certain that what is already a good source of leads would become a phenomenal source of leads. Moreover, once the Web site is up and running, the annual maintenance cost is a small fraction of the cost of Yellow Pages advertising.

You can extrapolate the Yellow Pages experience across all traditional forms of advertising and marketing. The key is to develop a content marketing mindset.

Because we know that saying this is much easier than doing it, in Part 3 we provide best practice success stories, and in Part 4 we give an in-depth case study that describes the process from beginning to end. But first, here is our B.E.S.T. formula, a simple way to begin your rethinking process.

The B.E.S.T. Formula: A Structured Approach for Creating a Content Marketing Road Map

We've found that even marketers who are willing and eager to move toward a content marketing strategy find the development and implementation of such a strategy difficult. Because there are few road maps to steer organizations safely through this marketing frontier, too few are willing to make the trek.

That's why we've developed the B.E.S.T. formula—so that content marketing can quickly become part of your corporate DNA. The process is designed to make it easier to make the transition to the creation of valuable and relevant content for your customers.

The B.E.S.T. formula for content marketing is a simple guide that you can use to develop and deploy a successful strategy. It also lets you take a critical look at what you're doing now, to determine whether you are mired in the swamp of traditional marketing malaise.

In a nutshell, the B.E.S.T. formula simplifies a complicated process. Apply it so that your marketing is

- *Behavioral.* Everything that you communicate with your customers has a purpose. What do you want them to do?
- *Essential.* Deliver information that your best prospects really need if they are to succeed at work or in life.
- *Strategic.* Your content marketing efforts must be an integral part of your overall business strategy.
- *Targeted.* You must target your content precisely so that it is truly relevant to your buyers.

Use the B.E.S.T. approach for all of your online, print, and in-person communications. That's how you can play the same role that newspapers, magazines, TV, radio, conferences, workshops, and Web sites have played in the past. Now it's your turn to become the trusted source that persuades prospects and buyers to become loyal, long-term customers.

First Understand, then Be Understood

You cannot hope to implement a successful content marketing strategy without understanding exactly what outcome you require. That means understanding what you want to get out of the initiative—sales increase, retention measures, cost savings, or something else. Equally important is an in-depth understanding of the needs and/or challenges of your targeted prospects. Only then can you craft a content marketing approach that will deliver more sales, more customers, and more measurable results.

The answers to these questions will guide you to a profitable content marketing strategy.

Behavioral

- How do we want our customers to feel?
- What effect must we achieve with them?
- What action do we want them to take?
- How will we measure their behavior?
- How will we put them on the path to purchase?

Essential

- What do our buyers really need to know?
- What will provide them with the most benefit, personally or professionally?
- How can we present the content so that it has maximum positive impact?
- What are the mandatory elements of the campaign?
- What media types must we include?

Strategic

- Does this content marketing effort help us achieve our strategic goals?
- Does it integrate with our other strategic initiatives?

Targeted

- Have we precisely identified the prospects we want to target?
- Do we really understand what motivates them?
- Do we understand their professional roles?
- Do we understand how they view the product or service we offer?

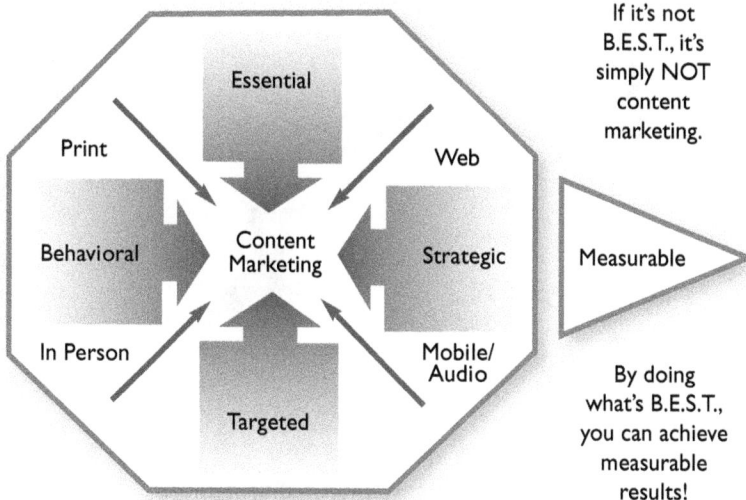

Figure 3.1 Going where few people have gone before—to the implementation of a content marketing strategy

The answers to these questions will help you define your marketing communications strategy. By taking the time and committing the resources to answer these questions, you will have the necessary information to create a content marketing plan that works (see Figure 3.1). Integrating the B.E.S.T. formula within your organization isn't easy, but as you have read and will see through the best practice success stories, content marketing isn't just something that's nice to do; it is imperative for growing and sustaining a profitable business.

CHAPTER 4

How to Select the Content Types That Best Match Your Strategy

Many information vehicles can connect you with prospective customers, but they don't all work equally well in every situation. Therefore, it's essential that you understand your choices—and when and how to use each of them. Here are brief descriptions of some of your options. We've also included at-a-glance charts to show what you can expect to achieve with the content marketing tool you select. Finally, we provide a quick best practice example for illustrative purposes.

You can find links to our examples online at the book's Web site, GetContentGetCustomers.com.

Print

Relevant, well-written, and well-designed print publications can make a dramatic impression on your target audience (see Figure 4.1). Unlike with a Web site, where visitors must find you, you have precise control over the outreach of a print publication (see Table 4.1). Print publications are highly portable and can be read anywhere (even with no Wi-Fi connection). It's important to note that printing and mailing costs are a significant investment that will certainly only increase over time. Nonetheless, if you create a terrific, well-targeted print publication, you can achieve measurable results.

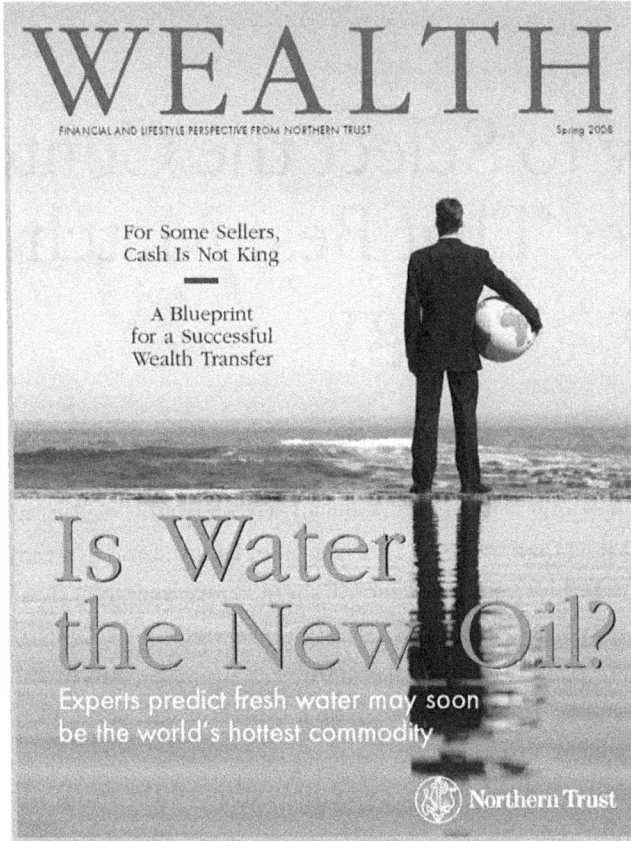

Figure 4.1 *Wealth* magazine from Northern Trust
engages wealthy clients with a diverse blend of
appropriate content

Magazines

The magazines we enjoy the most are those that match our interests most precisely. This applies in both our professional and our
personal lives. The same is true of magazines that you create for
customers. You must understand exactly what information is most
important to your target group—and the way in which the members of that group would like to receive it. In other words, you need
to pay attention not just to your subject matter, but also to the style
and length of the articles you write, as well as overall design and lay-

	Custom Magazines	Newsletters	White Papers
Lead Generation			✔
Brand Awareness	✔		✔
Customer Education	✔	✔	✔
Thought Leadership	✔		✔
Perception Modification	✔		✔
Customer Retention	✔	✔	
Internal Communications	✔	✔	
Sales Support	✔		

Table 4.1 Why and when to use print publications

out. Every element is critical to your success (see Figure 4.2). Generally, custom magazines tend to be a minimum of 24 to 32 pages and are most often mailed on a quarterly basis.

Points to Remember
- High-quality editorial content is consistently delivered to a targeted database in a magazine format.
- Magazines are generally 24 pages or more.
- The most effective frequency is quarterly or more.
- Some magazines contain partner advertising to help defray the investment.
- Be prepared to spend at least $40,000 for even a small initial distribution.

Key Objectives
- Creates and maintains key relationships.
- Positions the company as a thought leader.
- Helps to strengthen database efforts (use the direct mail list to update your customer database).
- Can be your company's key sales tool.
- Acts as an effective way to bypass gatekeepers.
- Should also be used as an excellent internal marketing tool.

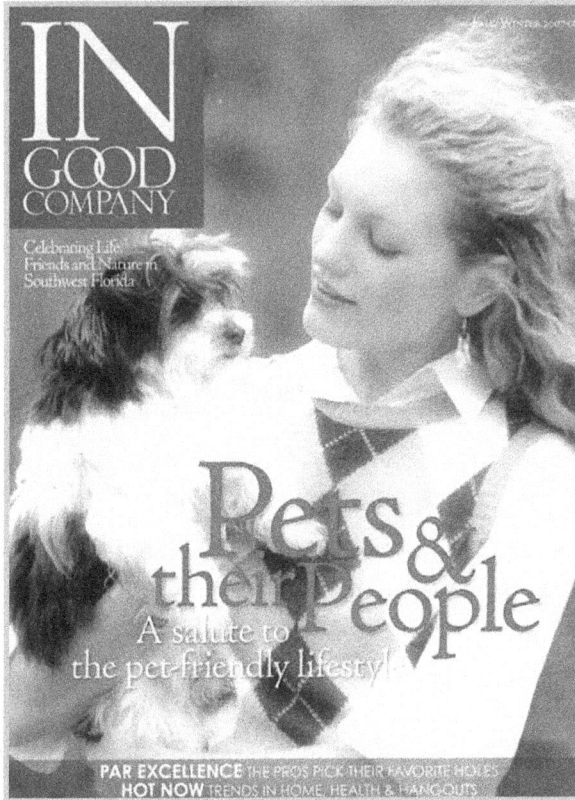

Figure 4.2 *In Good Company* magazine captures the flavor of the affluent lifestyle within a Bonita Bay community

Newsletters

Your newsletter may be just two sides of the page, meant to be folded and mailed, or it may extend to 16 pages or more. Whatever the length, newsletters are designed to be consumed quickly and should have attention-grabbing headlines with concisely worded articles. In terms of content, you must also focus on the precise information needs of your target audience. Beware: too many newsletters are glorified sales pitches—today's consumers know better. Newsletters, because of their more timely nature, are often sent more frequently than magazines and should also refer customers to your Web site for more information.

White Paper Series

White papers focus on topics or issues that require a lot of explanation. They tend to cover technical topics, but they may extend to any number of subjects. White papers are perfect for demonstrating thought leadership on issues that are vital to your buyers. They aren't meant to replace sales collateral, so don't use them as an excuse to promote your products and services. Technical or not, they should be written in a style that immediately captures the readers' attention and pulls them through to the final paragraph. In other words, white papers need to be educational, but they don't have to be boring.

Points to Remember
- High-quality editorial content is delivered to a targeted database in white paper format.
- White papers are generally between 8 and 12 pages.
- They can use a print, electronic PDF, or digital magazine format.

Key Objectives
- Integrates with the advertising program.
- Creates a clear call to action.
- Positions the company as a thought/education leader.
- Supports database efforts.
- Can generate leads.

Online

You have infinite reach across the globe when you establish a presence on the Internet. Even small companies can look like giants on the Web. As Guy Kawasaki indicated (see Chapter 2), in 2007 you could accomplish for $13,000 what would have required a half-million-dollar investment just a few years earlier. Even better, once you have made your initial online investment, your incremental costs will change little, even if your traffic skyrockets. Thanks to today's inexpensive and user-friendly Web tools, it's easy to get started, to add an additional

Web presence, or to keep improving what you have. Many of these tools enable you to begin an ongoing dialogue with your prospects and customers that will improve both acquisition and retention. Smart marketers are getting better and better at putting the Internet to work as part of a cohesive content marketing strategy (see Table 4.2).

	E-books	Web Sites and Web Portals	Webcasts
Lead Generation	✔	✔	✔
Brand Awareness	✔	✔	✔
Customer Education	✔	✔	✔
Thought Leadership	✔	✔	✔
Perception Modification	✔	✔	✔
Customer Retention		✔	
Internal Communications			
Sales Support		✔	

Table 4.2 Why and when to use online content marketing tools

Web Sites

Think of your Web site as your primary corporate presence on the Internet. If you are a small organization, it may be the only exposure you have. In that case, design it so that your visitors will be immediately engaged when they arrive. Make it easy for them to find exactly what they're looking for. You have less than 10 seconds to grab their attention before they head off somewhere else. Make it obvious how you can help your visitors achieve their personal or professional objectives. As your corporate Web presence, your Web site must provide complete information about your company, the products and services you provide, and why they should buy from you (see Figure 4.3). Be sure to use visuals that are closely connected to your written content. Mindjet (Mindjet.com), which we explore in Chapter 17, is a good example of a small company that combines content and corporate information effectively.

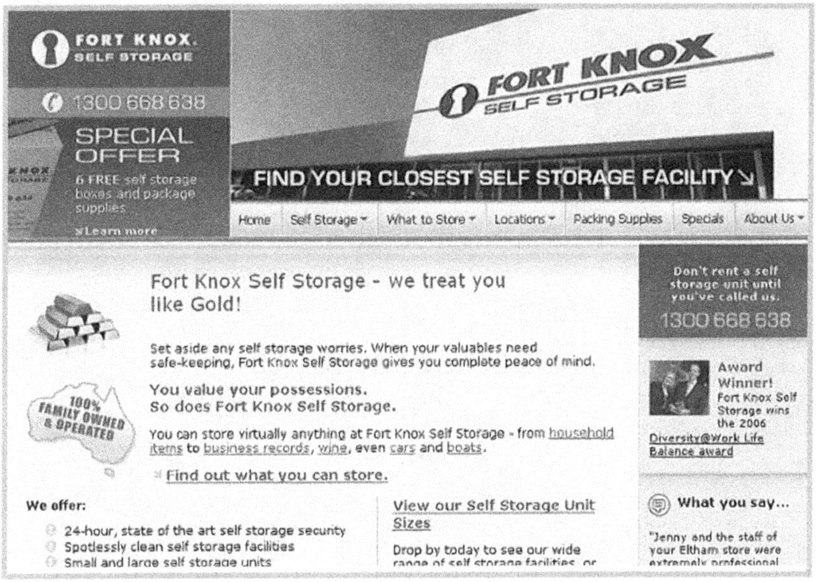

Figure 4.3 The Web site of Australian company Fort Knox Self Storage makes it easy for customers to buy

Content Web Portals and Microsites

Many larger organizations—and even some small ones—have multiple sites (or microsites) on the Internet. These typically concentrate on narrowly targeted areas of content. For example, check out HomeMadeSimple.com from Procter & Gamble (see Figure 4.4). It is P&G's content marketing Web portal dedicated to solutions for the home. It offers ongoing original content and a monthly e-newsletter, which has generated more than 1 million consumer sign-ups. You may have also noticed that many large brands, such as IBM and Shell, are leveraging traditional interruptive media such as magazines and billboard space to promote their microsites.

Points to Remember
- A microsite generally revolves around a key marketing objective or content area for the brand.
- Often, the microsite is created with a separate URL.
- The site is updated continually.

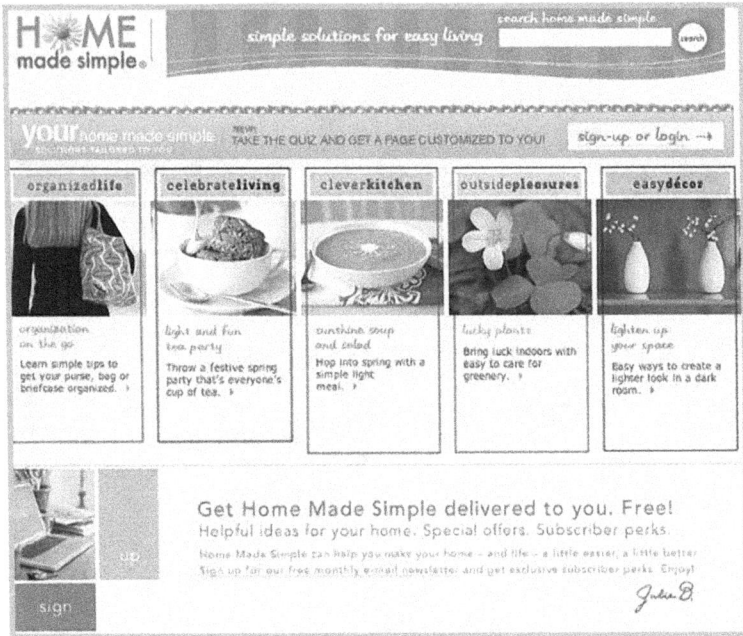

Figure 4.4 At HomeMadeSimple.com from P&G, it's all about living a nicer life, not about buying soap

- Best practices include integrating it with a blog to keep the site fresh with new content.
- Traditional marketing efforts are often employed to promote microsites.

Key Objectives
- Creates an online community for customers and prospects.
- Moves behavior through education.
- Can enhance database activities and generate leads (in concert with e-newsletters and white papers).

E-book Series

When you have a strong body of knowledge inside your organization that you want to share broadly across the Internet, e-books offer you the opportunity to reach out to customers and prospects. They, in turn, can pass along your e-books to friends and colleagues. E-books are typically 20 to 50 pages, designed in landscape format with lots of bullet points and helpful graphics. An e-book can be created and distributed in chapters or as an entire book. Excellent examples are Small Business 2.0 from the Web 2.0 guru Stephanie Diamond (tinyurl.com/hszxm; see Figure 4.5) and David Meerman Scott's *The New Rules of Marketing and PR*, which has generated more than 250,000 downloads since its release at the beginning of 2006. Some e-books are also broken into chapters and created as series, giving customers regular doses of content instead of receiving it all at once.

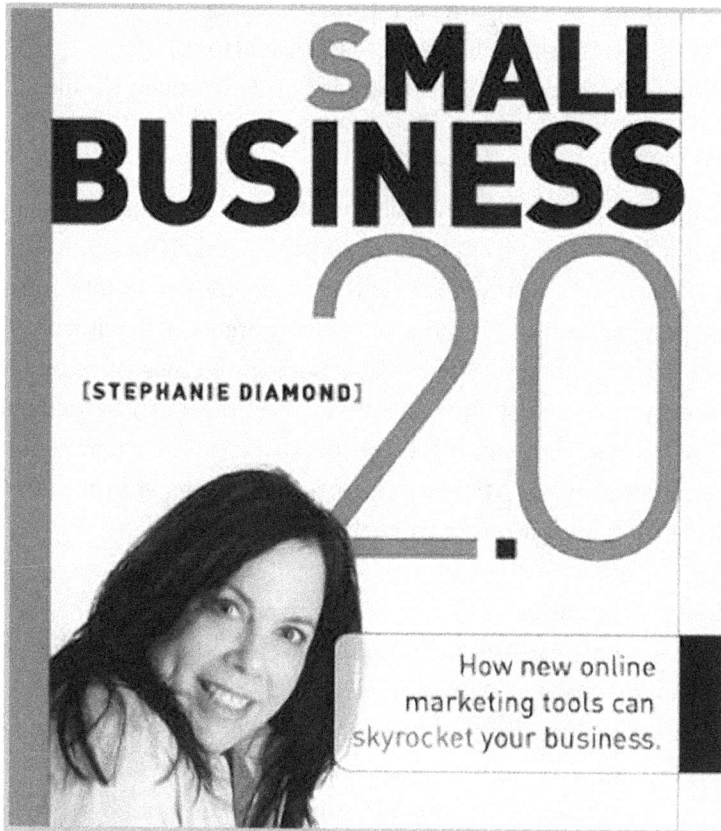

Figure 4.5 Small Business 2.0 from Stephanie Diamond; this free content helps marketers, thus proving her expertise

Points to Remember
- High-quality editorial content is consistently delivered to a targeted database in a chapter or book format.
- E-books are generally 20 to 50 pages or made up of 5 to 10 individual chapters of 8 to 12 pages each.
- E-book chapters should be at least monthly in frequency; weekly is better.
- E-books can use a PDF or digital magazine format.

Key Objectives
- Offers one of the best lead-generation tools.
- Provides the opportunity for viral exposure and pass-along.
- Positions the company as a thought leader.
- Helps strengthen electronic database efforts.
- Educates customer/prospect base on key industry issues.

Webcast Series

Looking for an interactive venue for content? Webcasts enable you to gather hundreds or even thousands of participants in a virtual room. One or more presenters deliver audio content combined with a slide presentation (or audio and video content). Participants typically have the opportunity to ask questions of the presenters and have them answered in real time. Archived Webcasts can be extremely valuable because they can reach prospective customers many months after the initial event. Microsoft is one of the kings of Webcasts (see Figure 4.6). Check it out at tinyurl.com/kdhv3.

Points to Remember
- Web events can be co-branded with a traditional media company or sponsored individually.
- Events are usually free to attendees, who must complete a registration form with qualifying information.
- Events run approximately 45 minutes to an hour.
- Webcasts through traditional business media outlets run from $7,000 to more than $40,000; the average is $12,000 in business-to-business markets.

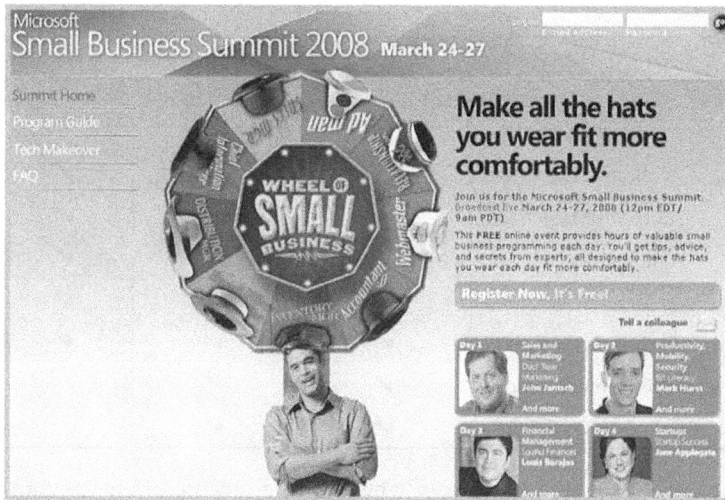

Figure 4.6 Small Business Summit from Microsoft: three days of compelling online content

- Webcasts produced on your own are extremely cost effective.

Key Objectives
- Acts as a powerful lead generator (sponsors receive all registration information from attendees).
- Brands the company as a thought leader.
- Gets the sponsor's products and services in front of key decision makers without sounding like sales.

Table 4.3 shows further examples of the use of online content marketing tools, described in more detail in the following discussion.

White Paper Series

As noted in the section on print, white papers are another way to provide thought leadership and deliver content that is vital to your customers. Even online, white papers tend to be very content-focused with relatively few graphics. Grant Thornton LLP does an excellent job of providing a targeted white paper series (tinyurl.com/3x6htg).

	Business Blogs	E-newsletters	Digital Magazines
Lead Generation	✔	✔	
Brand Awareness		✔	✔
Customer Education	✔		✔
Thought Leadership	✔	✔	✔
Perception Modification	✔		✔
Customer Retention	✔	✔	✔
Internal Communications	✔	✔	
Sales Support	✔	✔	

Table 4.3 Further examples of why and when to use online content marketing tools

Digital Magazines

Today, you can replicate the look and feel of a print magazine online, delivering every bit of the brilliant design and colorful graphics that its print cousin can provide. In many cases, companies that produce print magazines now have digital versions online to complement them. This provides a way to integrate your print content with your Web presence. Digital magazines combine the beauty of print with the interactivity of the Internet. They reside on, or are linked to, your Web site. Numerous software tools are available to create them. To see the possibilities, check out samples of digital magazines that Nxtbook has created at tinyurl.com/33vz4c. Marketers who don't like the confinement of a digital replica usually repurpose the magazine content using a microsite.

E-newsletters or E-zines

These tools can be used to communicate regularly with current and future customers by supplying relevant content that's carefully targeted to their information needs. With an e-newsletter, typically you provide a brief paragraph or two for a set of five to seven articles with links back to the complete articles on your Web site (see Figure 4.7). As long as you are providing valuable content, your readers will also be receptive to your request that they take action to sign up for a newsletter or white paper. A good example of this is Tendo Communications' *Tendo View* (Tendocom.com/view). E-zines are generally text-based e-mails that focus on one key story or concept. Shama Hyder produces an excellent e-zine series at her small business marketing site, ClickToClient.com.

Points to Remember
- High-quality editorial content is consistently delivered to a targeted database via e-mail.
- These are usually short, hard-hitting e-mails that link back to a Web content portal.
- They are distributed weekly or monthly.
- Get permission!

Key Objectives
- Creates and maintains key relationships.
- Generates feedback from customer base.
- Can be tracked to show behavior patterns.
- Can be a solid lead generation tool.
- Consistently keeps you in front of customers.
- Can be co-branded to gain third-party credibility.

Business Blogs

Blogs—or "Weblogs"—began as individual expressions of opinion about deeply felt topics or issues. Today they play a key content marketing role, enabling honest dialogue with customers who care deeply about your company, products, and content. Be sure to establish a blogging strategy that integrates with your content marketing strategy. Begin by asking the right questions: Why are you blogging? What will you blog about? Who will blog? Can you maintain frequent blog entries? Can you accept negative feedback

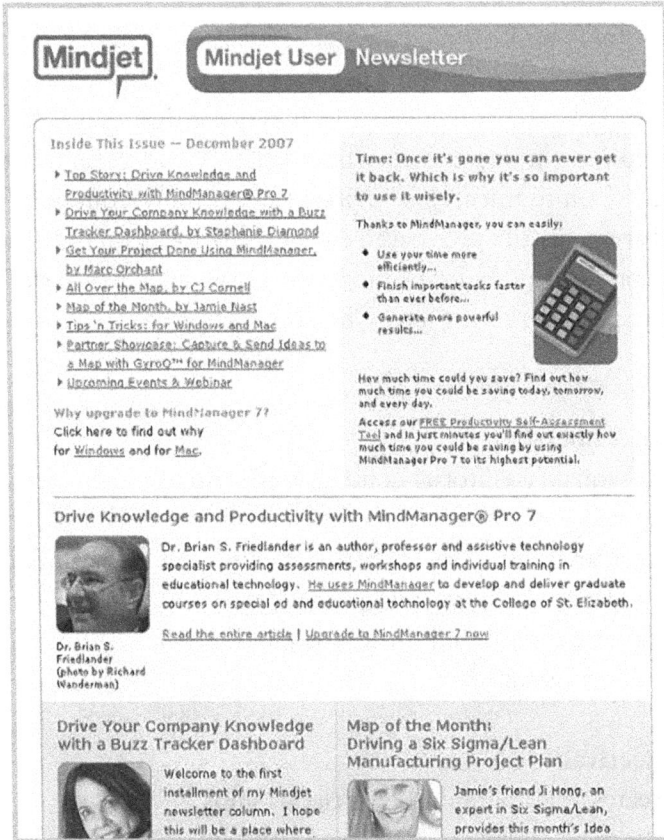

Figure 4.7 Mindjet's e-newsletter: chock full of content designed to make its customers more productive

and respond openly and honestly? If you can answer affirmatively, business blogging could be a core component of your content marketing strategy. Check out Sun Microsystems' CEO's blog for a cool example (blogs.sun.com/jonathan).

A February 2008 Forrester study found that more than half of corporate marketers do not have a blog and are still trying to figure out the medium. The survey also found that three-quarters of all marketers don't see blogging as key to the overall marketing mix. This represents a huge opportunity for marketers who do see the value of blogging as essential to their customer communication programs (see Figure 4.8).

Virtual Trade Shows and Conferences

Current technology and high-speed Internet connections enable the creation of lifelike happenings. Event managers can create Internet-based virtual trade shows and conferences to generate leads, increase event participation, drive revenue, and improve communication with current and future customers (see Figure 4.9). To learn more about the technology, go to Veplatform.com.

Video Series

It's easy today to add video to your Web site, digital magazine, or e-newsletter. Video enables you to convey even very complicated content simply and convincingly. It also gives you the chance to humanize

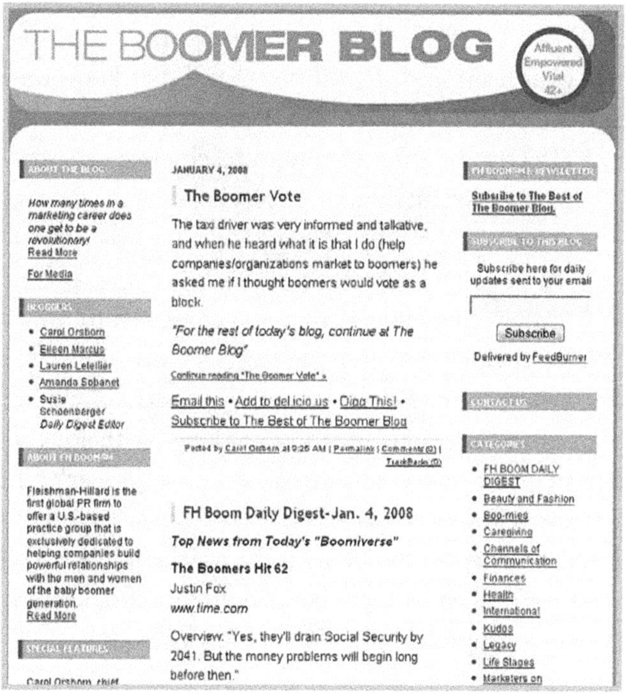

Figure 4.8 The Boomer Blog from Fleishman-Hillard demonstrates the firm's in-depth knowledge of the biggest generation

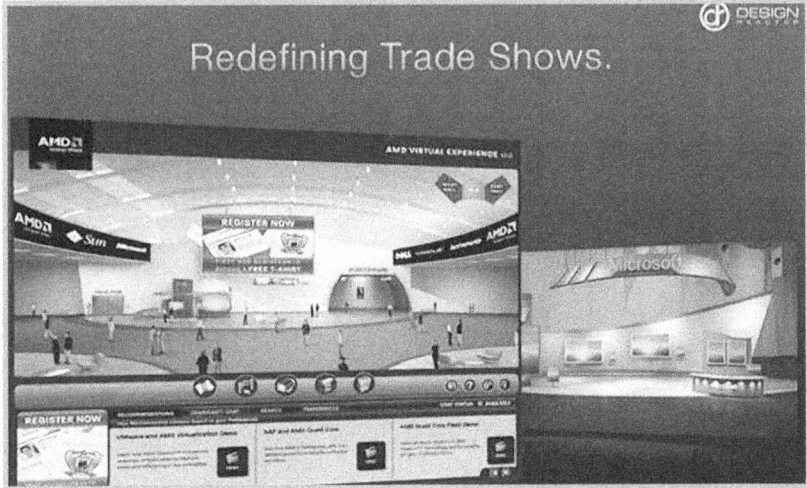

Figure 4.9 A virtual trade show online replicates the in-person experience

members of your team so that visitors feel as if they know them before they meet in person. As Blendtec has demonstrated, there may not be a more cost-effective or efficient way to reach prospects than with an interesting and creative method of displaying content through video.

Podcasts

A podcast is simply an audio file that you can listen to on your computer or MP3-type player. Often, podcasts are distributed as syndication feeds through RSS (Really Simple Syndication) or even iTunes. Podcasts are generally 5 to 30 minutes long, with longer podcast downloads becoming more popular. Paul Dunay, a marketing executive with BearingPoint, has a regular podcast series in conjunction with MarketingProfs on his blog, Buzz Marketing for Technology (BuzzMarketingForTech.blogspot.com). Some corporations are expanding their podcast programs into video podcasts (vodcasts).

In-Person Content Marketing

Although the popularity and effectiveness of trade shows and conferences is suffering from cost pressures and the effectiveness of the

Internet in some industries, most businesses still want and need to be physically in front of their target buyers. This is particularly true if you are selling complex, high-value products or services, where an in-person connection carries a lot of weight. Although live events require a great deal of work and a significant investment of both time and money, they will pay off if you make sure you target the right buyers and provide the right content (see Table 4.4).

Road Shows

Road shows are mini-conferences or tours that are typically conducted by a single organization, although related companies that don't compete will often participate. Usually, individual events last for a day or less and are conducted in cities where there is a high concentration of prospective customers. As always, it's essential that attendees walk away believing that they have received valuable, problem-solving information that positions your organization as a thought leader. Road shows often take the form of ongoing training for customers dealing with complex product issues. Large design software firms such as Autodesk and SolidWorks have been producing these types of events for years, and road shows have become one of their largest marketing initiatives.

	Road Shows	Executive Roundtables
Lead Generation		
Brand Awareness	✔	✔
Customer Education	✔	✔
Thought Leadership	✔	✔
Perception Modification	✔	✔
Customer Retention		✔
Internal Communications		
Sales Support	✔	✔

Table 4.4 Why and when to use in-person content marketing tools

Executive Roundtables

An executive roundtable is a gathering of industry executives who are experts in their field and have enough drawing power to pull in your prospects. Through brief presentations and interaction among roundtable participants, you have the opportunity once again to position yourself as a thought leader. You will also be perceived as an industry force that can bring many key influencers together. The best part? Your customers will have the chance to learn and improve themselves and their companies—all because of you.

Repurpose, Repurpose, Repurpose

Be sure to repurpose the best content that comes out of your road shows and roundtables. You will certainly have photography, transcripts, audio, and video from your in-person events that will serve as valuable content for magazine articles, newsletters, white papers, Web sites, podcasts, video podcasts, and other video productions.

CHAPTER 5

Making Great Content Happen

Many businesses, especially small businesses, may not have the financial resources to create a glossy custom magazine program, but all companies can initiate an effective content marketing program that works. By using the B.E.S.T. formula from Chapter 3 (Behavioral, Essential, Strategic, and Targeted), you can gather the information necessary to begin the content plan. Once that is complete, you can take that information and follow these four steps in detail to create your content plan.

1. Determine Which Organizational Goals Will Be Affected by the Content Program

To be successful, an effective content marketing program must be directly tied to your organization's overall objectives. Don't get into creating content because it's in style. Do it because it truly helps your customers and, in turn, your business. Here are some reasons we've actually heard before from marketing professionals who want to launch content programs:

- "We want to drive more traffic to our Web site."
- "Our competitors are doing it, so we need to do it too."
- "We'd really like to win an award for this."
- "We have tons of great information in this company—we need to tell the world about all the wonderful things we're doing."

Some of these statements may sound reasonable to you. The problem with all of them, however, is that they are not measurable and they don't consider the customer for a second. How does driving more traffic to your Web site accomplish your organizational goals? Just because your company has lots of "great" information, does that mean that telling your story will bring you more revenue? Not in and of itself. Remember, the ultimate goal here is a behavior change. Most of the key problems with a content program result from a clear misunderstanding of organizational goals. So, let's start there. Organizational goals must be two things: specific and customer-focused. Here are a few examples of organizational goals:

- Increase our number of domestic widget-line software customers by 20 percent.
- Generate an average of 10 percent revenue growth with our top 20 percent of customers in Latin America.
- Sell consulting packages to 10 new customers in 2010.
- Decrease customer service calls by 20 percent.

These may seem simple, but it's amazing how many marketing organizations don't bring these types of goals to the table when creating a content program. So, before you launch your content program, be sure to list your key organizational goals. Once that is complete, understand which ones you are trying to affect with your online or offline content program.

2. Determine the Informational Needs of the Buyer

Most people want to move directly into creating the tactics for the content program. It makes sense to do things that way, right? Now that you understand the organizational goals and have chosen the ones that will be affected by the content program, you can come up with some clear and measurable content marketing tactics. Right? Wrong.

Let us give you an example that is more personal. Let's say you want to shape your daughter into the next Tiger Woods. So, a reasonable goal would be for her to win the junior nationals. Since that is your goal, you create a plan of action that includes finding a personal golf coach for your daughter, signing her up for the junior league program, and buying her the latest in golf equipment. Sound reasonable?

Unfortunately, when you created the plan, you didn't consult your daughter (the customer) about what you wanted her to be—or what she needs for her success model. What if your daughter doesn't like golf? What if she likes golf, but doesn't want to be in competitive sports? What if she's built for basketball, or engineering? Worse yet, what if you were so busy planning the strategy that you didn't realize she was left-handed?

This may seem like a strange example, but this exact issue comes up in organizations all the time. Businesses create specific content so that customers react in very specific ways. Without a clear understanding of the customer's information needs, any reaction that is close to the end goal is pure dumb luck (see Figure 5.1).

Successful businesses already have a pretty good understanding of their core buyers. In order to create an effective content program,

Figure 5.1

however, you need to take this a step further. Businesses with content marketing programs create content that is supposed to do very specific things. Just think how pointless this would be if you didn't know what information customers need in order to make better buying decisions—buying decisions that ultimately lead back to the organization's overall goals.

Understand your customers by doing comprehensive research. Comprehensive research does not necessarily have to be expensive. Think of your research as including the following:

- Phone calls and in-person meetings with customers—including people that you think should be customers (what we call "shutouts")
- Zoomerang or SurveyMonkey e-mail surveys to customers and prospects
- Discussions with your customer service and sales personnel
- Listen to customers with Google Alerts (www.google.com/alerts and Twitter.com)

By doing these things, you'll be able to create a buyer persona (a vision of who your target customer really is) and a true understanding of what information that customer needs, which will effectively get you to your goals.

3. Determine What You Want Your Customer to Do and Why This Helps the Business

Have you ever asked someone who owns a company what her Web site is for? Most answers are scary and revolve around the ultimate response, which is, "Because you can't do business without one." Even companies that believe that their Web sites drive revenue can rarely define exactly how.

Content marketing programs are no different. Organizations create custom magazines, newsletters, microsites, podcast series, and other such material for all kinds of reasons. Many of these organizations know exactly what these programs do and what they are supposed to do. Unfortunately, many others do not. Before you initiate and create the content for your content marketing plan, make sure that

- The content plan specifically drives your organization's goals.
- The action(s) you want the customer to take is (are) in some way measurable.
- The content is based on your research concerning the buyers' informational needs.

If you have each of these components, you can create very specific goals for your content program. Some of these goals will be easy to link to your overall goals (e.g., achieving a business transaction). Others will just be pieces of the overall pie that keep you going in the right direction. Examples of these may be

- Downloading a white paper to extract more customer information
- Signing up for an e-newsletter or e-zine to begin creating a relationship with a prospect
- A trial offer or demo that begins a conversation between you and the customer

Today, most organizations call these actions conversions. Whatever you call them, make them specific and measurable in some way. Even print programs can measure conversions through group A/B testing and benchmarking studies, or through specific calls to action that drive customers to Web landing pages.

4. Determine the Product and Content Mix

As we discussed in Chapter 4, there are a number of content products to choose from, and this list is growing longer every day. By mixing your knowledge of the customer, your organizational objectives, and, frankly, your budget, you should be able to determine an appropriate content mix of products. Remember, even though there are leading content products (e.g., a custom magazine may take the primary role), your content marketing program should be well integrated with your Web site, microsites, ancillary content initiatives, and other collateral. Make sure all touch points speak to one another.

Now for the Hard Part: The Content

From our experience, the previous steps are challenging but can be accomplished by almost every company in the world. Variations of these steps are used to determine customer requirements as they pertain to new product launches or product extensions, so savvy companies should be able to breeze through them with no problems.

The real challenge comes at this stage, where we need to actually begin planning and developing content. The majority of organizations are set up to sell products and services, not to create and deliver consistently valuable editorial products. That's why the content execution seems so unnatural to most businesses.

Get Outside Help—Especially with the Content

According to the Custom Publishing Council, approximately half of all U.S.-based companies outsource a portion or all of their content activities to an outside expert publisher or journalist. Anything can be outsourced: project management, content creation, design, Web development, audience development, distribution, marketing, and more. Of all of these, the most important is content.

Many case studies are written by outside freelancers or editorial/content directors. David Meerman Scott, author of the book *The New Rules of Marketing and PR*, says that businesses of any size that are looking to create great content have a simple solution: hire a journalist.

David states, "A journalist skillfully creates interesting stories about how an organization solves customer problems and then delivers those stories in the form of e-books, white papers, content-rich Web pages, podcasts, and video. And consumers love it. How refreshing to read, listen to, and watch these products of journalistic expertise instead of the usual product come-ons that typical corporations produce."

Let's face it: marketers are so busy focusing on their products and driving demand that it's difficult for them to step back and think about customers' informational needs the way journalists do. Also, great writing is an art form and takes talent. If you have that talent in-house, great. If not, find an expert from the outside. Companies, no matter what their size, may not always be able to outsource the complete project, but they can always afford to hire a great writer.

The Editorial Plan and Schedule

Whether you decide to outsource your content or not, you need structure if you are to deliver high-quality content consistently. If you think and behave like a publisher, you should create a content schedule that works from the present to about a year out. That doesn't mean that you can't change things as you go depending on strategic objectives, product launches, or new customer information. What it means is that producing good content takes time. Whether you are creating content for a magazine, an e-book, or a video series, you need to plan ahead to get it done right.

Good content doesn't happen overnight. Most often, it takes research and revision to meet the needs of your customers. Therefore, two sets of plans are needed. First, create an ongoing editorial calendar with key milestones for content deliverables. Second, develop a production schedule for the project team to follow for each individual project. This is exactly what is done in traditional publishing companies. In order to keep meeting reader/customer demands, each product is timed to the day from every point in the process.

Where Does Content Come From?

The traditional route of creating content by completing a sound and reasonable content plan is always important. What's often forgotten, though, is that you can take advantage of content that can be found in and around your organization.

For example, do your executives and employees speak or give presentations on a regular basis? If so, get the rights to record them on video or audio. That's a piece of important content.

Do your engineers or process improvement personnel create industry documentation to substantiate designs or quality improvement measures? If so, rework the information to create a piece of valuable content for your customers and prospects.

How about white papers? Most companies have so many white papers they don't know what to do with them all. Could your white papers be packaged to provide resources for certain customer segments? What about a book or e-book version?

The list could go on forever, depending on your organization. The goal is to look at what is happening in your company and uncover gems of content that can be reworked by your editorial staff and produced as original and valuable content.

It's a Process Issue

When you find great content, you'll usually find a great process as well. Jim McDermott, a publishing executive who spent more than 35 years at Penton Media, Inc., continually stated one truth while he was a publisher and corporate director of quality at Penton: if there was a problem on a project—if there was a mistake, if the magazine was delivered late, if the customer was unhappy for some reason, if the content didn't meet the strategic goals—it was almost always the result of a process breakdown.

In publishing, this is the ultimate truth. Delivering great content to your customers is delivering a promise to them. Once you start, you need to keep that promise. If a company has one or two content products, the schedule should be pretty easy to keep. But as more and more companies deliver integrated and multiple content initiatives to customers, keeping the schedule becomes a challenge.

Assign a Project Manager

Superior execution is the core of a successful content program. One person in your organization should be responsible for and "own" the content initiative. Consider this person the "publisher" for your content efforts. Ultimately, this person is responsible for executing the goals you set out to accomplish. When content programs fail, it's usually not because of a lack of high-quality content, but because of poor execution. That's why a project manager may be your most important content asset, even though this person most likely won't be creating any of the content. The project manager must ensure excellence in every content marketing tactic, including:

- Content/editorial
- Design/art/photography
- Web development/integration
- Content-specific marketing
- Project budgeting
- Contract negotiation with freelancers
- Print/Web production and maintenance
- List/audience development and maintenance
- Research and measurement
- Responsibility for accomplishing the goals of the project

Sometimes, just a little up-front work can make all the difference. This is true with content marketing. With a little planning, a few processes, and ownership within the organization, any size business can make an important impact on the lives of its customers.

Setting Up the Plan for Measurement

If you're thinking about launching a content program without having a process in place to measure its effectiveness, stop right now. Content marketing and custom publishing programs have been talked down for years, much like traditional media, because of a lack of measurement formulas.

The great news is that content marketing can always be measured if you have a clear understanding of your strategic communication objectives. Just keep it simple and answer the question, "How will we know that the content plan is working?" This should lead you directly back to your organizational goals.

Return on investment (ROI) has always been dicey at best when it comes to marketing. The Holy Grail has been (and always will be) to link your marketing initiative directly to sales. That's easier said than done. We've seen more than a few marketers determine ROI after the fact, taking whatever measurement they could find to prove that something indeed worked.

Return on Objective

Perhaps a better way to judge the effectiveness of a content plan is to analyze return on objective (ROO). ROO was popularized while we were at Penton Media, Inc., in 2003 by Penton Group Publisher Bill Baumann. Bill, like the rest of us, grew tired of advertisers constantly barking about less than adequate ROI measures when it was impossible for us to measure sales lift—at least not without access to the advertisers' CRM databases for tracking purposes.

It was at that point that we put our measurement energy into ROO, which was something that we could define in conjunction with our clients and use to keep both sides accountable. Before signing any final agreement, we would ask the question: "One year from today, how will you know whether or not the project was successful?" In most cases, we already knew the answer, but it was important to hear what the client said. The answer to that question was ultimately what we planned to measure—that was the return on objective.

The measurement of sales lift, impact, retention, and other such goals is key to any ROO program. The "measurement picture" comes into play when sales data are missing or challenging. Sometimes ROO can be determined with one statistic, while other times four or five are needed to show an impact on the organization's business goals.

ROO measurements come in all shapes and sizes, and usually include multiple items to give you the complete answer to your question. The important thing to remember is, this is not measurement for the sake of measurement. The tools and tactics given here are used to directly answer what the project's objective is. If you keep that in mind, you'll get your ROO.

Here are a few measurement initiatives to get you started:

- *Tracking sales lift* among those who receive the content program vs. those who do not.
- *Tracking conversions* for online content products or print subscriptions, and measuring new or increased sales.
- *Online readership studies* to determine the impact of the content project, as well as the acquisition of customer informational needs and trends.
- *Measuring engagement* (time spent) through online research or by using analytic measures on e-newsletter or Web portal products.
- *Pre-/post-awareness study* to measure the impact of the program. If possible, separate out a control group that does not receive your content initiative. Without that, it's challenging to tell whether it was the project that made the impact, or if it was something else in your marketing arsenal.

There are also a number of new online measurement tools that can give you some insight into how your content is performing, both with search engines and with customers themselves. Here are a few that you might want to check out.

Traffic Comparison Sites
- Alexa.com
- Compete.com
- Quantcast.com
- Trafficestimate.com

Blog Impact
- Technorati.com
- Icerocket.com
- Feedburner.com (blog RSS feeds)
- Google Blog Search

Finally, here are some additional tactics to consider when integrating the measurement picture into your content marketing:

- Using distinct 800 numbers for print and online initiatives
- Using individual URLs for different content projects
- Ensuring that every print or Web page has some type of call to action
- Using print and online versioning tools to send more precise content to customers and prospects based on their individual needs, and measuring the difference in impact

Ultimately, we are only scratching the surface here when it comes to content marketing measurement. The key comes down to this: you have to plan for measurement. It is almost impossible to measure the content vehicle after you've already begun. An organization that invests in content without investing in the measurement of that content doesn't truly believe in the content initiative.

Don't forget these questions:

- What is the true purpose of the content marketing effort?
- What are the underlying marketing objectives?
- What do you really want to tell your customers?
- Once you have their attention, what do you want your customers to do? What is the desired behavior?
- What vehicle best meets the needs of your customers?
- In order to meet your customers' informational needs, how should you integrate your content marketing efforts with other media?

The days of vanity custom publications are over. For today's content marketing to be successful, it's all about customer behavior. Once you understand what the desired behavior is, the rest can fall into place—so start there.

CHAPTER 6

Putting the "Marketing" in Content Marketing

mar·ket·ing [mahr-ki-ting]–noun–The act of buying or selling in a market.

— DICTIONARY.COM

ontent marketing, taken at face value, is simple terminology for a complex process. *Content*, as in creating information that meets your customers' needs, and *marketing*, as in distributing and promoting that information to a targeted group of people, inherently make sense. This portion of the book is about all the ways to distribute and promote your content. But, distribute it to do what exactly?

This book is not a marketing theory book; it's an action book. It was designed for you to take pieces and parts and insert them into your marketing and content plans tomorrow. That said, it's important to understand why you are undertaking content marketing, why you are creating all this great content in the first place.

Go back to the definition of marketing at the beginning of this chapter. Marketing is all about behavior. It's an action. It's not about generating buzz, or Web site traffic, or press mentions—unless those things lead to profitable customer behavior.

Don and Heidi Schultz, in their book *IMC, the Next Generation*, state, "For all the complexity of marketing and communication plans, firms want only four outcomes from them." Those four outcomes are

- To acquire new customers
- To retain and maintain present customers
- To retain and grow sales volume or profit from existing customers
- To migrate existing customers through the firm's product or service portfolio

What this means is that every bit of your content marketing focus must affect customers' or prospects' behavior. If this becomes the cornerstone of your content, the distribution and promotion of that content take on a different meaning from just creating traffic or buzz. Every word and every page you create has a purpose: to drive the ultimate customer action.

Basic Principles of Content Promotion

Segmentation Is Key

Almost all businesses have different types and levels of customers. To be most effective, the ultimate distribution of your content should not be one-size-fits-all. Group your customers into different buying groups (also called buying personas), and treat both the content and the marketing to each group as separate.

Permission Marketing

Anything that you deliver to your customers or prospects that they have not specifically requested could be considered spam. That is why it is imperative, for both your print and your e-mail content programs, that you have your customers opt in to your programs. Opting in means that they have specifically requested your print magazine, e-newsletter, e-book, or other similar materials.

According to the CAN-SPAM law, you have a right to use e-mail correspondence to communicate with your customers, as long as you have some kind of working relationship with them. But that doesn't mean that you can send them unsolicited information on an ongoing basis. Use e-mail information to get their permission to send them more. Use new offers to get them to sign up for your content. You must also give your customers the option of opting out or unsubscribing to anything you send them as well.

Content without Promotion Is Nothing

Lee Odden, one of the leading marketing bloggers in the country, posted this about the content vs. promotion debate:

> *If you create great content and no one knows about it to link to it, you're spinning your wheels. A combination of content as well as social networking, link networking, public relations, and gaining editorial visibility as well as viral and individual link solicitations will all work together synergistically. Building a community of consumers of your content as well as relationships with the media in your industry is the distribution network necessary to gain the most link value out of creating great content.*

Almost all organizations believe that they create, or can create, great content on a continuous basis. All too often, a brand will engage in a content project, not see positive results, and halt the initiative, thinking that the content didn't meet customer needs. The majority of the time, the problem was not necessarily in the content, but in the marketing of the content.

Meet Your Customers Where They Are Plus One

As we have discussed, your choice of media depends on your customers. You wouldn't need to roll out an iPhone digital magazine version if none of your customers had iPhones. That said, you need to help your customers take the next step. Yes, you should give them content in media that they already use, but you also have to be cutting-edge.

Just because your research indicates that only a small percentage of your customers engage in online video doesn't mean that you can't get them there. It's not like the iPhone example, where they have to have an iPhone. If you create a valuable video on a topic that your customers need to hear about, they have the PCs and Internet connections to get there. As long as the content is truly important, you have the opportunity to be seen as an innovator just by the type of media you use to distribute your content.

Consistency in Communication

The old rule of thumb in print advertising is that it takes seven impressions of an ad per year to make an awareness impact on a decision maker. The situation is much the same with content marketing.

Behavior change doesn't happen overnight. Content must be delivered consistently in all the media you use. That means that one white paper should be part of a white paper series. One video should be part of a video series. One magazine issue does not a magazine make. Whatever you decide to use, send it to your customers frequently and stay on schedule. If you can't commit to a schedule, don't do the project. While great content can make a difference, going dark for a period of time or delivering your content inconsistently will damage the perception of your brand.

Let Your Content Go

If you love your content, you must learn to let it go. In the past, brands had complete control over their content message and the medium. This is still basically true with custom magazines and newsletters. But the rise of the Internet and social media has changed the rules forever. Once your content goes online, it could end up anywhere. Let it. Regardless of where it ends up, the goal is to get your message out to the right types of people. If that happens and you see action, you've accomplished your goal—it doesn't matter whether people engaged with the content on your site or someone else's.

Why Does Marketing Content Feel So Awkward?

In the past, the majority of companies (yes, including media companies) that were creating high-quality content for years didn't have to worry about using their content as a marketing tool. They had targeted databases and targeted direct-mail lists, and they knew exactly where their prospects and customers were at most times. Today, customers can opt out of just about every type of marketing they receive. Even though we may know more about our customers, they are becoming more elusive—elusive because they can choose to ignore our message at any moment.

Up until now, marketing time and resources have been used for brand advertising, sales initiatives, event marketing, direct marketing, and similar activities, *not* for marketing content. But today, since the average company spends a quarter of its marketing budget on content initiatives, it is imperative that organizations focus a large portion of their resources on the marketing of content.

Mediaweek recently featured a story called "Is Social Media Killing the Campaign Microsite?" This brought attention to the fact that the microsite (or content Web portal/content microsite) might be going the way of the 30-second spot. The author, Brian Morrissey, states that social media is changing behavior so much that marketers can't expect their customers to search actively for their products or services.,

Social media are just one aspect of this issue. Ever-changing buyer behavior and expectations are another. Regardless of the reasons, custom content cannot be marketed the way it was in the past.

Let's take a look at the traditional custom publishing or content marketing campaign:

1. Create glossy magazine or newsletter.
2. Mail magazine or newsletter to targeted list of customers and prospects.
3. Upload content to the magazine microsite or newsletter page of the Web site just before the print copies are delivered.
4. Repeat the process in three months.

We may be simplifying just a bit, but this is how 99 percent of the custom projects were produced. While this used to be more than acceptable, it just doesn't work anymore.

It's Not All about You

We've been keeping up with the postings from the folks at PandemicBlog recently and picked up on this review of an article by Kevin Nalts—one of the experts in viral marketing with video—on best practices for using viral videos. Kevin's thoughts struck us as so simple, yet the premise is something that most content marketers have not yet realized. Kevin says:

> *Would you go to Hersheys.com to watch funny videos? Probably not. Would you watch Hershey-sponsored videos via You-Tube? Much better chance. It's based on when pharmaceutical marketers wanted their brand site to be the "ultimate destination for people who have condition x." Puleez—just go syndicate or advertise on WebMD.*

This is true not just for video, but for all your content that can be "Webified." Heck, we're huge fans of the microsite. *The microsite is not dead;* it's simply just one way out of many that you need to connect and communicate with your customers.

Less Content, More Marketing

This statement is essentially the key, and there is no better example of this than in blogging. Successful blogging, to most people, is about frequency. That couldn't be further from the truth. As said best by Eric Kintz at mpdailyfix, blogging is not about "how often," but about how the blogger participates in the community. For example, is the blogger just adding noise to the already cluttered marketplace, or is he providing a filter and a voice of reason that elevates the conversation? The same can be said for all your Web content. However your company is involved in physical communities in your industry, you need to double those efforts on the Web.

Right around the time we were finalizing this book, we had conversations with three industry experts—two marketers and one media professional—about their Web content. None of them could figure out why they weren't getting more traffic. Outside of the basic search engine optimization (SEO) fixes, the majority of it came down to poor marketing, not poor content. When we asked, "How are you marketing your content?" it was as if we asked them if they were the missing gunmen on the grassy knoll.

Here's the point: before you create any more "great content," figure out how you are going to market it *first*. Let's discuss some strategies for how to do that effectively.

New Media Promotion Strategies

As technology continues to change on a daily basis, so do the opportunities for marketing your content. Here are several promotion and distribution activities that you should consider integrating into your overall content plan.

Search Engine Optimization

Search engine optimization (SEO) is the process of improving your "organic" search engine rankings on Google, Yahoo!, MSN.com, Ask.com, and other similar sites. On a search engine results page, these are generally the results on the left side of the page (the right side is usually for paid listings).

One of the biggest reasons why companies are starting to pay attention to content is that content scores well in organic search engine listings. So, if part of your business strategy is better visibility within the search engines (it better be!), you need to develop a content strategy to create inventory for possible placement.

Content and SEO are tied at the hip. It's tough to have one without having the other. As you launch your content strategy, you would be wise to work with an SEO expert to make sure you are getting the maximum exposure for your content through the search engines.

Search Engine Marketing

Search engine marketing (SEM) generally refers to the pay-per-click (PPC) listings on the right side of a search engine results page. Many companies use PPC to generate conversions (to a direct sale, download, or free trial promotion) or to buy traffic when organic listings are nonexistent.

Google AdWords and Yahoo! Search Marketing are the largest providers of PPC keywords. A PPC system is a live auction that updates every second, featuring those listings on the right that bid the most and score well (more clicks) for that particular keyword. Advertisers who purchase keywords pay only when the ad is clicked on, making the ad's effectiveness incredibly easy to measure when it is tied to an online event such as an online registration form. PPC is an effective method for driving target prospects and customers to your white papers, e-books, subscriptions, or other content conversion pages.

Social Media Marketing

Content can play a large role in your overall social media marketing strategy. Social media sites can be broken out into social media networks (e.g., Facebook), social Web applications (e.g., Digg.com), and even virtual worlds such as SecondLife.com.

Depending on the goals of the content program and the target audience, sites such as Facebook and YouTube can be leveraged to promote your content initiative. For example, your company could launch a branded Facebook fan page where your employees can share content with customers on a regular basis. With regard to YouTube and other video-sharing sites, the Blendtec example we've discussed in previous chapters shows that with the right message, video can have a significant impact on the profitability of a business.

Twitter, a microblogging tool (140 characters per post maximum), is an excellent combination play between social networking and content distribution. Not only has Twitter been embraced by the blogging community, but businesses such as Starbucks, Kodak, and Whole Foods Market also employ successful Twitter strategies. Dell leverages Twitter for customer service purposes as well as to promote refurbished Dell computer offers through @DellOutlet. Try this: mention that you are having a problem with your Dell computer while using Twitter and see how fast you receive a note from a Dell employee.

Even though social media marketing is increasing its influence daily, most marketers are still just dabbling in it. This creates an opportunity for you to test which social portals provide the best return for your objectives and which sites your customers seem to be affiliating with.

Content Syndication—RSS

RSS, or Really Simple Syndication, is fast becoming a mainstream technology. RSS is a format that allows you to syndicate your Web content to individuals with an RSS reader application or to other sites that wish to carry your content.

Organizations need to make their Web content available through RSS feeds, including blog content, article content, and even news content. There are a number of services that provide RSS tools for free, including Google's FeedBurner.com.

Leveraging Social Bookmarking Sites as Content Syndication Tools

Search engines such as Google, Yahoo!, and Ask.com allow each domain a maximum of two results on a search page. To dominate a particular keyword and receive more listings, you need to leverage social bookmarking sites.

According to Wikipedia.com, social bookmarking is "a method for Internet users to store, organize, search, and manage bookmarks of web pages on the Internet with the help of metadata. In a social bookmarking system, users save links to web pages that they want to remember and/or share."

Social bookmarking sites are generally used to drive significant amounts of traffic by people voting for a particular article (such as "digging" a Digg.com article). We believe that for most businesses, the benefits revolve mostly around search engine optimization.

Most social bookmarking and news sites receive high visibility with search engine providers. So, when you submit your article or story to a bookmarking site, that individual listing has an opportunity to be indexed by a search engine. The result: depending on the keywords used, you could dominate a particular keyword with listings coming from multiple bookmarking sites.

Some of the most popular social bookmarking sites include:

- Digg.com (news)
- Propeller.com (news)
- Reddit.com (news)
- Mixx.com (news)
- Shoutwire (news)
- Del.icio.us (bookmarking)
- StumbleUpon.com (channel surfing)
- Furl.com (news)
- SmallBusinessBrief.com (small business/small business marketing)
- Sphinn.com (SEO-related)
- Junta42.com (content marketing)

News Releases

David Meerman Scott's book *The New Rules of Marketing and PR* rewrites the rules for using press releases. The "new" news release is now more effective than ever. David's "New Rules of News Releases" include:

- Don't send news releases only when "big news" is happening; find good reasons to send them all the time.
- Instead of just targeting a handful of journalists, create news releases that appeal directly to your buyers.
- Write releases that are replete with keyword-rich copy.
- Include offers that compel consumers to respond to your release in some way.
- Add social media tags so that your release can be found.
- Drive people into the sales process with a news release.

What this means for your content efforts is that news releases should be integrated into every part of those efforts. If you recognize and understand that your target audience can find you today in new and unique ways, including search engines and social media sites, news releases become all-important tools in promoting your great content. This includes issue launches, cover stories, key case studies, white papers, e-books, video launches, and more. Remember, the old goal of a press release was to get media coverage. The new rules of news releases tell you to promote your content so that it can be found by the right people.

Putting the New Promotion Techniques to Use

Let's end this section by going back to the traditional custom magazine example. For the basic quarterly magazine project, here are some ways to get the most "bang for your buck" out of your content, and to create multiple avenues for qualified prospects and customers to reach you:

1. Make audio and video recordings of interviews for the magazine or newsletter for later repurposing (we'll use magazine for the rest of this discussion).
2. Develop a news release schedule before the magazine comes out. Target three or four key topics that affect your customers and the industry (based on the magazine content). The release link should take people to the magazine subscription or digital magazine subscription page. An incentive could be a free subscription to the print magazine or newsletter.
3. Discuss the magazine on your corporate blog. Get your editor to post some of the key findings or issues. If you don't have a corporate blog, create one on your magazine microsite.
4. Send out news releases through a keyword-optimized service such as PRWeb.
5. Post videos of interviews on YouTube and other targeted video portals specific to your industry. Upload audio to microsites. Research podcast directories that may be relevant to your industry.

6. Print the glossy 32+-page magazine and mail it to your targeted database.

7. Send the digital magazine version to the international audience or to a domestic audience that you didn't want to spend printing and postage on (possibly a secondary customer target).

8. Make sure that all articles have their own HTML pages on your microsite. Be sure that each article has social media capabilities, such as letting people add it to Facebook, Digg, or StumbleUpon, to name a few.

9. Be sure to Stumble noteworthy articles and choose the proper category for the article. For example, if your article goes best in agriculture, those people who have tagged agriculture as a keyword may see it when they use StumbleUpon.

10. Provide something remarkable and different on your microsite for downloading. This does two things: (1) it continues the conversation with your current customers, and (2) it gives you information on prospects so that you can begin a conversation with them. Something remarkable may be a free e-book about the 10 trends in your industry or a free white paper on a new, cutting-edge technology. Keep the sales pitch out. Seek only to educate at this point.

11. Use PPC, targeting specific keywords to drive people to your downloadable content offering.

12. Be sure to make RSS feeds available for your Web content. Integrate your RSS feeds to promote your content through Twitter (try Twitterfeed.com).

13. Continue the news release program, pushing the audience to the videos, an e-book, or key articles. Remember, news releases aren't for getting press; they are for building key links and for helping bloggers and influencers find your site. *Industry bloggers can be key to your magazine effort.*

14. Upload articles to key vertical and social bookmarking sites, such as SmallBusinessBrief.com for small business, Sphinn for SEO/SEM, or Digg.com for wider exposure.
15. And if you are really on the cutting edge, create a Facebook fan page around your magazine or your company and promote within that vehicle. Invite your key customers to join the Facebook group.

There is more that you can do, but this gives you an idea of how you should be marketing your relevant and valuable content. Think of it this way: how much valuable content have you or your organization created that has been seen only by one group of people—or, worse yet, has not been engaged with at all? It's a marketing problem, not a content problem.

PART THREE

Learning from Smart Marketers— Best Practice Success Stories

Chapter 7

Best Practice Success Stories Overview

You may be surprised at the range of organizations that have implemented successful content marketing strategies. In the following chapters, we will examine how 14 organizations and 3 "solopreneurs" are using content marketing to connect with their customers.

These organizations range from multibillion-dollar publicly traded multinationals to single-person companies run from bedrooms. Regardless of their size, you will find that the most important common threads are their customer-centric focus, a content marketing mindset, and a determination to create content that is relevant and valuable to their customers.

Although some of the success stories involve projects with huge budgets, others were undertaken with almost no monetary investment at all. There are key takeaways from every success story. No matter what the size of your organization, you will find ways to apply the lessons gleaned from a fascinating array of content marketing implementations.

You will learn from a welding equipment company, a retail giant, a manufacturing media powerhouse, a bank, a chamber of commerce, a solo kitchen designer, an Australian Web company, a British law firm, and many others.

Each organization has managed to bring an understanding of its most important customers to the creation of print, online, and in-person content. The net result of these efforts is a strong connection to both new and old customers. Each organization has become a trusted vendor, based in large part on the high-quality content that it provides consistently to its customers.

CHAPTER 8

Yes, Content Marketing Can Make Welding Cool

MillerWelds.com exemplifies how new-generation Web sites can deliver content that connects with current and future customers.

Type of organization: Welding equipment supplier; subsidiary of the publicly traded company Illinois Tool Works.

Major marketing objective: To achieve an in-depth understanding of its customers so that it can provide content that is relevant to helping them with critical welding-related issues.

Content types:

- Print magazine
- Digital magazine
- Web site
- Microsites
- Blogs
- RSS feeds

Unique element: In addition to providing excellent content, the Miller Welds.com Web site makes it very easy for customers to select and buy exactly the right products for their needs.

Results: Intense customer focus in the creation of broad-range content marketing underlies strong multiyear, double-digit revenue growth.

Miller Electric Mfg. Co.'s powerful online presence shows that you can be both fun and informative. The company has a broad-based constituency, ranging from hobbyist welders to professionals working on skyscrapers, race cars, and airplanes. Amazingly, Miller manages to appeal to all of them online through its main Web site, several microsites, its blog, its e-newsletter, and discussion forums. This is truly the very best of content marketing.

Miller was founded in 1929 to provide welding solutions at a time when blacksmiths were still earning a good living doing metalwork. It employs more than 1,500 people in its headquarters town of Appleton, Wisconsin. It also has an expanding presence overseas, including offices in China. The company is a midrange manufacturer that has been a wholly owned subsidiary of Illinois Tool Works since 1993.

Over the last three years, Miller has managed to achieve double-digit annual growth. The company might well have achieved this level of success without its leading-edge online presence, but those online efforts have certainly added significant value to its offline efforts. Central to everything the company does is the need to understand its customers in order to deliver relevant content and, ultimately, precisely appropriate solutions.

As Vickie Rhiner, corporate marketing communications, emphasizes:

The "overarching" objective in all our marketing strategies is to understand our customer. Our research with the customer is what motivates us to provide information/content that is relevant to them. For many of our customers, the welding operation in their business is important to their very livelihood. As the manufacturer of the equipment they depend on day-in and day-out, they look to us for information that may help them with their most critical business issues, e.g., reducing welding costs, increasing productivity, operator efficiency, and equipment purchase justification (ROI).

You don't have to be involved in welding to get a feel for the enthusiasm that Miller exudes. One look at a recent cartoon from its e-newsletter will give you a pretty good idea: "You know you're a welder when your welding helmets cost more than your car." Miller's customers love what the company does—and the site reflects that.

Many online elements create a sense of community for several different market segments. At the same time, it's also obvious that this is a Web site designed to sell products and services.

At its best, compelling online content begins an ongoing dialogue with your best buyers from the very first moment they land on the site. That's exactly what Miller accomplishes.

MillerWelds.com Is Anything but a Typical Industrial Web Site

As we will discuss in Chapter 19 (which focuses on ThomasNet), most industrial Web sites still fall far short of what's required to do business successfully in the twenty-first century. They simply don't provide enough information to make it easy to buy products and services. Moreover, most of them also miss the opportunity to provide content that enables them to build a trusted relationship with current and future customers.

MillerWelds.com is as good a Web site as you would expect to find from one of the major consumer packaged-goods companies. In fact, it generates a level of traffic that many consumer companies would envy—250,000 visitors per month.

This site and others like it are also beginning to take on the role that trade and special-interest publications have traditionally played. That is, they are providing highly focused, intrinsically valuable content that helps their customers do their jobs more effectively— or pursue their hobbies with more skill. While their media company counterparts are suffering through big budget cutbacks, they are pouring on the content steam.

Today, even small companies can offer their prospects and customers a rich experience, with lots of content that is relevant to their particular interests. In this new generation, content marketing drives the online experience. That is, by first understanding exactly who your customers are and what they need to know, you can provide them with content that leaves them smarter and more knowledgeable. Content marketing enables organizations of every size to attract and retain more customers.

Now That's Content Marketing!

Miller is well ahead of its peers in its understanding and application of content marketing. And, yes . . . it makes welding cool!

In fact, one of its competitors, Lincoln Electric, has a perfectly credible Web site. But when it comes to delivering an outstanding customer experience, Miller beats Lincoln hands down. Although the Lincoln folks do provide good product information, at the time of this writing they weren't offering much beyond that.

MillerWelds.com provides customers and prospects with a rich, relevant, and fun experience by providing microsites devoted to welding applications and interests such as racing, manufacturing, and construction. Miller has made its Web site the "go-to" site for welding information (see Figure 8.1). In so doing, it has become a company with which you would love to do business.

In more recent years, MillerWelds.com has become an information source for hobbyists and instructors. Vickie Rhiner relates:

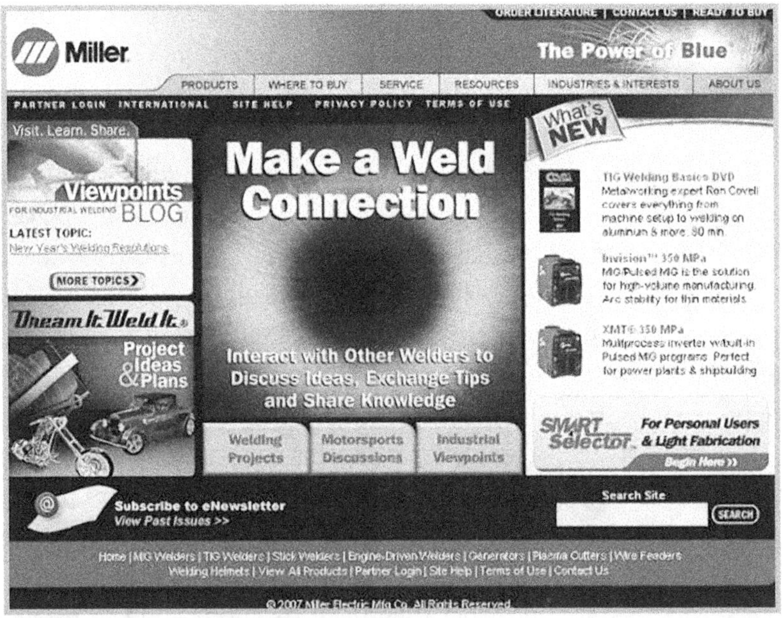

Figure 8.1 MillerWelds.com is the go-to site for everything anyone would want to know about welding

After Miller appeared on the cable TV show American Chopper, *we were the recipients of calls, e-mails, and letters from instructors around the country looking for help with their welding curriculum because their class enrollment was soaring. Many of the areas you now find within our website are in direct response to what the customer has asked us for.*

At MillerWelds.com, it's easy to find information that relates to your particular industry or interest. For example, if your welding work relates to construction, you can find a dedicated microsite with a wealth of information, including well-written articles that will help you solve some thorny problems (see Figure 8.2).

You can also browse an article archive to find information on the particular problem you're facing (see Figure 8.3). Thus, if you need

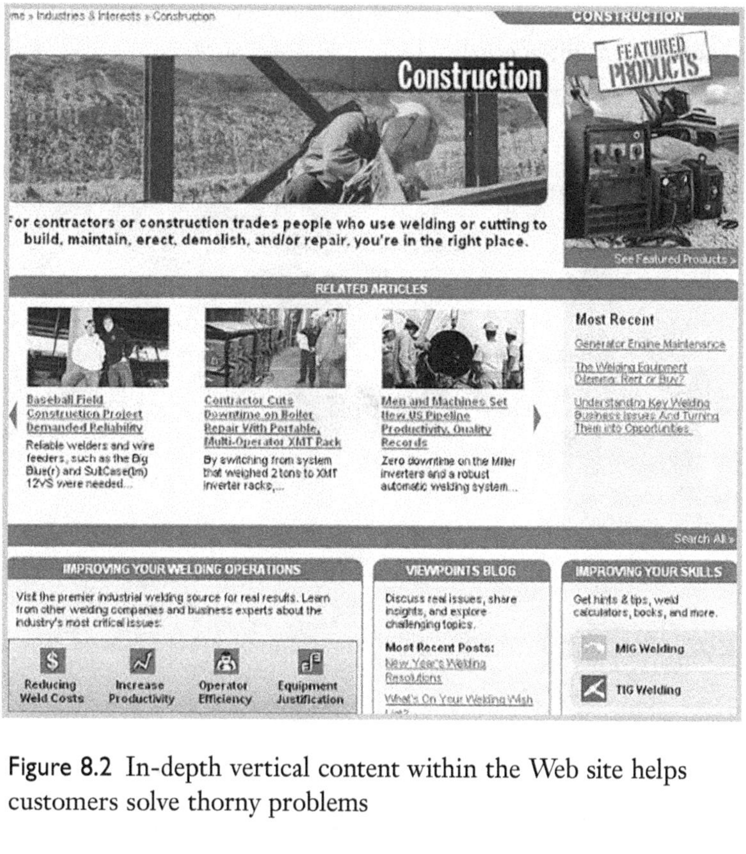

Figure 8.2 In-depth vertical content within the Web site helps customers solve thorny problems

to cost-justify an investment in upgrading your pickup-truck-mounted welding equipment, the site tells you exactly how to do the analysis and provides you with a cost comparison that will justify the upgrade.

You can stay current on all new articles that are posted in your area of interest by signing up for the site's RSS feed. For example, if all you care about is the motor sports industry, you can sign up for motor sports information. The Miller e-newsletter, *Power Click*, is another useful resource that directs recipients back to the Web site for even more information (see Figure 8.4). The e-newsletter is carefully customer-focused, with only a small product item included.

The goal of the e-newsletter, according to Sue Feldkamp, manager of interactive marketing, is to "engage our customers and bring them back to the site often. We accomplish this by understanding what they are looking for and making it easy to find. Continuous evaluation of what they're doing on the web allows us to monitor and adjust content accordingly."

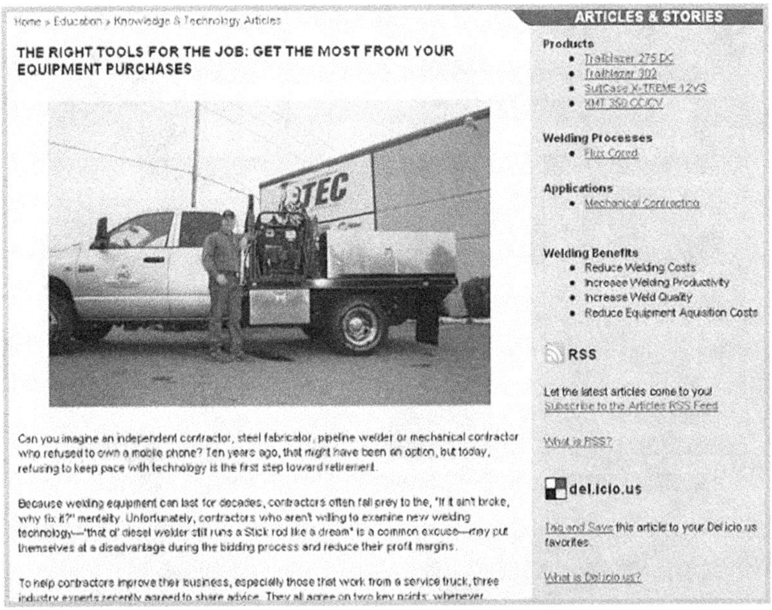

Figure 8.3 Easy-to-browse article archive helps with both problem solving and purchasing decisions

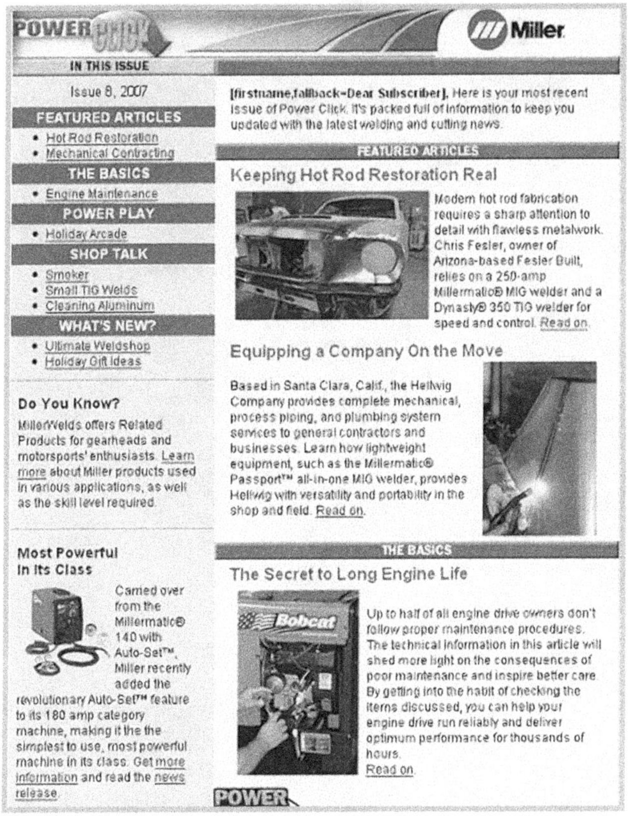

Figure 8.4 The Miller e-newsletter, *Power Click*, engages customers and keeps them coming back to the Web site

The Miller blog, Viewpoints (see Figure 8.5), is prominently featured on the home page. Its tagline, "Visit. Learn. Share.," reflects the spirit of the blog, in which the most popular posts draw dozens of comments. For example, posts that relate to solving the problem of the critical shortage of professional welders are both highly rated and much commented on.

Cool factor aside, this Web site is both comprehensive and easy to use. Plus, you can find exactly what you want to buy with very little effort. But, that's pretty cool, too.

Since the company sells through a vast network of distributors, the "ready to buy" page is optimized for that process (see Figure 8.6). First

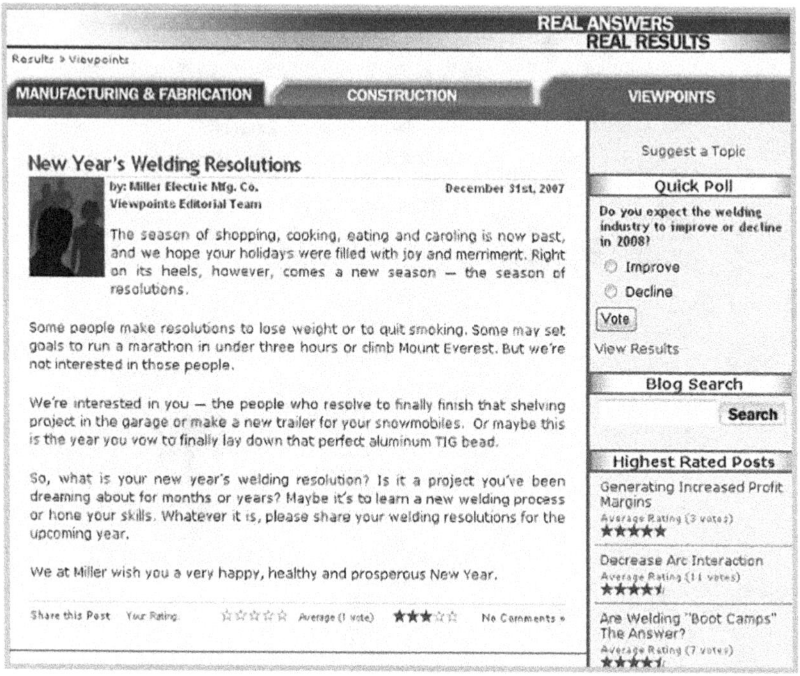

Figure 8.5 Miller blog invites customers to "Visit. Learn. Share."

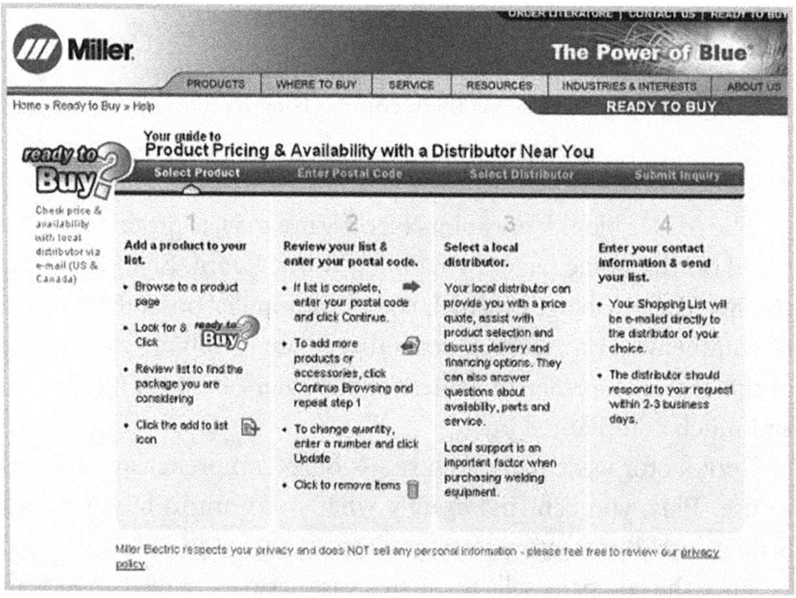

Figure 8.6 Miller makes it easy to find exactly what you want to buy

MULTIPROCESS SELECTION GUIDE												Summary	Features	Typical Applications
Multiprocess Welder	Class	Stick	MIG	MIG-P*	DC TIG	DC TIG -P*	Flux Core**	CAC-A	SAW	Pro-Pulse™	RMD™ Pro	Portability	Weldable Metals	Welding Output Range
1-Phase														
Shopmate™ 300 DX	●	●	●		●		●					Lift eye, optional running gear	All metals	10-35 V, 5-400 A
XMT® 304 CC/CV	●	●	●	●	●	●	● 1/4"					Handles, optional cart, MIGRunner	All metals	10-35 V, 5-400 A
1&3 Phase														
XMT® 350 CC/CV	●	●	●	●	●	●	● 5/16"					Handles, optional cart, MIGRunner	All metals	10-38 V, 5-425 A
XMT® 350 MPa	●	●	●	●	●	●	● 5/16"					Handles, optional cart	All metals	10-38 V, 5-425 A
XMT® 350 VS	●	●	●	●	●	●	● 5/16"					Handles, optional cart	All metals	10-38 V, 5-425 A
PipePro™ 450 RFC	●	●	●	●	●			● 3.6"	●	●	●	Lift eye, optional cart	All metals	10-44 V, 5-600 A
XMT® 455 CC/CV	●	●	●	●	●	●	● 3.8"					Handles, optional cart	All metals	10-38 V, 5-600 A
3-Phase														
Dimension™ 302	●	●	●		●	●	1/4"						Most metals	10-32 V, 15-375 A
Dimension™ 452	●	●	●		●	●	5/16"					Lift eye, optional running gear	Most metals	10-38 V, 20-565 A
Dimension™ 652	●	●	○		●	●	3.6"	●					Most metals	10-65 V, 50-815 A
Dimension™ NT 450	●	●	●		●	●	5/16"						Most metals	10-38 V, 5-500 A

Class Key:
● Light Industrial
○ Industrial
● Heavy Industrial

Quality Key:
● Excellent
○ Good/Fair
(Indicates performance within rated output range of unit)

* With optional controls.
** If using self-shielded wire, use CV weld output.

Figure 8.7 Intuitive product selection tools simplify your buying decisions if you don't know exactly what you want

you select your products, then you narrow down your geographical location so that you can select the appropriate distributor.

What if you're not quite sure which products to select? There's a Web site solution for that, too (see Figure 8.7).

You begin by first choosing a broad product category. This opens up a page providing detailed tabular information that enables you to compare possible choices based on a detailed set of criteria. Once you make a possible selection, you are taken to a very detailed product page that includes everything (including the price). One of the multiprocess products even has a page that lets you open a product simulator to show you exactly how it works.

Content Marketing Takeaways

Miller thoroughly understands this content marketing lesson: although the Internet provides unique ways to connect with your customers, if you are to make that connection, your content must be vital to your customers' information needs while simultaneously serving your underlying marketing objectives.

If you deliver great stuff, you'll get permission to capture critical data (name, company, and e-mail address), and then to connect with your target buyers regularly. Regular interaction with your best clients will enable you to provide the product and service solutions they really need. By caring about your buyers' information needs first, you can count on a growing stream of devoted customers.

The MillerWelds.com Web site reflects the passion for welding that the company shares with its customers around the world. By having segmented its Web site to appeal to both professional welders and hobbyists, the company demonstrates how well it understands its buyers.

CHAPTER 9

Creative Content Marketing Enables a David to Compete Successfully against Goliaths

There's a small hotel in a very nice place, and it leverages online brains versus big company brawn.

Type of organization: Very small, privately owned hotel and resort company.

Major marketing objective: To dramatically increase reservations made directly from its Web site, rather than through travel agencies, to improve profitability.

Content types:

- Web site
- E-newsletter
- Blog

Unique element: The strength of the content is highly dependent on the visual allure of the site, which turns visitors into virtual vacationers.

Results: A 400 percent increase in online bookings and significant profit improvement.

How does a small, charming hotel compete against corporate giants? Successfully, if you use the Web as effectively as the 'Tween Waters Inn on Captiva Island does. That's what sparked our attention in a September 13, 2007, article in *Gulfcoast Business Review*. Although we had actually stayed at the waterfront boutique hotel, we had no idea how smart its managers (and its marketing partner, Noise Inc.) were about content marketing.

By fully embracing an online content marketing mindset, 'Tween Waters Inn has achieved dramatic bottom-line results through the use of creativity rather than the spending of big bucks. It has established the clear objectives of increasing direct online reservations while building an impressive e-mail marketing list. This drops dollars to the bottom line, because the inn now pays only 6 percent commission on nights booked on its Web site—versus 10 percent on various travel sites.

It's important to add that the team has been brilliant at using ongoing promotional efforts to create a very large e-mail list that is very receptive to its regular messaging. In particular, it has cross-promoted with a new airline, USA3000, to do joint list building.

Southwest Florida is blessed with two beautiful barrier islands: Sanibel and its slightly more remote next-door neighbor, Captiva. The 'Tween Waters Inn is a charming reminder of the gentler last century. But its current marketing needs are all about twenty-first-century global realities.

Although it is a very small hotel (137 rooms and 19 cottages), the 'Tween Waters Inn is located in an idyllic setting. It is the largest hotel in the stable of its parent company, New York–based Rochester Resorts, so it lacks the national clout of the big brands and the big reservation systems. It is also at a local disadvantage because its nearest competitor is three times larger and just three miles down the road. In addition, 'Tween Waters competes with two Ritz-Carltons and a Hyatt resort less than 35 miles away. Of course, it also has to compete with the rest of Florida—Miami, Palm Beach, Orlando, and so on.

With a very limited marketing budget of just 2.5 percent of revenues, 'Tween Waters can't outspend the competition—it has to outflank it.

Transformation of the Old Web Site in 2005 Was Critical to Content Marketing Success

You have only a few seconds to capture your visitors' attention and persuade them to linger on your Web site. You won't make that happen without a combination of outstanding design and compelling content.

For a resort, the appeal of its Web site may derive more from how it looks than from how it reads. The 'Tween Waters Inn is a lovely small hotel beautifully situated on pristine Captiva Island in southwest Florida. Resting between San Carlos Bay and the Gulf of Mexico, the inn is exactly the sort of romantic getaway that refugees from the frozen North seek as an escape from the pressures of work and winter weather. Before deciding on a stay, visitors will want to imagine themselves as guests at the resort before they actually arrive. Elegant design carefully integrated with compelling content conjures up a virtual stay at the resort.

The resort's old Web site (Figure 9.1) was fine for its time, but it became inadequate as time went by. Because it was essentially unchanged since October 1997, it did not measure up to the current standards. What had been more than acceptable in 1997 looked very old-fashioned and out-of-date years later.

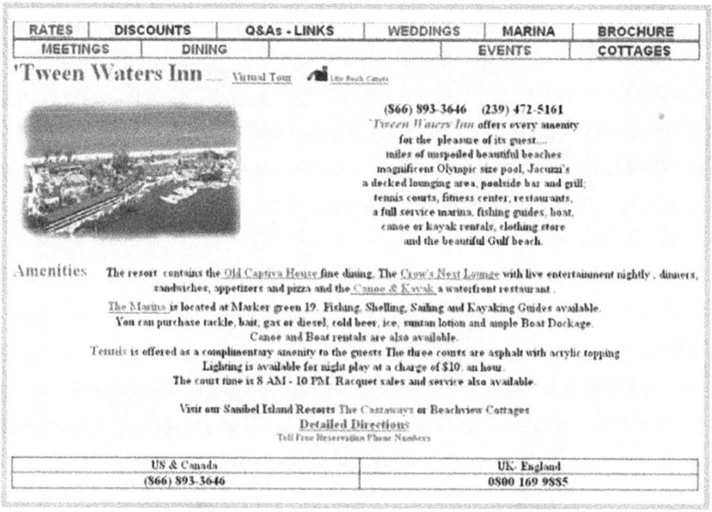

Figure 9.1 The old Web site had content but lacked an elegant design and reservation functionality

This is not to say that the old Web site lacked content. In fact, all the basic content elements from 1997, such as information about weddings, the marina, meetings, and dining, have been posted at the current site. The old Web site also provided a toll-free number front and center so that potential guests could call for reservations. However, what they *couldn't* do was book a reservation directly at the Web site. That became a major disadvantage for the inn.

What the 'Tween Waters Inn had going for it was endless charm and a perfect location on the Gulf of Mexico. It would be a wonderful place for a wedding. But the look and feel of the wedding page on the old Web site (Figure 9.2) failed to convey the charm and beauty that the inn offers.

Back when the Web site was launched, there was just one Ritz-Carlton Naples, and the gulf-front Hyatt Regency Coconut Point had not yet been built. In fact, the Ritz-Carlton Web site was mediocre at best in 1997.

However, in 1997, a compelling Web site wasn't all that important because most travelers were not using the Internet to plan and book travel. In fact, Harris Interactive research showed that only 16

Figure 9.2 The 1997 version of the wedding page failed to show the charm and beauty of the inn

percent of consumers used the Internet at home in 1997, compared to 70 percent in 2006.

Today, travelers surf the Internet before they do any actual surfing anywhere else. According to Pew Research, almost two-thirds of Internet users booked travel online in 2006. Therefore, a well-designed, content-rich Web site is probably the single most valuable travel marketing weapon. This is doubly true if you are a small, charming resort with a limited budget and very little national exposure.

Everything changed with the launch of the inn's new Web site and a creative, but inexpensive, marketing campaign.

Creative Content Marketing Trumps the Big Boys' Budgets

'Tween Waters Inn General Manager Jeff Shuff partnered with a creative agency, Noise Inc., with offices in Wisconsin and Florida. John Sprecher, chief creative officer, worked with Jeff to brainstorm the new Web site (see Figure 9.3).

Figure 9.3 The new Web site captures the sensuous island feeling of both Captiva and the resort

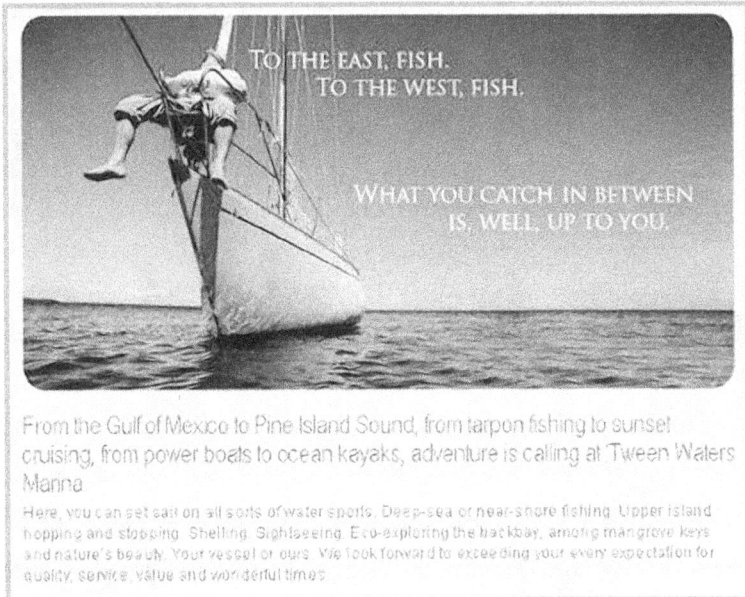

Figure 9.4 The site is organized both by activity and event so that you can find just what you want

The site captures the sensuous island feeling of Captiva and of the resort with 30 content-rich pages. The large, seductive images contain alluring text such as: "The perfect place for the active enthusiast . . . or the enthusiastically inactive."

But the 'Tween Waters Inn site isn't just beautiful. It's also designed to sell, with a reservation link on each and every page. Of course, it's also search engine optimized, taking advantage of Captiva Island's well-deserved reputation as a very special place.

The site is organized by both activity and event (see Figure 9.4). Thus, if you are a boater, a golfer, a tennis player, or just a loafer, you can find out exactly what's available.

If you need to plan an event, 'Tween Waters makes it very easy to envision what's possible through the use of relevant graphical elements and well-written descriptions of the facilities and the staff's capabilities. For example, if you're a bride-to-be, the delightful visuals will help you imagine what it would be like to have your big day on the edge of the Gulf of Mexico at a charming and intimate resort (see Figure 9.5).

Figure 9.5 Delightful visuals on the new wedding page call out to brides-to-be for a destination wedding

The Cost of the Web Site? Just $20,000.
The Return on Investment? Priceless

'Tween Waters Inn has gone from 5 percent online booking in 2005 to 20 percent online booking in 2007. The commission savings go right to the bottom line. Although the hotel doesn't share its financials, you can mentally calculate the positive profit impact of adding 4 percent more net revenue from all those online reservations.

"This year we're running 24 percent ahead in online booking," Jeff says. His immediate goal is to get 30 to 40 percent of reservations via the Web site.[1]

This successful content marketing strategy continues to pay off in very measurable ways. This early-twentieth-century inn has embraced very twenty-first-century content marketing strategies.

Content Marketing Takeaways

You can successfully compete against bigger competitors who can easily outspend you if you leverage every bit of creativity you have with your content marketing strategy.

For a travel destination, a great Web site with outstanding design and compelling content is essential. The quality of its Web site enables the 'Tween Waters Inn to compete successfully with much bigger hotels and resorts. Most importantly, the Web site is designed not just to look good, but to transform visitors into hotel guests.

You can create or recreate a strong brand by integrating online and offline marketing tactics. This integration dramatically increases the overall impact of your content marketing efforts.

By using customer-friendly ways to grow a large e-mail database, you can then communicate meaningfully and consistently with your best customers and prospects. In this example, ongoing communication strengthens the bond with guests, thereby increasing their lifetime value to the hotel.

CHAPTER 10

Finally, a PR Agency That Understands both Boomers and Blogging!

Genuine thought leadership from Fleishman-Hillard, built on blogs with personality and substance.

Type of organization: Huge global public relations firm with highly focused internal practices.

Major marketing objective: Establish thought leadership through targeted blogs that make prospective clients smarter about, and more effective in going after, hot markets.

Content types:

- Blog
- E-newsletter

Unique element: These blogs have strong personalities that match their topics and target readers. They look and sound nothing like the corporate Web site.

Results: Fleishman-Hillard has been able to establish such strong thought leadership in its target areas that it's the natural choice for companies looking for PR help in cracking those markets.

This global PR firm proves that you can use blogging to grow your business. Its people have become both boomer- and youth-marketing mavens.

Boomers Are Still Very Big Business

Baby boomers have been an incredibly important element in society ever since they first showed up in 1946. As the oldest boomers turned 62 in 2008, they began having yet another seismic effect on the economy.

First, they overcrowded elementary schools. Then they overcrowded Washington, D.C., with peace protests. And soon they may overcrowd the social security and Medicare systems.

Boomers were scary when they were young. They may be even scarier now that they're older. One thing's for sure: they will continue to have a dramatic impact for decades to come. And they will almost certainly continue to be among your most important customers.

In the United States, we tend to think of boomers as an American phenomenon. In fact, the population explosion occurred globally—in Canada, Europe, and the Asia-Pacific region as well. Everywhere that young men were off serving their country saw the birthrates soar when they returned home to begin long-delayed families.

For a global PR firm like Fleishman-Hillard, this offers the potential for global thought leadership. A highly motivated group of roughly 100 employees from around the world launched the "FH Boom" practice group in 2006.

Because Fleishman-Hillard had worked with AARP for years, it was clued in to the association's research on the coming boomer tsunami. While most marketers mistakenly underestimated the looming cultural and economic impact of the baby boomers as they neared retirement age, Fleishman-Hillard did not.

Eileen Marcus of the company's Washington, D.C., office had a vision for a boomer-specific practice within the company. Partnering with California-based Carol Orsborn, Ph.D., she launched the FH Boom practice. They understood that they had to break through to a younger generation of marketers who still failed to appreciate the economic impact and buying power of the 78 million baby boomers born between 1946 and 1964. A blog would hit these skeptical marketers where they lived (see Figure 10.1).

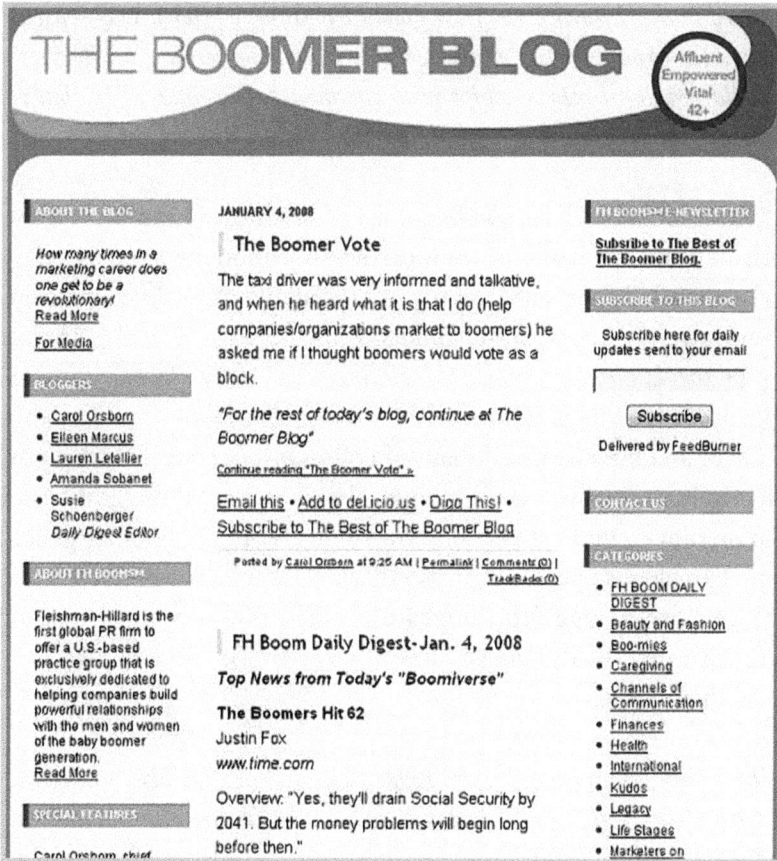

Figure 10.1 The Boomer Blog Web site demonstrates the company's thought leadership

As Orsborn says, "We didn't want to start a practice that didn't have thought leadership, and it was clear that a great blog would be essential to help achieve it."

For content marketers of any age who are trying to stay current with the latest gyrations of this generation, TheBoomerBlog.com from Fleishman-Hillard is a wonderful place to explore.

Unlike so many of their peers, who hide their thought leadership under virtual bushels, the Fleishman-Hillard folks are front and center with an enjoyable and insightful blog. They describe themselves simply and precisely:

Fleishman-Hillard is the first global PR firm to offer a U.S.-based practice group that is exclusively dedicated to helping companies build powerful relationships with the men and women of the baby boomer generation.

Guest blogger Carol Orsborn has now ventured out on her own with an online presence at www.carolorsbornphd.com and as a blogger at www.VibrantNation.com, a site targeting upscale women aged 50 and over. She is also the coauthor of the book *BOOM: Marketing to the Ultimate Power Consumer—the Baby Boomer Woman.* Appropriately, she is described as a thought leader.

Carol and her energized team of colleagues use content marketing effectively to establish their individual and collective thought leadership on how to understand and how to market to the boomer generation. The blog is updated daily, so there is always a reason to check in.

They also manage to integrate the FH Boom brand inside the blog with the "Daily Digest" (see Figure 10.2).

As they put it:

This time, smart marketers, regardless of their age, are joining in with their own "aha's," courageously overturning the status quo that reflexively favored younger consumers in order to connect with our era's largest and most lucrative segment: men and women 42+.

The Boomer Blog is our solution, capturing our thoughts, discoveries, and growing intelligence of a multi-generational team as we grapple with, report on, and respond to the barrage of daily research, case histories, and news that is rushing to catch up with this fast-moving generation.

TheBoomerBlog.com contains loads of invaluable content on the "affluent, empowered, vital 42+" boomers, such as:

- The FH Boom "Daily Digest" to keep marketers current on the latest in boomer coverage online
- Buying patterns

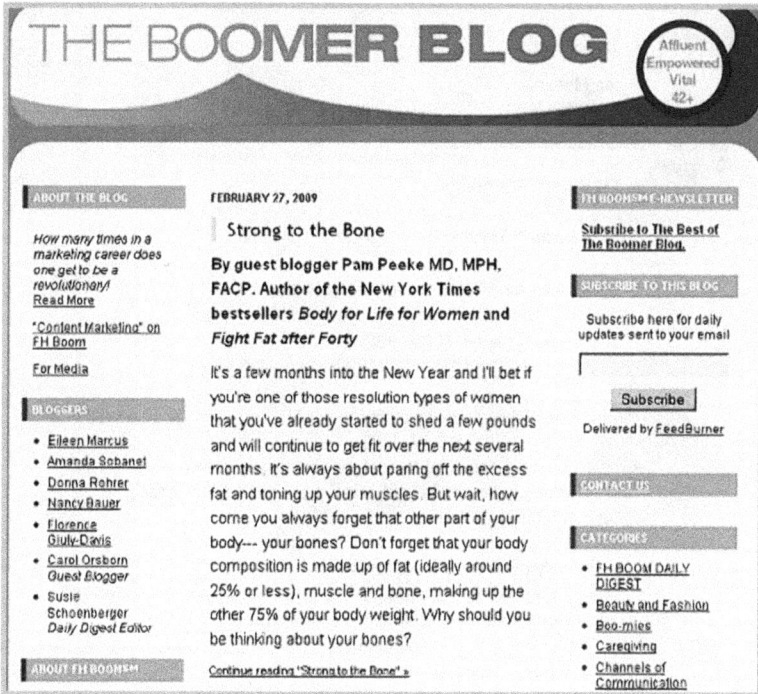

THE BOOMER BLOG — Affluent Empowered Vital 42+

ABOUT THE BLOG

How many times in a marketing career does one get to be a revolutionary! Read More

"Content Marketing" on FH Boom

For Media

BLOGGERS

- Eileen Marcus
- Amanda Sobanet
- Donna Rohrer
- Nancy Bauer
- Florence Giuly-Davis
- Carol Orsborn *Guest Blogger*
- Susie Schoenberger *Daily Digest Editor*

ABOUT FH BOOM™

FEBRUARY 27, 2009

Strong to the Bone

By guest blogger Pam Peeke MD, MPH, FACP. Author of the New York Times bestsellers *Body for Life for Women* **and** *Fight Fat after Forty*

It's a few months into the New Year and I'll bet if you're one of those resolution types of women that you've already started to shed a few pounds and will continue to get fit over the next several months. It's always about paring off the excess fat and toning up your muscles. But wait, how come you always forget that other part of your body— your bones? Don't forget that your body composition is made up of fat (ideally around 25% or less), muscle and bone, making up the other 75% of your body weight. Why should you be thinking about your bones?

Continue reading "Strong to the Bone"

FH BOOM™ E-NEWSLETTER

Subscribe to The Best of The Boomer Blog.

SUBSCRIBE TO THIS BLOG

Subscribe here for daily updates sent to your email

Subscribe

Delivered by FeedBurner

CONTACT US

CATEGORIES

- FH BOOM DAILY DIGEST
- Beauty and Fashion
- Boo-mies
- Caregiving
- Channels of Communication

Figure 10.2 The FH Boom Daily Digest delivers the latest news from the "Boomiverse"

- The unique nature of boomer women
- Boomers and the printed word
- Case studies on successful approaches to influence/benefit boomers—much of this is very definitely content marketing
- Links to boomer-specific online resources

The FH Boom team also reaches several thousand RSS subscribers who receive daily updates (see Figure 10.3).

The Web site's striking, somewhat edgy look was driven by the boomer members, who had to convince the younger IT and design folks at the firm that a stodgy, boring look wouldn't be appropriate to appeal to Gen X or Y marketers. And it wouldn't reflect the vital, energetic nature of the boom generation.

To contact:

Eileen Marcus
202-828-8886
marcuse@fleishman.com

FH Boom^{SM} Offerings:

The FH Boom^{SM} Training, Keynotes and Consulting

- Training for marketers, senior leadership and executives on connecting positively with boomers based on the latest research
- Keynotes, speeches and retreats on related topics

The FH Boom^{SM} Communications Inventory

A review process designed to analyze campaigns already existing or on the boards in light of our proprietary intelligence about marketing-to-boomers

- Identify overlooked possibilities and missed opportunities for initiatives directed towards boomers
- Customer 'persona' analysis, development and implementation by segmentation
- Motivational analysis and prescription: illuminating the interface between boomer responses to life events and resulting shifts in consumption and value-based behaviors and attitudes in light of the latest adult development and ritual studies theory

---

Figure 10.3 The FH Boom team makes it easy for marketers to understand what it does and how to contact team members in order to learn more

While they are busy generating a treasure trove of insights on the biggest generation, the FH Boom practice within Fleishman-Hillard doesn't forget that it also needs to do some serious rain-making. The blog provides a complete range of information on the services that FH Boom provides.

It does a great job of highlighting FH Boom achievements and capabilities. TheBoomerBlog.com definitely makes it easier for blog visitors and RSS subscribers to take the next step—to become clients. In fact, Orsborn notes that the team can directly track new business from prospects who started out as regular subscribers.

Three Big Boomer Aha's

If you're marketing to boomers (and/or if you are a boomer yourself), you need to understand their social and economic impact. Here are three important aha's from Carol Orsborn:

- Eight out of ten boomers are online every day.
- Eight out of ten boomers say that they have no plans to retire.
- Most boomers have no idea how popular they are going to be with employers as the "baby bust" generation behind them leaves huge holes within organizations.

Blog-Based Thought Leadership for the Youth Market, Too

Illustrating that it understands the direct connection between blogging and thought leadership in multiple markets, Fleishman-Hillard also tackles the tech-savvy younger generation with its NextGreatThing (NGT) blog (see Figure 10.4). This is the creation of Alan Rambam, who leads the company's youth marketing team.

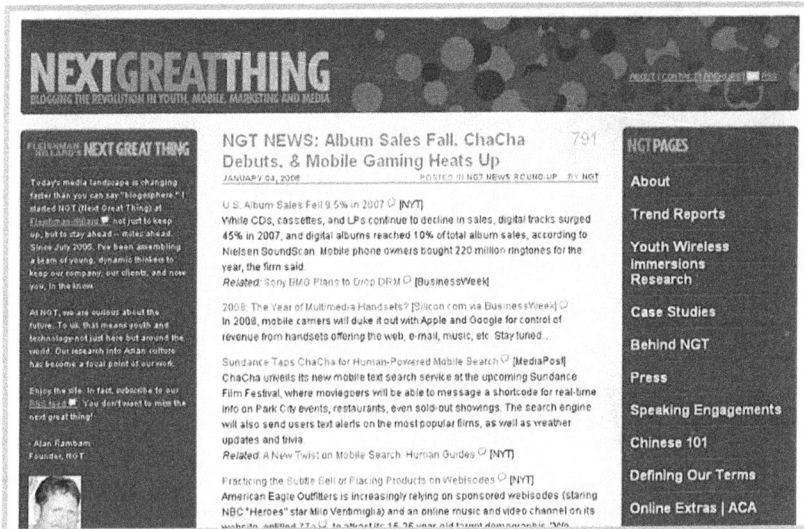

Figure 10.4 Targeting a younger, tech-savvy generation with the NextGreatThing blog

Here is how he describes what NGT is all about:

Today's media landscape is changing faster than you can say "blogosphere." I started NGT at Fleishman-Hillard not just to keep up, but to stay ahead—miles ahead. Since July 2005, I've been assembling a team of young, dynamic thinkers to keep our company, our clients, and now you, in the know.

At NGT, we are curious about the future. To us, that means youth and technology—not just here, but around the world. Our research into Asian culture has become a focal point of our work.

NextGreatThing.com couldn't be more different from The-BoomerBlog.com in the topics it covers, but it shares the enthusiasm, depth, and utility of its corporate cousin. NGT offers plenty of timely and insightful content, including trend reports, case studies, research, and an incredibly cool "Chinese 101" section (see Figure 10.5). This is really great stuff.

Once again, Fleishman-Hillard has established thought leadership within a universe that is critical for marketers to understand. It

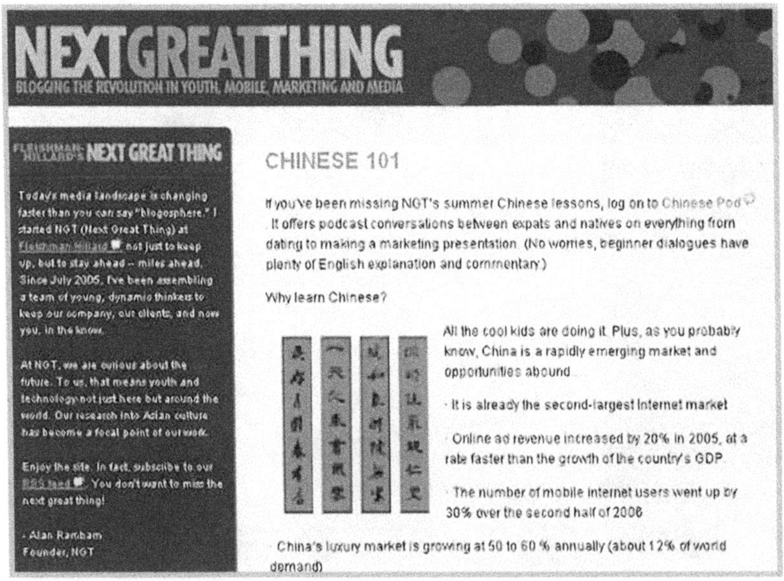

Figure 10.5 An incredibly cool "Chinese 101" section is included

has used a blog-based content marketing strategy to create thought leadership that ultimately drives revenue.

The Bottom Line

If you need to stay current on the "never say die" baby boom generation, TheBoomerBlog.com is the place to go.

If you want to understand youth culture, you need to hang out at the NextGreatThing.

Even better, if you're looking for a blogging role model, these are great ones to emulate. Fleishman-Hillard has precisely focused on illuminating supremely important markets. Not only are the blogs informative and insightful, but they are also fun to read.

As Carol Orsborn sums it up:

It is essential that our firm's people be perceived as thought leaders. This elevates all of our practice groups. We are demonstrating that we really do have detailed knowledge and that we are deeply committed to our markets.

Content Marketing Takeaways

Giving away genuinely valuable content that helps potential clients market to boomers and to the millennial generation ultimately brings business to Fleishman-Hillard. As the firm has demonstrated, an informative, insightful, and interesting blog may be an organization's single best way to develop thought leadership.

Define a content area that will benefit from regular reporting and commentary. Provide plenty of substance. Don't be afraid to take a stand. You need to stand for something.

Make sure that your blogging team is passionate about the content that is covered. Be timely, and update your posts frequently.

Make it easy for visitors to subscribe. Offer plenty of information that demonstrates your capabilities and encourages a phone call or e-mail to make the first step toward becoming a customer.

CHAPTER 11

How to Create a World-Class Web Site for a Superb Nonprofit—without Breaking the Bank

A content-rich Web site and newsletter perfectly reflect the David Lawrence Center's mission: "restoring and rebuilding lives."

Type of organization: A nonprofit mental health and substance abuse facility offering affordable services to everyone in need.

Major marketing objectives:

- To encourage prospective clients to take the next step and seek help directly, by phone or in person.
- To make a persuasive case for supporting the center as a donor or volunteer.

Content types:

- Web site
- E-newsletter
- Print newsletter

Unique element: Shifting of major resources to online marketing in order to replace limited advertising content with in-depth, client-centric, actionable content.

Results: A dramatic 200 percent increase in the number of monthly page views on the new Web site.

Connecting with Prospective Clients and Donors through Rich Online Content

Traditional marketing avenues have become both more expensive and less effective as basic buyer behavior has changed dramatically. This new reality requires a dramatic shift in the marketing mindset within nonprofits just as much as it does in business organizations. In fact, as nonprofits face tough economic times, they must make the most of every marketing dollar. As the David Lawrence Center illustrates, a content-rich Web site and e-newsletter can make a dramatic and measurable difference in marketing results while staying within very limited budgets.

Fortunately, a shift to content marketing enables resource-constrained nonprofits to connect with their clients effectively, efficiently, and inexpensively. By providing their current and prospective clients with relevant and compelling information, nonprofits can make a powerful connection with these clients before they ever pick up the phone or walk through the door. This is critically important for clients who are understandably reluctant to take the first step toward getting help.

Moreover, engaging with potential donors and volunteers online is vital for an organization like the David Lawrence Center that counts heavily on active community support and participation. The same warm, positive messaging and imagery that appeal to prospective clients exert an equally powerful pull on the generous community members who enable the center to thrive.

The David Lawrence Center's outstanding Web site and newsletter demonstrate just how well content marketing can work (see Figure 11.1).

The David Lawrence Center is a nonprofit mental health and substance abuse facility that provides affordable services for anyone in

Figure 11.1 The colorful new David Lawrence Center Web site is all about positive outcomes

need. Located in Naples, Florida, the 40-year-old center serves all of Collier County.

It is the only not-for-profit treatment center in Collier County providing affordable mental health and substance abuse services. In addition to helping children with behavioral, emotional, and substance abuse challenges, the center provides counseling and rehabilitative services to adults in crisis and individuals with persistent mental illness. Each year, 16,000 individuals take advantage of more than 50 prevention, intervention, and treatment services.

The center's Web site derives its power primarily from great thinking and design rather than from a big budget. What's even more impressive is that the new Web site was driven by a very small team: the communications director, Trista Meister, in partnership with a local Web development firm, Exploritech.

Old Site Better than Many, but Limited and a Bit Gloomy

Actually, the old Web site wasn't bad (see Figure 11.2). In fact, it was much better than many Web sites that have been created to promote "marketing professionals." But it took only limited advantage of the power that a great Web site could bring. The old Web site failed to provide comprehensive information about the wide range of services offered by the David Lawrence Center (see Figure 11.3).

In addition, although it contained a few fairly strong visual images, those images represented the sorrow of mental illness or addiction rather than the joy of recovery. For example, in Figure 11.2 we just see a pair of somewhat haunted-looking eyes at the top of the page. A very brief description of the center's substance abuse programs follows. There is only a slight suggestion of positive out-

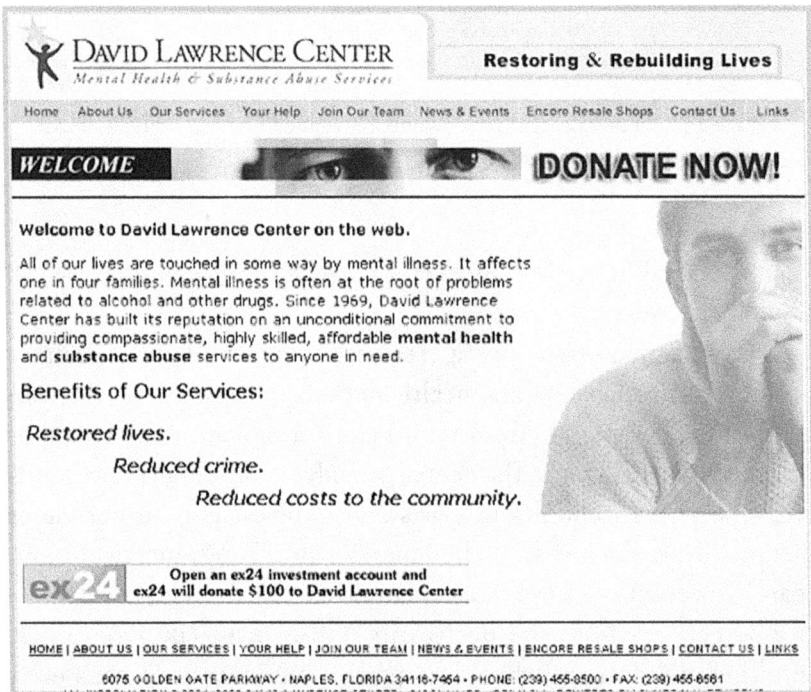

Figure 11.2 The old site was not bad, but was a bit gloomy and light on content

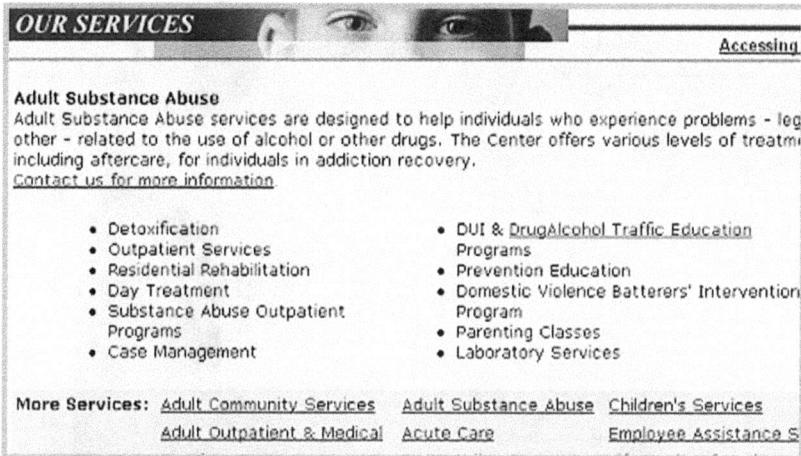

OUR SERVICES

Accessing

Adult Substance Abuse
Adult Substance Abuse services are designed to help individuals who experience problems - leg other - related to the use of alcohol or other drugs. The Center offers various levels of treatm including aftercare, for individuals in addiction recovery.
Contact us for more information

- Detoxification
- Outpatient Services
- Residential Rehabilitation
- Day Treatment
- Substance Abuse Outpatient Programs
- Case Management

- DUI & DrugAlcohol Traffic Education Programs
- Prevention Education
- Domestic Violence Batterers' Intervention Program
- Parenting Classes
- Laboratory Services

More Services: Adult Community Services   Adult Substance Abuse   Children's Services
Adult Outpatient & Medical   Acute Care   Employee Assistance S

Figure 11.3 The old site offered only bullet points and brief descriptions rather than a meaningful level of detail

comes. There are no success stories to illustrate just how clients could benefit from taking advantage of the many programs offered at the David Lawrence Center.

New Web Site Adds Content and Color to Engage Visitors Quickly and Comprehensively

The new Web site and e-newsletter take a completely different approach (see Figure 11.4). Not only do they add more powerful visual images with vivid colors, but they also share with us a host of stories that celebrate positive outcomes for patients young and old. Prospective patients will feel that they may well be able to achieve comparable success in dealing with their individual problems.

This is equally important for donors and volunteers who want to be part of a successful nonprofit operation. The consistent message that is delivered both verbally and visually is that contributing either money or time to the David Lawrence Center will enable many more wonderful outcomes for the young people and adults who take advantage of its services.

Here's why the new site is so successful:

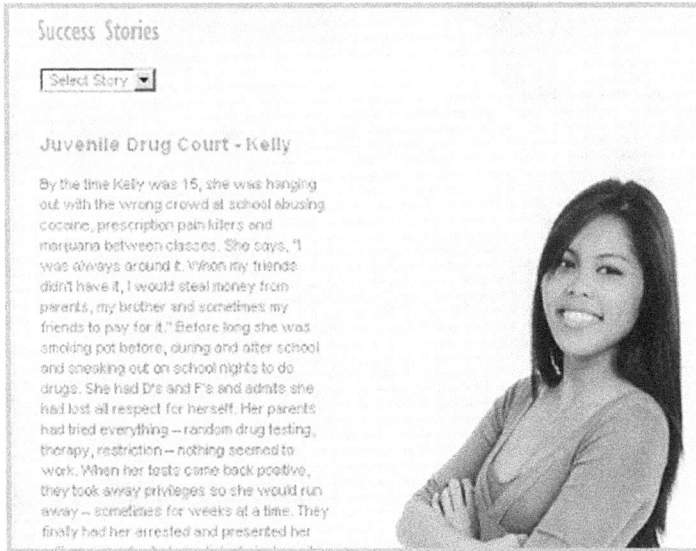

Figure 11.4 Upbeat success stories warm up the new Web site

1. The pervasive theme of the site is that successful outcomes can be found when you seek treatment at the David Lawrence Center. This is very important because individuals who are seeking help may well have hit rock bottom. When they arrive at the site, it's uplifting to view positive results.

2. The Web site offers comprehensive information on all the services provided by the David Lawrence Center. The broad accessibility of information makes it very comfortable to take the first step of asking for help. Visitors with serious problems can discover likely solutions online before they ever have to talk to someone on the phone or in person.

3. Powerful and positive visuals pervade the Web site. For individuals who may well be surrounded by clouds of gloom and sadness, these images offer a wonderful antidote.

4. Dozens of success stories reinforce the idea that the David Lawrence Center can provide assistance, not in the abstract, but in the real world. Success stories are tied to specific programs, giving them even more relevance. Brief lead-ins with good visuals and strong headlines take you to a page dedicated to the great outcomes achieved by the center's patients.

The site fully utilizes the power of storytelling to reinforce the strength of the center's services.

5. Just like a commercial Web site, the David Lawrence Center's online home makes it very easy to take the next step by calling just the right number or sending an e-mail asking for help. On the old site, you had to work pretty hard to figure out how to take the next action.

6. Visitors are also offered the opportunity to make a donation, just as they had been on the old site. But the rich visual and the call to action are both more positive and less intrusive than they had been (see Figure 11.5). The "Your Help" page describes in detail all the ways in which community members can offer help. They are also offered the chance to volunteer. And who wouldn't want to volunteer after learning about the many wonderful things the David Lawrence Center does for the greater Naples community?

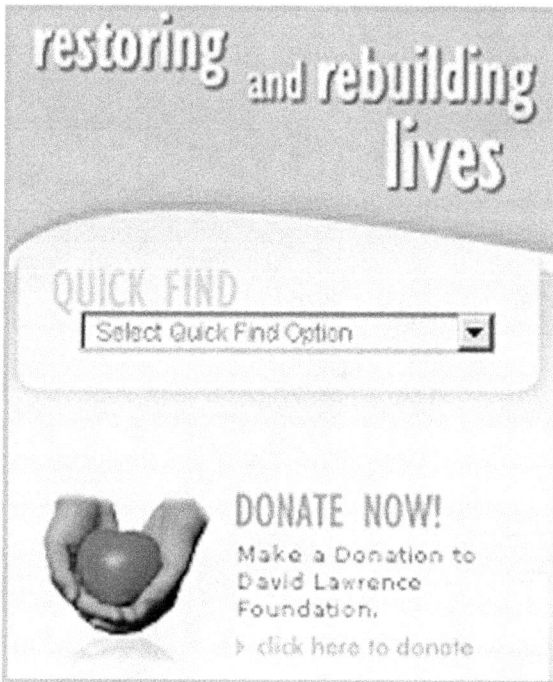

Figure 11.5 They make it easy and appealing to donate money or just time

Newsletter in Print and Electronic Form Extends the Reach of the Web Site

The positive imagery and language of the Web site are carried through in the monthly newsletter (see Figure 11.6). The lead story in the October 2008 edition tells how the center was able to keep a suicidal teen out of harm's way. The newsletter keeps interested community members up-to-date on what's going well—or what's not going so well—with the center. Thus, it describes some serious funding challenges related to some of the center's children's services while sharing the good news about its ability to expand many of its children's outpatient services.

Relevant e-newsletter content may be the most cost-effective way to strengthen the relationship with those folks who really care about

Figure 11.6 The positive imagery and language of the Web site is carried through in the monthly e-newsletter

the success of the David Lawrence Center. For a resource-con-strained nonprofit, e-newsletters enable regular personal outreach that would be impossible in person or on the phone. Of course, the e-newsletters also link to the Web site, generating a consistent spike in visitors when the e-newsletter hits cyberspace.

The Most Cost-Effective Marketing Tool Ever Deployed by the David Lawrence Center

Before embarking on the transformation, Trista Meister did exten-sive research online. She examined a wide range of health-related sites, many of which were awful, but many of which illustrated the path that the David Lawrence Center's Web site should take. After interviewing many potential Web developers, she settled on Exploritech because it understood the importance of content—and how to integrate that content with powerful visual elements. Even better, Exploritech was affordable.

The one-time cost of creating the new Web site was approxi-mately 50 percent of what the center spent each year on Yellow Pages advertising. But the ongoing monthly cost is very modest. Because the center's Yellow Pages advertising is so fragmented, it has been very difficult to determine any kind of return on this investment. Because the Web site is very measurable, the center is able to track exactly how it is delivering tangible results.

Visitors Increased Modestly, but Page Views Increased Dramatically

By transforming its site from a content-challenged and somewhat depressing Web presence into a client-centric, content-rich, and beautifully designed resource, the David Lawrence Center has increased its page views by 198 percent. It has gone from just over 16,000 monthly page views to almost 49,000.

The number of visitors also increased, but not as dramatically—just 14 percent. This is not too surprising because the center is lim-ited in its ability to promote the site. Nonetheless, traffic did grow. But what stands out is that the average visitor spent much more time and viewed many more pages on the new site. There's only one reason for that: relevant and valuable content kept visitors on the site and encouraged them to stay and explore.

The center's newsletters provide a natural outreach that reminds the community of the great work that the center does—and of the significant challenges it faces in serving some of the most vulnerable citizens in the region. The image-rich and colorful newsletter design matches that of the Web site, reinforcing the center's branding.

Thus, the David Lawrence Center achieved one of its most important objectives: to demonstrate online how it could help solve tough mental and substance abuse challenges—before its clients ever called or came for a visit. Excellent content marketing worked exactly as it should to build a trusted relationship with prospective clients and donors before they ever decided to commit to seeking help or offering it.

Content Marketing Takeaways

You must have a thorough comprehension of your customers and what is most important to them. If you do not understand the problems and challenges that they face, you cannot hope to create content that is truly relevant to them. Trista and her colleagues have a very clear understanding of what is most important to their clients and to their donors. This knowledge informed every aspect of the site.

Only content that is intrinsically valuable to your customers will work as a core component of your content marketing strategy. Building on their understanding of their clients' needs, Trista and her team were able to create content that showed just how they could help their clients achieve positive outcomes for a broad range of mental, emotional, and substance abuse issues.

A comprehensive content marketing strategy may be either a complete or a partial replacement for traditional advertising and marketing. Such a strategy can be both more effective and less expensive than doing things the old-fashioned way.

Great design adds significant value to content marketing by making it more accessible, more appealing, and more actionable for your customers.

Great content marketing is really about developing the right mindset without needing a huge dollar investment. In this case, the shared mindset between Trista and the Exploritech team demonstrates that a relatively small investment in content marketing can result in a big payoff.

Relevant and valuable content is just the first step in turning a prospect or visitor into a customer. You must then make it easy for that person to buy. Just like a commercial Web site, the David Lawrence Center's online home makes it very easy for people to take the next step by calling just the right number or sending an e-mail to ask for help or to offer donations of money or time.

CHAPTER 12

Solopreneur Sagas—Even Microbusinesses Make Content Marketing Pay Off

Three very different owners of small businesses are delivering content just as creatively as—perhaps more creatively than— many of their peers in much larger organizations.

Type of organization: Single-person businesses.

Major marketing objectives: To use content marketing to increase visibility, credibility, and revenues.

Content types:

- Web sites
- Blogs
- In-person content marketing

Unique element: Content marketing has replaced traditional marketing for each business.

Results: Each business has received a tangible return on its marketing investment.

An author, a kitchen designer, and a seller of smoothies are all making the most of limited budgets to increase their revenues and grow their businesses. Although they're using a diverse combination of online and in-person techniques, they share one common thread: each entrepreneur is providing content that makes it easier for his target audience to make a positive buying decision. In each case, the entrepreneur is substituting big doses of creativity for a big budget.

Canadian Single Mom May Beat the Odds to Become the Next J.K. Rowling

A multipronged content marketing strategy—online and in person—is helping this self-published author sell books.

Creating a successful business book is difficult. Creating a bestselling work of fiction is even more challenging. Creating a blockbuster children's fantasy novel is probably the most difficult of all.

But, thanks to equal doses of determination, creativity, and showmanship, Kamilla Reid of Edmonton, Alberta, is starting to sell a lot of books.

Her fantasy novel, *The Questory of Root Karbunkulus*, is the first in a series of six. It involves the ultimate scavenger hunt by 14-year-old Root, whose very life may be at stake in the adventure. The mystical quest involves a cast of fantastical characters, beasts, and perilous situations.

Kamilla's eclectic background ranges from banking to theater, and now to the writing of children's fiction. For the first time in her life, Kamilla believes that she's doing exactly the right thing. Although she's up against some very steep odds, the early results of her content marketing efforts look very promising indeed.

Kamilla is working with BookSurge, which is owned by Amazon.com, to produce the book. In fact, BookSurge featured Kamilla in its November 2007 e-newsletter. BookSurge works with authors by taking their manuscripts and turning them into professionally finished books that are printed on demand using state of the art digital technology. Authors' books are automatically placed on Amazon.com and made available to the authors at very affordable prices.

Going Way Beyond Amazon.com

The BookSurge connection gives the *Questory* an automatic place within Amazon.com and makes it eligible for all of Amazon's special merchandising and marketing opportunities. Perhaps more importantly for Kamilla, Amazon will also sell volume quantities of its books to its authors at a very low price. This is perfect for Kamilla because it gives her complete freedom to sell and market the book in any way she chooses. In fact, she is going way beyond what a traditional author would do to promote a book. She is also going way beyond Amazon.com.

Doing What Ernest Hemingway Couldn't or Wouldn't Have Done

With a small budget, you can't hope to replicate the efforts that the publishers of Harry Potter made on behalf of their blockbuster hit. However, as Kamilla has proven, you can make things happen with a big dollop of creativity and intelligent use of all the tools available on the Web. Her highly imaginative in-person and online content marketing has already taken her well beyond the ranks of typical first-time novelists. She has begun to build a buzz for her book by thinking way outside the binding. She's done several innovative things that may very well take her from Edmonton to New York City to the rest of the world.

Kamilla did not sit demurely behind a desk ready to sign books for parents and children. Instead, she invented a mini-fantasy drama with all kinds of mystical things going on (see Figure 12.1). She

Figure 12.1 Kamilla created a mystical miniature play that replaced traditional book signings

wore a special red cloak that plays a big role in the book. She had magic. She had a big, creepy statue. She had mystical mist. It was only after setting the stage brilliantly that she did a wonderfully dramatic reading from the book. The kids who were lucky enough to be there absolutely loved it. Best of all, Kamilla sold more than 1,000 books in just seven weeks.

Various types of videos (Figure 12.2) are a major component of the *Questory* Web site (RootKarbunkulus.com). Here's what you'll find:

- A fun video of the book launch that fully conveys the excitement of the kids who had the good fortune to be part of the event.
- An exciting video book trailer that does a great job of capturing the spirit of this fantastical novel. You wouldn't know it, but Kamilla shot the video in her basement. And for those of you who know the story of Baby Einstein, that's exactly

Figure 12.2 Vibrant videos bring the book, its author, and its young fans to life

the way it started—on a bare-bones budget, with the first video shot in the basement.

- Video captures of television interviews that show Kamilla dressed in the famous red cloak talking about the book, sharing her enthusiasm, and building awareness among thousands of TV watchers in her home province.

Figure 12.3 Kamilla's Web site creates a sense of drama that captures the essence of the book

The look and feel of the site itself (Figure 12.3) are absolutely wonderful. The site conveys a sense of drama and mystery, and hints of the secret world that we won't know about until we start reading the book. It's exactly the kind of mysterious world that will draw kids in for the first novel—and probably for the next five as well. The *Questory* world looks just scary enough to intrigue kids, but not so frightening as to put them off. In addition to the look of the site, there is an accompanying audio track that reinforces the element of mystery and drama.

You can find complete reference information on the Web site about all things *Questory*:

- A sample chapter
- The complete storyline
- A complete list of the characters (both human and nonhuman)
- All the new words you'll need to learn if you are to understand the book
- A fascinating bio of Kamilla, complete with pictures
- A press section—entitled buzz—that shows all the great coverage she's gotten
- Plus—a store where you can buy the book

Kamilla Reid is selling books, making money, building buzz, and establishing a foundation that will make it possible for her to achieve bestseller status. In fact, her creative content marketing efforts generated sales of 1,000 books in just seven weeks. That's more than most first-time authors ever sell in a lifetime. In fact, only 5 percent of books published in the United States each year sell more than 1,000 copies.

Is it certain that she will achieve her bestseller ambitions? No. But we certainly wouldn't bet against her.

Kitchen Design Expert's Three-Pronged Web Strategy

This solopreneur takes word of mouth to the Web.

In many ways, Ann Porter, the owner of Kitchen Studio of Naples, Florida, is a traditional solopreneur. At the same time, she is also a compelling and creative content marketer. Ann manages to maintain three separate online channels that connect her to current and future customers.

As a traditional solo practitioner, she is an indefatigable networker who relies very much on word of mouth to promote her kitchen design business. She belongs to a number of professional and community organizations that connect her to business and consumer prospects. In other words, she does all the things that smart small business owners must do to succeed by connecting one-on-one.

Like many small business owners, she has found that other forms of traditional marketing have been ineffective in building her business. For example, she advertised with the major lifestyle magazines in the greater Naples area, but she saw very little return on her substantial investment. She also advertised in the Yellow Pages, but found that the caliber of the responses did not balance the cost of the advertising. So . . . she has taken it to the Web.

An Integrated Approach

Ann's three-pronged online strategy includes a standard, well-designed Web site, her own blog, and a blog that she writes on the *Naples Daily News* Web site. In each case, she does a great job with text and graphics, clearly explaining what she can accomplish for her clients.

Ann launched her Web site, KitchenStudioOfNaples.com (see Figure 12.4), in 2002—since then, it has remained virtually unchanged. It is visually appealing and reflects her strong aesthetic sense. It shows her sense of style and the type of kitchen she would design. Like

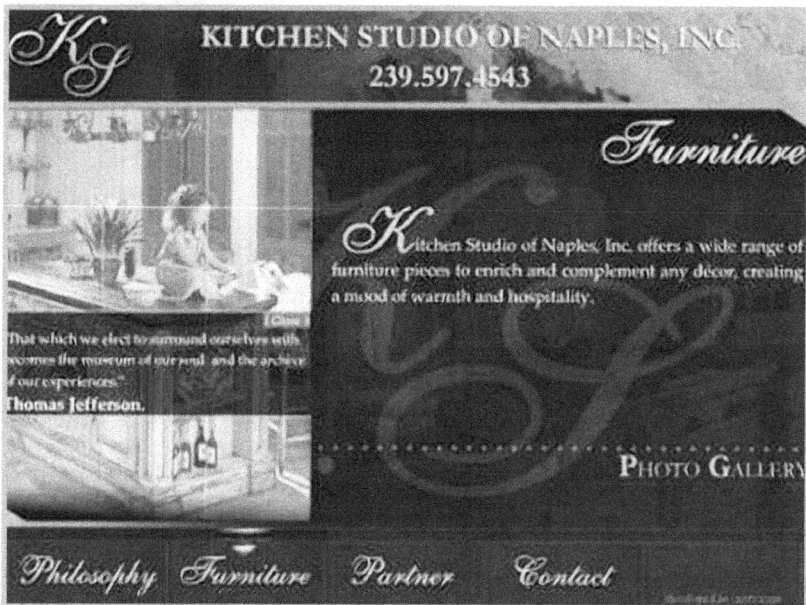

Figure 12.4 Ann's elegant Web site, with its rich colors and imagery, reflects her design sense

many small business owners, she hired a talented but transitory Web developer who no longer lives in the area. What's even more challenging is that the Web site was built using Flash, which makes for great visuals but requires expert Web designers to maintain and update. So she has begun to rethink the Web site in terms of a non-Flash design. She knows that optimizing search engine marketing results will be a future priority.

Ann recently launched her blog, KitchAnn Style (Figure 12.5), using the content management system inside WordPress, which has gone well beyond its blogging roots to become a complete Web site creation tool. Ann has done 100 percent of the work herself. Her

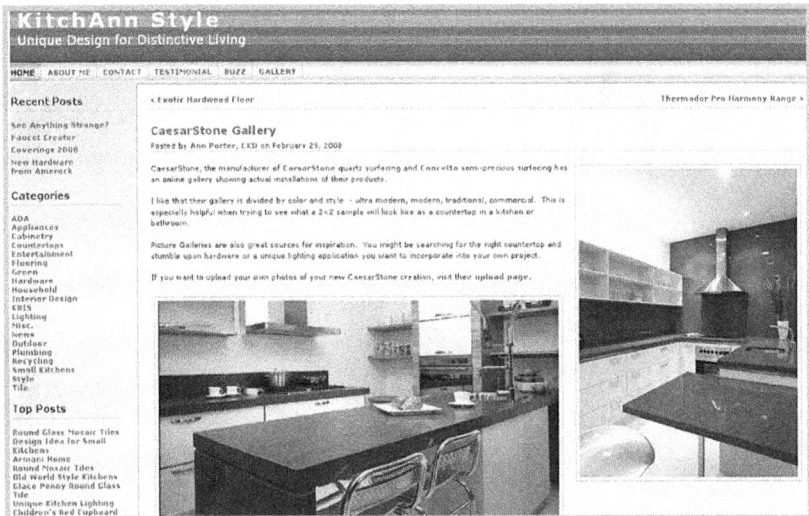

Figure 12.5 Ann's timely, interactive blog offers great design tips and visual examples

version of WordPress is absolutely free. Her blog requires time and thought, but no money.

Ann's blog has a clean, sleek look. It's well organized by category, top posts, and links to external design resources. She uses excellent-quality visuals to illustrate the points she makes about kitchen design issues (see Figure 12.6). Both current and prospective customers will find her blog useful and informative.

Figure 12.6 The WordPress-based blog is well organized and highly visual

In a recent post, Ann illustrated the use of glass panels in the kitchen with the example of a gorgeous contemporary Stuttgart apartment. Because the visual makes the point so well, she didn't need a lot of explanatory text.

Traffic to Ann's blog has been increasing steadily. In fact, it is significantly expanding the word of mouth that has been so much a part of her in-person marketing strategy. Ann relates the story of a builder she recently met. He had actually visited her blog before she had time to follow up on that first meeting. Not surprisingly, he was impressed. Her substantive and well-designed blog gave her instant credibility with the builder after just one meeting.

Pioneers in the User-Generated Content Revolution

The *Naples Daily News*, like many newspapers around the country, is experimenting with user-contributed editorial material. One of its most fruitful experiments has been its user-generated blog section (see Figure 12.7). Ann was an early contributor to the section with her Ask Ann weekly blog post.

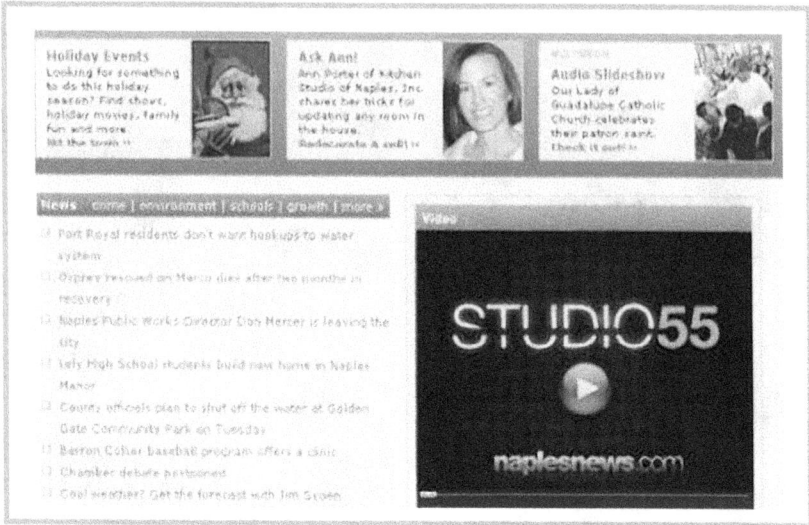

Figure 12.7 The *Naples Daily News* blog reaches more than 200,000 visitors

According to *Naples Daily News* statistics, its weekly reach, both in print and online, is 215,460. Its average household income is $87,482. More than 80 percent of its readers own their own homes. That's an ideal target audience against which to build a personal and professional brand.

Ann is beginning to receive slow but steady increases in referral traffic as visitors go directly from the *Naples Daily News* to her blog. This is a perfect example of creative content marketing and, in this case, article marketing. She offers solid kitchen and home design advice to *Naples Daily News* readers with a fresh post each week. She reaches an affluent audience through a trusted newspaper without having to advertise or count on the newspaper to pick up her press releases.

Multiple Avenues Pay Off

Ann Porter has maximized a limited budget, done a lot of hard work, exhibited plenty of creativity, and developed a consistent approach in order to establish a steadily improving content marketing strategy. The net effect: she has global reach, instant credibility, and a 24/7 sales presence. Word-of-mouth marketing is essential. Taking word of mouth to the Web is making a measurable difference for Kitchen Studio of Naples.

Simple Visual Blog Delivers Dollars for Maui Wowi Franchisee

Small can be beautiful and profitable when it comes to content marketing.

Although he comes from a sophisticated billion-dollar media company background, Mitch York has left that complex baggage behind. On the Web, he keeps it simple. In fact, he delivers just the right amount of information—most of it visual—on his Web site, CoffeesAndSmoothies.com.

Mitch learned from experience that two key factors were making it more difficult than it needed to be to sell his smoothie services:

- Prospects weren't exactly sure what his company did.
- Prospects didn't feel comfortable working with an organization that they didn't know or trust.

His blog has solved those problems. He now has credibility, and his offerings are easy to understand. He has gotten content marketing exactly right, and for the right price—free!

When prospects arrive at Mitch's blog (CoffeesAndSmooth ies.blogspot.com), they find pictures of happy customers enjoying their smoothies, coffee concoctions, or hot chocolate in a festive environment (see Figures 12.8 and 12.9). Simple captions show the names of customers, such as St. John's University, City College of New York, Bailey Arboretum, and the Fashion Institute of Technology, along with tidbits about the events. The visuals make it clear not only that Mitch is for real, but that his customers have a lot of fun while enjoying his smoothie socials.

Figure 12.8 The Maui Wowi blog offers a visual demonstration of the company's credibility

On the right side of the blog, Mitch describes exactly what his company does and how to get in touch with him.

Mitch's Web site looks great. It tells us exactly what we need to know about what Mitch does and why we can trust him to do it. Wouldn't it be great if some big-time marketers understood content marketing as well as Mitch York does?

Mitch built his blog for free using Google's Blogger. He proves that content marketing can be simple, visual, effective, and free. Check out his site—and, if you live in the New York City area, you may want to hire his company to liven up your workplace with a tropical event!

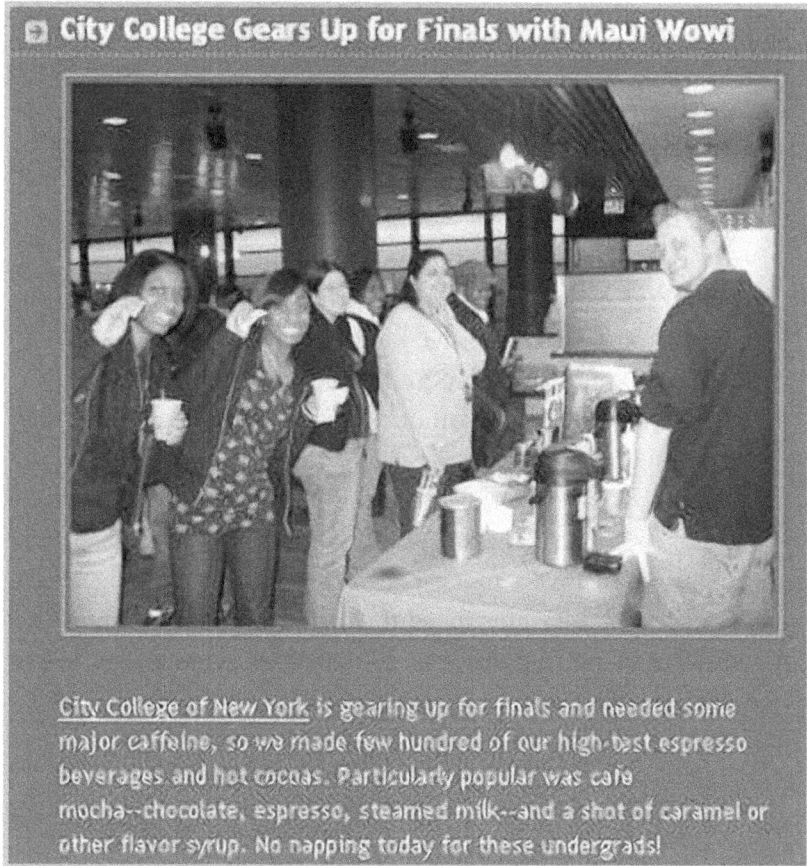

> **City College Gears Up for Finals with Maui Wowi**
>
> City College of New York is gearing up for finals and needed some major caffeine, so we made few hundred of our high-test espresso beverages and hot cocoas. Particularly popular was cafe mocha--chocolate, espresso, steamed milk--and a shot of caramel or other flavor syrup. No napping today for these undergrads!

Figure 12.9 Mitch's blog illustrates that you don't have to be huge to be a big hit

Content Marketing Takeaways

Kamilla, Ann, and Mitch demonstrate the importance of effective content marketing for even very small businesses. For each of them, content marketing plays a vital role because they don't have a sales force or a marketing department or a big budget for traditional advertising.

These creative solopreneurs demonstrate that you can establish credibility with your target audience through effective content marketing strategies. Because their situations are so different, the type of content they provide is also very different:

- Children's author Kamilla Reid is creating an online and in-person fantasy world in which her prospective readers can immerse themselves.
- Ann Porter needs to build the perception that she is an established expert in her field, with the ability to deliver on sophisticated and expensive kitchen projects.
- Mitch York must paint an online picture of the types of events he delivers by promoting actual events that prove that his company is for real.

For each of these solopreneurs, the initial content marketing investment was relatively modest. Better yet, their ongoing investment is very, very low. They need to keep putting in the time—but not additional marketing dollars—to make their content marketing strategies pay off.

CHAPTER 13

Content Marketing Pays Off on the Bottom Line in Australia

B itemark teaches small and medium-sized businesses to reinvent their online presence in order to achieve dramatic increases in sales, leads, and profits.

Type of organization: Web site and e-newsletter developer in Melbourne, Australia.

Major marketing objective: To attract new clients with its Web site, blog, and e-newsletter.

Content types:

- Web site
- Blog
- E-newsletter

Unique element: Unlike many Web developers, Bitemark has done an in-depth study of what types of content and design will produce tangible sales results for clients.

Results: Online content marketing works for Bitemark because most of its growth comes from clients who have discovered the firm online.

"We are really thinking like publishers," says Brett Gilbertson, Bitemark's director of marketing. In terms of content marketing, he says, "It's been a complete mind shift." This applies equally to Web sites, blogs, and e-newsletters. Brad and his team are recognized today as online marketing experts Down Under. They would be just as effective if they were headquartered in San Francisco or New York City.

Bitemark didn't start out to teach its Australian customers how to create Web sites that prompted action, leads, and sales. But it wound up filling a void that it didn't know existed.

Bitemark first offered software solutions that enabled Web professionals to build sophisticated Web sites. But technology wasn't the answer to creating results-driven Web sites.

Today, Bitemark provides a full range of online services that enable its clients to transform old-fashioned, brochure-ware sites into content-rich Web sites and to create e-newsletters that turn visitors into buyers.

For Brett and his clients, it's all about driving measurable results. Bitemark has studied what works and what doesn't. It is continually fine-tuning its efforts to be certain that it drives sales and profits on behalf of its clients.

Bitemark's content creation expertise evolved only after it realized that Web developers did not understand the need for relevant content. Nor did the developers' clients. Bitemark also realized that the vast majority of businesses were clueless about creating Web sites that produced leads and sales.

Brett estimates that fewer than 10 percent of small to medium-sized businesses understand the importance of content marketing. "Great content isn't just about making prospects smarter and better informed," he says. "Great content is really about delivering sales and marketing results."

Brett reiterates this idea on his blog. His company makes its living by building Web sites. But not just ordinary Web sites. Although its Web sites look great and typically have strong visuals combined with clear, intuitive navigation, that's not the point. The company's objective is simple: it builds sites for clients that generate plenty of leads and plenty of sales. It does this through results-oriented content marketing.

Brett stresses:

Effectively dealing with the infinite choices consumers have on the web involves a mind shift from old marketing where commercial messages are thrust on people. The messages that work best on the web are those that consumers choose. There's a huge benefit to making this mind shift—it then becomes easy to create the kind of content that your customers are looking for.

In other words, make sure that your content is customer-centric.

Brett's team is very clear about why most Web sites get it all wrong. It doesn't pull any punches on the firm's Web site, which says

Unfortunately, most of the time . . . businesses do this with their websites:

- *Talk about themselves more than their customers*
- *Use jargon that their customers don't understand*
- *Make it difficult for their customers to find them*
- *Distract them with unnecessary sizzle and clutter*
- *Hide behind their websites by not giving out contact details*
- *Leave their customers wondering what to do next*
- *The list goes on . . .*

It's not confidence-inspiring. The upside for you is that it's not hard to stand out with your web marketing.

Brett emphasizes that the ideal solution integrates a solution-oriented Web site, effective search engine optimization, and a blog. "This is a very powerful combination," he says.

Brett adds that it's essential to understand what problems your target customers are trying to solve—and then to make it obvious on your Web site that your company is ready, willing, and able to solve those problems.

Leading by Content Marketing Example

The Bitemark Web site (Figure 13.1) immediately grabs your attention with a strong visual—and an equally strong challenge question: *"Is it time to fire your website?"*

Figure 13.1 The bold Bitemark Web site gets right down to business with an attention-grabbing headline

One of the Web site's strengths is that it doesn't waste words. With typical Aussie directness, it gets right down to business, using lots of brief sentences in bullet points accompanied by relevant graphics. The Bitemark site is also full of case studies, examples, and testimonials.

Bitemark also makes it clear that you can expect a certain level of service and performance from the company. If it fails to perform, Bitemark expects you to call it on this.

You come away trusting that the company knows what it's doing, that you can benefit from its help, and that you can count on it to do the job.

Bitemark's Conversion Rate Blog: Guaranteed to Make You a Better Content Marketer

Brett himself writes the popular Conversion Rate blog (Figure 13.2), which typically tackles complex online marketing issues. Recently, he provided an in-depth examination of good and bad e-mail marketing practices. Regular readers of the blog benefit from his cogent analysis, which is based on a significant amount of research.

While examining e-mail marketing issues, he put together a rogues' gallery of terrible preview pane examples, as well as a winner's circle of great e-mail examples.

In another recent blog series, he evaluated how it might still be possible to use the online Yellow Pages for affordable lead generation. He determined that if you invest in the top level of advertising and make sure that your ad content is solution-focused (rather than being all about your company), you can expect to generate a

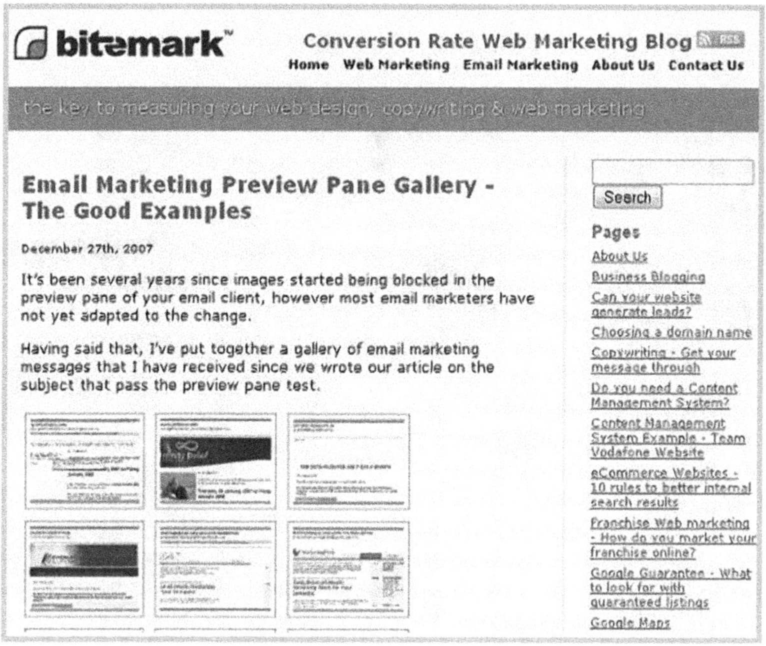

Figure 13.2 The Conversion Rate blog is chock-full of valuable online marketing content

solid return on your advertising investment. Even though he was talking about advertising rather than content marketing in this case, it still goes back to being customer-centric in your messaging.

Brett's blog is valuable because it provides thoughtful content that deals with universal problems that online marketers face when they try to generate tangible results from their efforts.

Like all great blogs, by providing real benefit to its readers, Conversion Rate provides just as much benefit to Bitemark.

Delivering Tangible Results for Customers with Limited Marketing Budgets

Bitemark's single-minded focus on content, which assures visitors that it can provide solutions, is delivering measurable results for clients such as Fort Knox Self Storage (see Figure 13.3) and Ace Mobile Mechanics. Both of these clients were struggling with typical first-generation Web sites that offered little incentive for visitors to move toward a purchase.

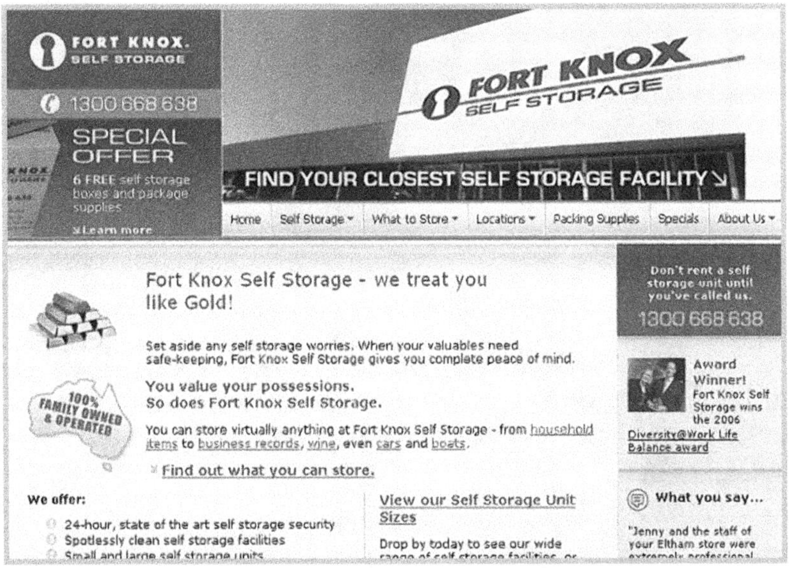

Figure 13.3 Customers like Fort Knox Self Storage can count on measurable results from Bitemark

Fort Knox Self Storage now has a visually appealing, action-oriented site that makes it obvious why you would want to store your possessions there. The new site has increased the number of leads substantially, with an impressive 4 to 5 percent conversion rate.

Ace Mobile Mechanics' previous Web site presented it as "the cheapest in town" and didn't even provide a phone number. At the time, the company's primary source of leads was the Yellow Pages, where it was spending $100,000 per year. Ace invested $10,000 with Bitemark for a 10-page Web site (Figure 13.4) that is delivering an

Figure 13.4 Ace Mobile Mechanics gets a 19 percent conversion rate from its Web site

astonishing 19 percent conversion rate. Ace's Web presence is now its lowest-cost source of leads. In 2008, the Web site will edge out the Yellow Pages in the total number of leads.

Relatively small online investments are producing dramatic results for Bitemark's clients. Its biggest challenge—and perhaps yours as well—is convincing traditional marketers to change the way they think about marketing. Doing so has not been easy, but it has been well worth the effort given the bottom-line results that Bitemark's clients are achieving.

Content Marketing Takeaways

Thinking like a publisher is fundamental to developing and executing a successful content marketing strategy. As we explained in Chapter 3, thinking like a publisher means figuring out what information is essential to your customers and then delivering it in a compelling way. Typically, this means helping them solve a problem or giving them ways to live a more successful professional or personal life.

When it comes to great Web sites, pure good looks and spiffy technology are meaningless if they don't reinforce relevant content.

If you are in any kind of marketing business, you must provide persuasive examples of content marketing that prove that you can actually generate results for your customers. As traditional marketing avenues diminish in value, your Web site should become your single best source of qualified leads and sales.

If you're writing a business blog, bring benefit to your customers first. Then benefits will naturally flow to you.

CHAPTER 14

You Can Trust Northern Trust to Deploy a Great Content Marketing Strategy

Northern Trust's implementation mirrors the excellence of its customer care and understanding.

Type of organization: Global bank catering to wealthy clients, with $63.1 billion in banking assets.

Major marketing objective: To use print and online content to reinforce its "wealth" thought leadership with its very wealthy clients and important third-party wealth advisors.

Content types:

- Print magazine for clients
- Web site for clients
- Microsite for wealth advisors
- E-newsletter for wealth advisors

Unique element: Targeted content for outside advisors who influence current and future Northern Trust clients.

Results: Client-centered content combined with impeccable execution of its financial services has helped Northern Trust maintain a dominant market position as the private bank that even its competitors concede is the best in the business.

The Northern Trust folks have always been good marketers—particularly when it comes to in-person events and community involvement. For example, each year they bring in their top investment professionals to present their best investment advice to capacity crowds of clients. They also provide custom events for the wealth advisors who look after their clients.

Northern Trust's people-to-people focus accurately reflects the way it cares for its clients—and the in-depth knowledge that its people are willing and able to convey. But it's not all about the money. In fact, each year the company hosts hundreds of clients on wonderfully unique vacation trips all over the world. Sometimes a client's just got to have fun.

Applying Client Understanding to a Content Marketing Strategy

Recently, Northern Trust began to extend the reach and quality of its content to print and online products. In fact, in their presentations to financial analysts, Northern Trust representatives discuss the company's fully integrated marketing program, as Figure 14.1 shows. This people-to-people implementation of content marketing reinforces already strong relationships.

Northern Trust is very clear about its mission, which is to "provide comprehensive, customized, and innovative financial solutions for successful individuals, families, and their businesses."

Three outstanding content marketing implementations illustrate Northern Trust's clear understanding of what is truly important to its clients:

- A content-rich, beautifully designed quarterly magazine entitled *Wealth*
- A client Web site that is much more client-centric today than it was just two years ago
- Interrelated content products that target the expert independent wealth advisors who serve Northern Trust clients

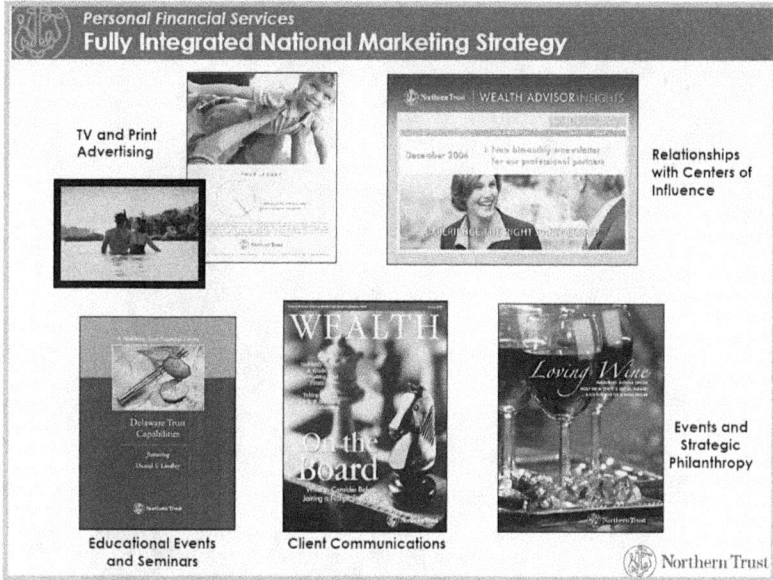

Figure 14.1 Northern Trust now adds content marketing in print and online to its integrated strategy

Wealth: Sophisticated Advice for Northern Trust Clients

Creating a magazine that genuinely reflects the passions and interests of its affluent clientele came naturally, because Northern Trust understands its clients so well. *Wealth* (Figure 14.2) is beautifully designed on high-quality, heavy paper stock. The articles are substantial, precisely targeted, and highly informative. Because there is no advertising, the amount of content delivered is equal to that of a magazine twice its size (Figure 14.3).

Here are some things its affluent readers learned in a recent issue:

- Understand wealth transfer planning so that you can count on leaving a legacy
- How to invest in a volatile market—avoid making major changes that could hurt your portfolio's performance

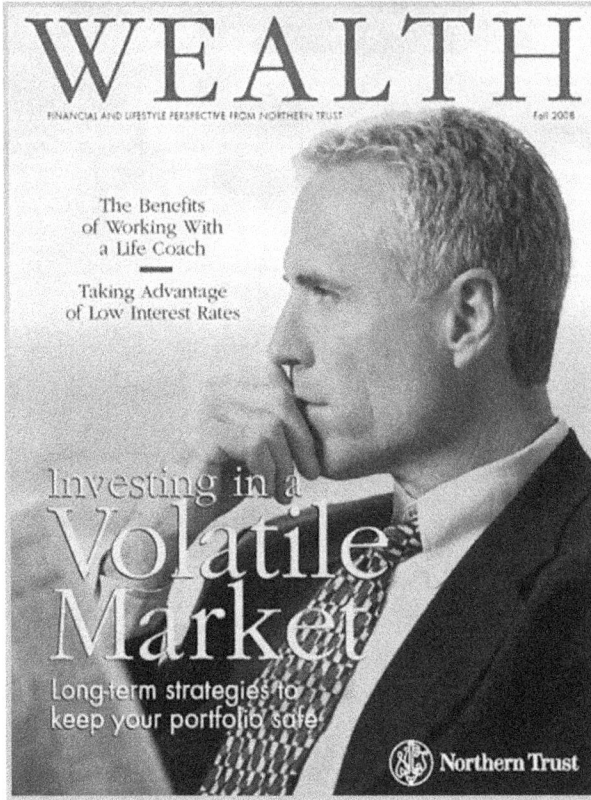

Figure 14.2 *Wealth* magazine engages the passions and interests of its affluent audience

- Consider working with a life coach to manage life's major transitions
- Size up exchange-traded funds (ETFs) as an investment strategy
- Why near-record low interest rates impact valuations of certain gifts
- Let a professional image consultant keep you current on fashion trends without needing to leave home

In this issue of the magazine, there are no feature stories that talk about Northern Trust. Wealth Magazine's content is completely customer-centric.

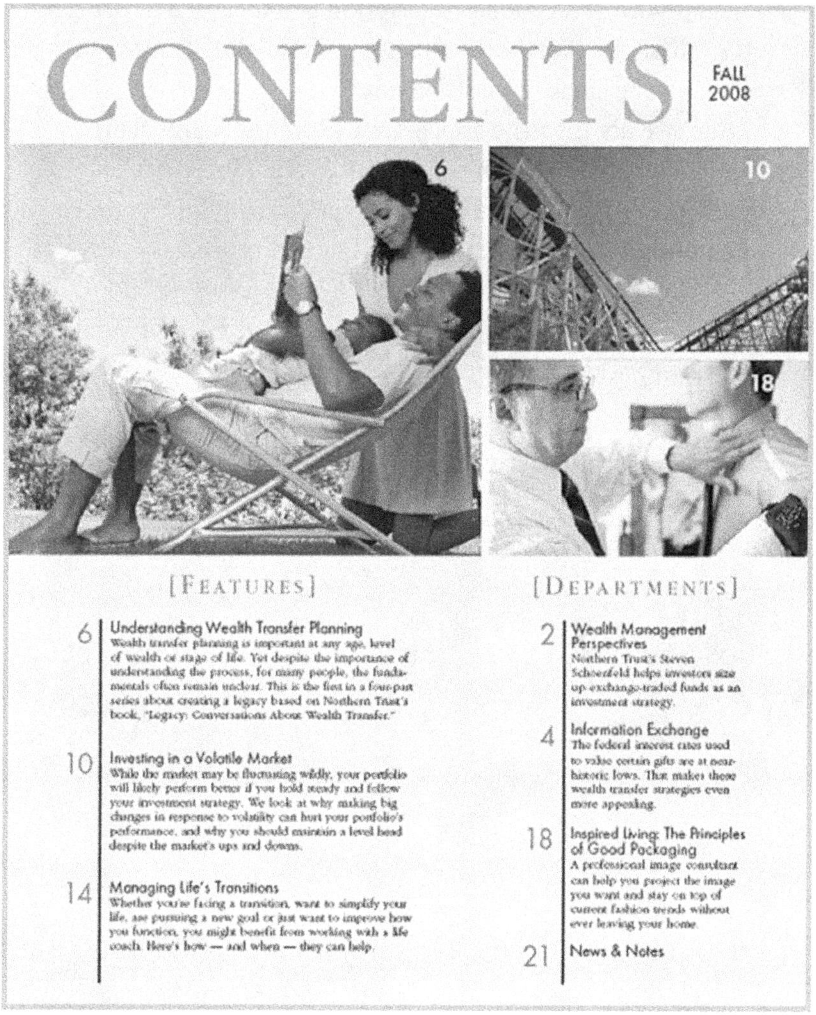

CONTENTS

FALL 2008

6 10 18

[FEATURES]

6 **Understanding Wealth Transfer Planning**
Wealth transfer planning is important at any age, level of wealth or stage of life. Yet despite the importance of understanding the process, for many people, the fundamentals often remain unclear. This is the first in a four-part series about creating a legacy based on Northern Trust's book, "Legacy: Conversations About Wealth Transfer."

10 **Investing in a Volatile Market**
While the market may be fluctuating wildly, your portfolio will likely perform better if you hold steady and follow your investment strategy. We look at why making big changes in response to volatility can hurt your portfolio's performance, and why you should maintain a level head despite the market's ups and downs.

14 **Managing Life's Transitions**
Whether you're facing a transition, want to simplify your life, are pursuing a new goal or just want to improve how you function, you might benefit from working with a life coach. Here's how — and when — they can help.

[DEPARTMENTS]

2 **Wealth Management Perspectives**
Northern Trust's Steven Schoenfeld helps investors size up exchange-traded funds as an investment strategy.

4 **Information Exchange**
The federal interest rates used to value certain gifts are at near-historic lows. That makes these wealth transfer strategies even more appealing.

18 **Inspired Living: The Principles of Good Packaging**
A professional image consultant can help you project the image you want and stay on top of current fashion trends without ever leaving your home.

21 **News & Notes**

Figure 14.3 The table of contents reflects the magazine's richly varied customer-centric content

The implicit message that Northern delivers? "We care about your well-being, and we have the knowledge and resources to protect it."

A Client-Centric Web Site

Northern Trust's client-centric Web site is visually appealing, well organized, and chock-full of content. It is better in several important ways than its predecessor of just a few years ago. The previous version

- Began with a very long description of Northern Trust that was all about Northern Trust, not about the client.
- Had a very small visual element.
- Didn't really give the appearance of being client-centric.
- Required a fair amount of work to access information.
- Had a lot of information, but included many disparate elements that lacked an easy-to-follow structure.

The new Web site—both client-centric and client-friendly—is better in every way (see Figure 14.4).

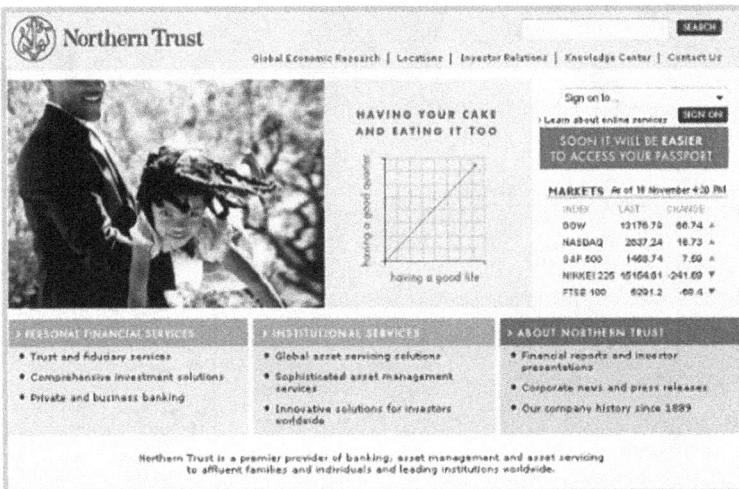

Figure 14.4 The new Web site is visual, content rich, and all about the customer

It gives the impression of a bank you can trust and enjoy doing business with. The new site

- Leads with a wonderfully warm visual of a father swinging his young daughter on a sunny day; to the right of the photo is a graphic, titled "having your cake and eating it too," that illustrates the balance between having a good quarter and having a good life.

- Has a very simple, three-column division between personal services, institutional services, and the "About Northern Trust" section.
- Features a "Knowledge Center" that gives clients access to an incredible amount of financial and economic information—all of which is logically organized.
- Offers podcasts of weekly discussions by Northern Trust experts on topics such as unique approaches to institutional investing, global pension plans, and timely tax tips.

What about that long description of Northern Trust that used to appear so prominently? It's still on the site, but instead of being in giant green letters at the top, it now appears in small black type at the bottom.

Northern Trust Delivers Targeted Content to Wealth Advisors

Northern Trust understands that if advisors don't understand its culture and mission, there is no way that they'll be able to convey that information to end customers. That's why advisor communication is one of the most important aspects of Northern Trust's integrated marketing plan.

Northern Trust's visually appealing microsite, NorthernTrust.com/wealthadvisor, was designed specifically for this audience (see Figure 14.5). Here, advisors can find

- Detailed information on client solutions
- A broad range of in-depth information relating to financial and wealth services
- Podcasts that they can listen to at their convenience
- A series of white papers that offer content to help advisors deal with specific client needs
- Access to *Wealth* magazine in PDF or HTML format, including hyperlinks to even more resources

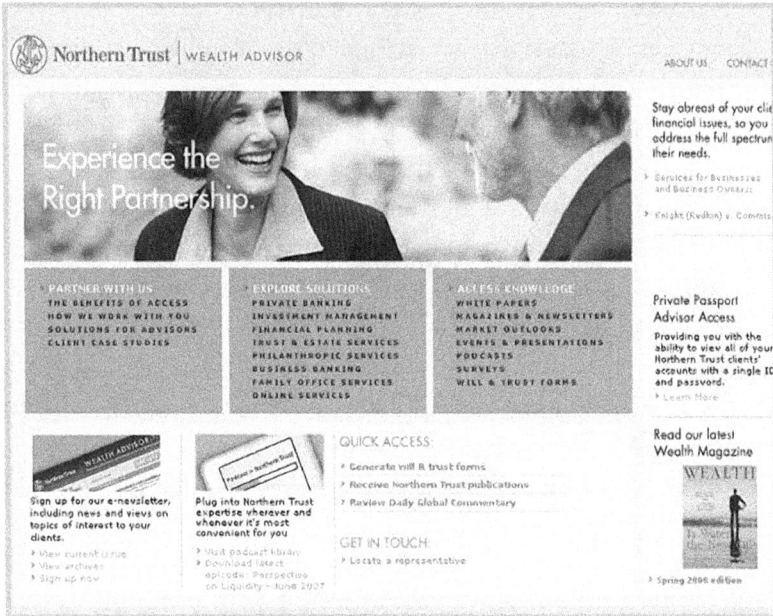

Figure 14.5 Wealth advisors are critical to Northern's success and thus merit their own microsite

Northern Trust also produces a bimonthly e-newsletter that provides up to-date information on many of the complex issues that wealth advisors must understand in order to best advise their affluent clients (see Figure 14.6). This e-newsletter, in turn, reminds them to connect back to the dedicated microsite.

Content Marketing Takeaways

Northern Trust has always had an in-depth understanding of its wealthy clients, which has enabled the organization to shape a culture of trust that has inspired long-term client relationships. This understanding made the development of a comprehensive content marketing strategy a natural extension of the way the company cares for its clients. Without it, Northern Trust would have failed to create relevant and valuable content.

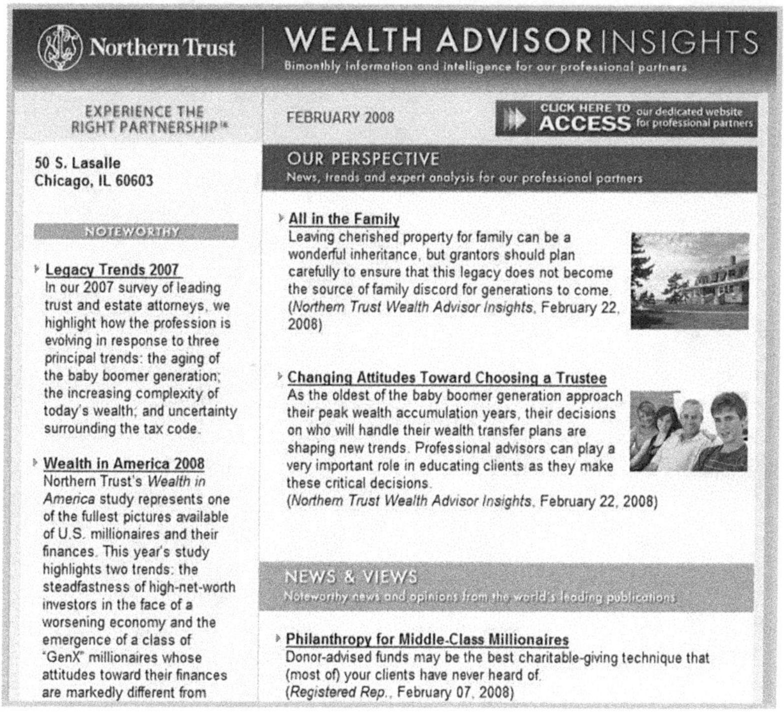

Northern Trust

WEALTH ADVISOR INSIGHTS

Bimonthly information and intelligence for our professional partners

EXPERIENCE THE RIGHT PARTNERSHIP℠

FEBRUARY 2008

CLICK HERE TO ACCESS our dedicated website for professional partners

50 S. Lasalle
Chicago, IL 60603

NOTEWORTHY

Legacy Trends 2007
In our 2007 survey of leading trust and estate attorneys, we highlight how the profession is evolving in response to three principal trends: the aging of the baby boomer generation; the increasing complexity of today's wealth; and uncertainty surrounding the tax code.

Wealth in America 2008
Northern Trust's *Wealth in America* study represents one of the fullest pictures available of U.S. millionaires and their finances. This year's study highlights two trends: the steadfastness of high-net-worth investors in the face of a worsening economy and the emergence of a class of "GenX" millionaires whose attitudes toward their finances are markedly different from

OUR PERSPECTIVE

News, trends and expert analysis for our professional partners

All in the Family
Leaving cherished property for family can be a wonderful inheritance, but grantors should plan carefully to ensure that this legacy does not become the source of family discord for generations to come.
(*Northern Trust Wealth Advisor Insights*, February 22, 2008)

Changing Attitudes Toward Choosing a Trustee
As the oldest of the baby boomer generation approach their peak wealth accumulation years, their decisions on who will handle their wealth transfer plans are shaping new trends. Professional advisors can play a very important role in educating clients as they make these critical decisions.
(*Northern Trust Wealth Advisor Insights*, February 22, 2008)

NEWS & VIEWS

Noteworthy news and opinions from the world's leading publications

Philanthropy for Middle-Class Millionaires
Donor-advised funds may be the best charitable-giving technique that (most of) your clients have never heard of.
(*Registered Rep.*, February 07, 2008)

Figure 14.6 Wealth Advisor Insights is a regular e-newsletter that keeps advisors current on complex issues

Additionally, Northern Trust has always excelled at providing in-person content for its clients in small- and large-group settings. The information it provides has a single objective: to make clients smarter and better informed about managing substantial individual, family, and business assets. This tradition of in-person content marketing was the natural precursor to print and online products.

Providing valuable content for third-party advisors positions Northern Trust as a trusted partner. By delivering focused content—with no expectation of immediate return—that enables these advisors to better serve their wealthy clients, Northern Trust becomes the logical source for a broad range of financial services.

CHAPTER 15

Leveraging Content Marketing to Strengthen Member and Community Relationships

The Greater Naples Chamber of Commerce improved its publications and, in turn, increased revenue.

Type of organization: Chamber of commerce with nearly 2,000 members.

Major marketing objective: To improve the quality of its publications in order to maximize member benefits and increase chamber revenues.

Content types:

- Monthly magazine
- Web site
- E-newsletter

Unique element: The chamber manages the content of its publications internally, thus improving quality while reducing cost and growing revenues.

Results: Revenue and membership growth, both of which can be attributed directly to content-driven products that provide value to members and the community.

All associations and chambers of commerce succeed based on their ability to deliver measurable value to their members. However, many of their efforts are intangible and therefore hard to measure. As a result, members often wonder whether they're getting their money's worth.

One of the best ways to transform the intangible benefits that a membership organization provides is to create information products that communicate effectively with members—and with targeted members of the business community in which the organization operates.

Although generating printed or online publications is relatively easy, making them relevant and compelling is much more difficult. That was a challenge that the Greater Naples Chamber of Commerce faced in the spring of 2006. In addition, as with most membership organizations, generating non-dues-related income is essential to the viability of the organization. That means that sponsorships and advertising can make a significant difference. So, too, can high-quality events and publications.

The Naples Business Community: Lots of Very Small Companies

Although the greater Naples business community includes a number of very large companies, the vast majority of local businesses have fewer than 25 employees. Chamber membership reflects this reality. Large organizations may join a chamber of commerce because they think it's the right thing to do or because they believe that they must be involved with the larger business community. Smaller companies with very limited budgets take a much more pragmatic view of things.

Although dues for small companies may be less than $300 per year, that's a significant expenditure for most such businesses. Therefore, these companies want to know that they are getting measurable value from their investment.

If the owners participate actively in chamber events and on chamber committees, they will probably feel that they are getting full value from the connections they make month after month. However, many owners spend most of their time focusing on their business operations and may have little time left over to allocate to chamber events or other business-related organizations.

In order to retain these busy business owners as members, keeping them at least virtually engaged with the chamber is all-important. This boils down to regularly providing them with content that matches their most important information needs. If this content is delivered in a format that permits members to advertise affordably, so much the better.

In addition to its Web site, the Greater Naples Chamber of Commerce offers *Business Currents*, a monthly business magazine, and *Leadership Link*, a monthly e-newsletter.

Providing Vital Content Creates Tangible Value for Members

In 2006, the Greater Naples Chamber of Commerce was making a significant monthly investment in multiple publications. But it was uncertain whether these content marketing efforts were truly serving members' information needs. In addition, it had to add or improve non-dues-related revenue in order to fund its many business, community, and public policy initiatives.

One of its first undertakings was to transform the chamber's publications from "good" to "great." The Naples chamber had always been deeply committed to providing essential information to its members but, like most smaller chambers, it had never had staff members with extensive publishing experience who could create truly great publications.

Its monthly newsprint-style publication had always had a number of good articles, but there was no consistent editorial structure. Nor was there an annual editorial calendar to give it focus and consistency. Moreover, the chamber was outsourcing much of the work of producing its print newsletter, which was fine, but the integration of customer needs and vendor support was disjointed.

In addition to the monthly publication, the chamber maintained a Web site that served as a central point for its membership directory and for event management. In theory, it was also an outlet for current news. But because it was so difficult to manage (there was no simple content management system), keeping the Web site current was almost impossible.

Let's take a look at how the chamber became more content marketing–oriented.

Step 1: Understand the Business Information That Is Most Important to Your Members

As of spring 2006, the chamber had not done a recent study to determine what topics and issues were most important to its members. This made it quite difficult to provide relevant content on any kind of consistent basis.

Therefore, the first step in the transformation of the chamber's publications was to figure out what members really wanted to know. This was part of a broader effort to make the chamber more customer-centric.

The chamber surveyed its members to determine

- What they thought about the content that the chamber was currently providing
- How relevant they found that content, in terms of their information needs
- What types of articles they preferred
- What business-related issues they most wanted to receive information on
- How they rated the design of the current publication

The chamber learned that the newsletter, *Currents*, was well read. That was the good news. The bad news was that it was not highly rated in terms of relevance to the members' information needs. The study also uncovered exactly what types of information members would really find relevant. This provided the data needed to reinvent the newsletter so that it would become a "must-read" publication.

The chamber took the production of its monthly publication in-house because it finally had the staff resources and expertise to create a great new monthly magazine. Catherine Dentino, the new communications manager, was a talented writer and editor as well as an outstanding graphic designer.

Step 2: Translate Research into a Publication That Is Genuinely Relevant to Business Owners and Executives

The chamber team was able to translate the research findings into the beginnings of a high-quality monthly magazine. The key elements were as follows:

- Research indicated that a glossy 8.5" × 11" magazine with full color throughout would significantly increase the perception of quality.
- Chamber members had given extensive rankings of the topics and issues that were most important to them. This enabled the team to create an editorial calendar that was a real road map to significantly enhanced editorial content.
- A design prototype was created so that key decision makers, including the chamber CEO, Mike Reagan, and members of the board of directors, could give constructive feedback.
- The publication was renamed *Business Currents* to more accurately reflect its core business focus.
- A media kit that focused on the "research-driven" nature of the improved publication was created.
- A low-cost, high-quality offset printing company was selected to produce the magazine each month.
- It was determined that chamber staff members would be able to edit and design the publication each month.
- Respected business leaders and subject matter experts would also contribute content regularly on a voluntary basis.
- A detailed production schedule was created so that the magazine would come out on time each and every month.
- The chamber's sales staff was trained in how to sell advertising to appear in the new publication.

Although the initial level of effort required to bring the magazine in-house was daunting, the chamber was able to produce a high-quality monthly magazine that premiered in October 2006. By instituting detailed editorial processes and schedules, the chamber has been able to deliver a high-quality publication consistently.

As a bonus, the new and improved magazine was less expensive to produce—plus it generated significantly more advertising revenue in support of chamber activities.

More than one year later, *Business Currents* continues to thrive, tackling tough business and community issues that have a significant impact on chamber members. Despite staffing changes, the chamber continues to maintain the quality of both design and content.

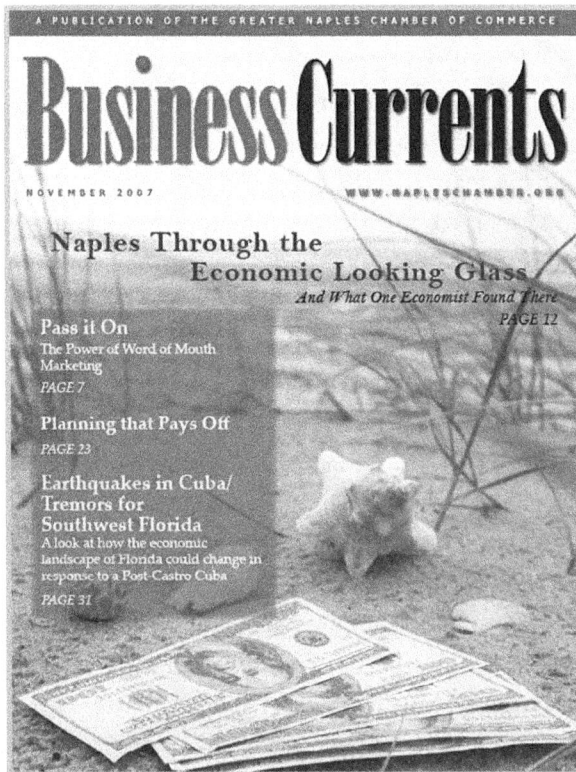

Figure 15.1 *Business Currents* delivers relevant content monthly, based on research about what information is most important to members and business executives

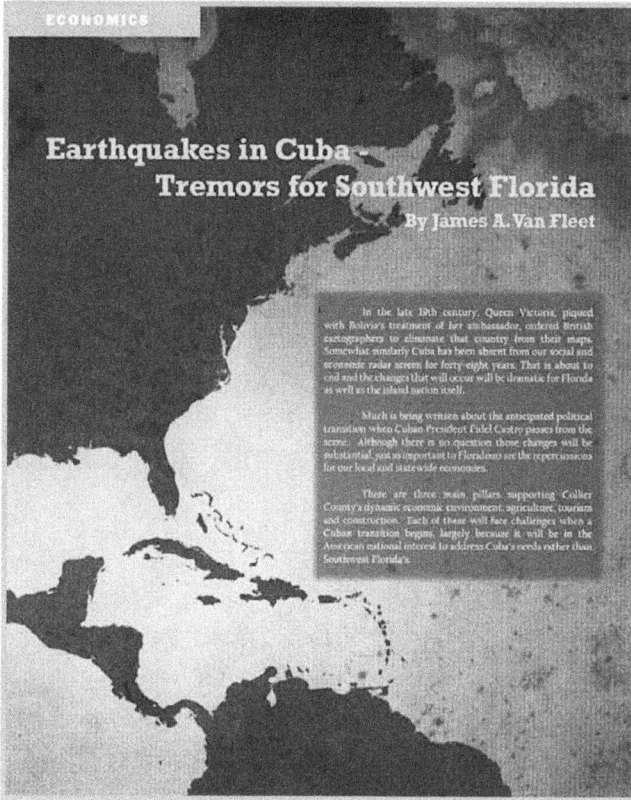

ECONOMICS

Earthquakes in Cuba – Tremors for Southwest Florida

By James A. Van Fleet

In the late 19th century, Queen Victoria, piqued with Bolivia's treatment of her ambassador, ordered British cartographers to eliminate that country from their maps. Somewhat similarly Cuba has been absent from our social and economic radar screen for forty-eight years. That is about to end and the changes that will occur will be dramatic for Florida as well as the island nation itself.

Much is being written about the anticipated political transition when Cuban President Fidel Castro passes from the scene. Although there is no question those changes will be substantial, just as important to Floridians are the repercussions for our local and statewide economies.

There are three main pillars supporting Collier County's dynamic economic environment: agriculture, tourism and construction. Each of these will face challenges when a Cuban transition begins, largely because it will be in the American national interest to address Cuba's needs rather than Southwest Florida's.

Figure 15.2 The magazine is not afraid to tackle tough issues that affect the region

Unlike many chamber and association publications, *Business Currents* doesn't gloss over significant challenges that face the business community.

In the November 2007 issue, for example, it included a stark but objective assessment of the local economy (see Figure 15.1). Another hard-hitting article explored the implications of a reopening of Cuba, which poses a serious threat to the vital tourism segment of southwest Florida (see Figure 15.2).

Although *Business Currents* also does a great job of covering chamber events, the real heart of the publication is its solid coverage of business, public policy, and community issues. In addition, it's chockfull of practical advice on how to run your business better.

This critical mass of compelling content generates excellent readership. Readership, in turn, is what makes advertising effective. Because advertisers know that they're getting to the right business buyers in a publication that is valued by those buyers, they know that they're in the right magazine.

Business Currents's high-quality content is significantly enhanced by its excellent design—beginning with memorable covers that motivate business executives to pick up the magazine the moment it lands on their desks (see Figure 15.3).

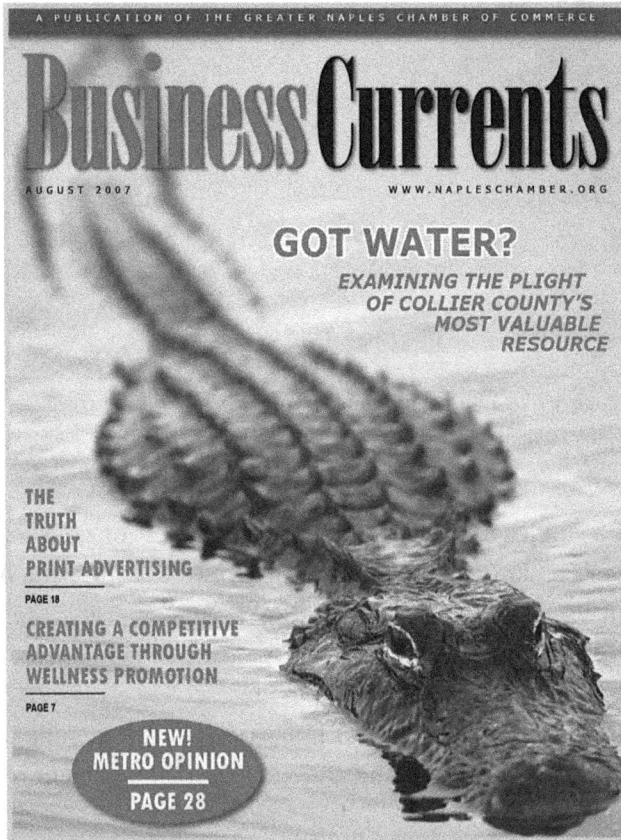

Figure 15.3 High-impact covers entice busy executives to pick up the magazine as soon as it arrives

Step 3: Create an Invaluable Web Site for Members, Business Owners, and Visitors

The chamber's next major content task was to upgrade its Web site, NaplesChamber.org, which was built on antiquated technology, was hard to manage, and offered good but limited content.

The biggest challenge in creating a great chamber Web site is that it must serve multiple constituencies: chamber members, prospective members, business owners and executives, tourists, and visitors (see Figure 15.4). Moreover, although much of the content is relatively timeless, a significant portion of it must be kept current. In addition, because it is an event hub, the site must provide e-commerce capabilities.

The chamber partnered with a Naples-based advertising and Web design firm, ISOOSI, that fully understands the importance of first-rate content and a user-friendly interface. ISOOSI is unusual in that

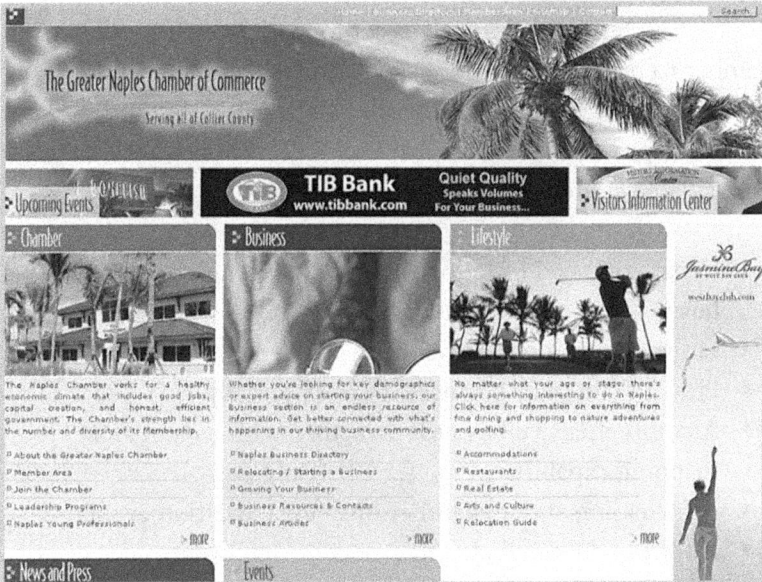

Figure 15.4 The chamber's Web site delivers a broad range of content serving multiple constituencies

its understanding of content marketing is just as strong as its ability to design great Web sites.

To provide robust transactional capabilities, the chamber also licensed Web-based software technology from WebLink. This provides excellent back-end capabilities that integrate with the chamber's accounting system, providing an easy-to-use management system. In addition, it provides all the e-commerce tools required to manage dozens of yearly events. Very importantly, the Web site is easy and inexpensive for chamber staffers to maintain.

Today, NaplesChamber.org draws a broad range of traffic. After the redesign, Web traffic increased dramatically as members, residents, and tourists accessed the much-improved content more frequently. Within 12 months of the launch of the new site, monthly visitors had increased to 45,729—an increase of 600 percent from a year earlier.

The redesigned Web site has a simple and intuitive design that, when you reach the home page, makes it obvious exactly where you should go for the type of information that you need. In addition, the Web site is now the go-to spot to learn about and register for chamber events. This makes it much easier to manage events, allowing the chamber to provide even more events that benefit its members.

The chamber continues to work closely with ISOOSI to maintain and improve NaplesChamber.org. The Web site has a great deal of invaluable content, including

- What you need to know if you're planning to relocate a business to southwest Florida
- How to start a business locally
- How to run your business more effectively
- A comprehensive business directory with e-mail and mapping capability
- Information about chamber business education events
- Information about chamber networking events
- The ability to sign up and pay for chamber events online
- Comprehensive tourist and visitor information
- Comprehensive relocation information
- And on and on and on

In short, NaplesChamber.org not only provides a treasure trove of information for its current and prospective members, but also serves as an extraordinary resource for the community.

Step 4: Retool the Monthly E-newsletter to Address both Business and Community Concerns

The chamber significantly improved the quality of its e-newsletter, *Leadership Link*. Its monthly content now includes coverage of both community and business topics—particularly focusing on the importance of leadership skills (see Figure 15.5).

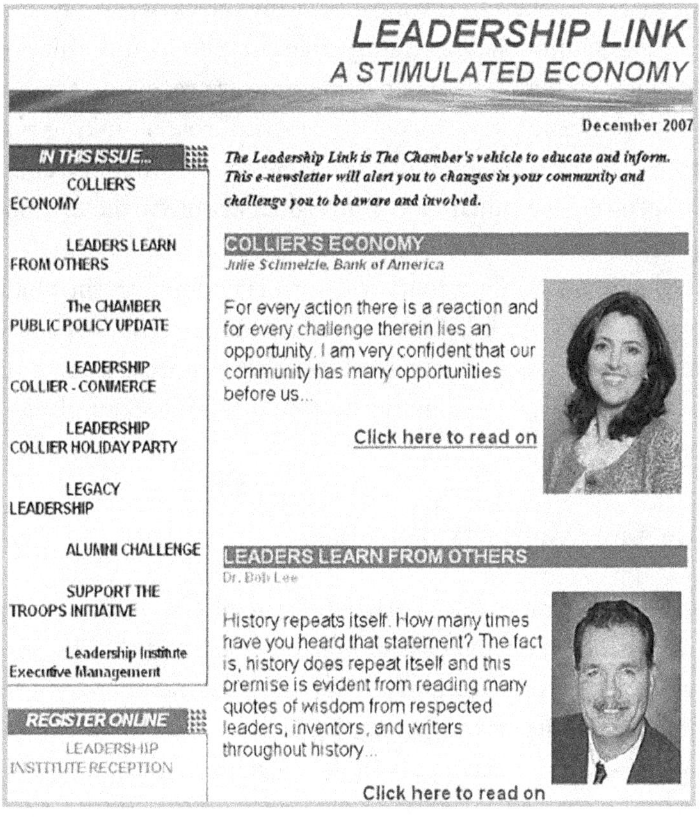

Figure 15.5 The monthly e-newsletter was retooled to address business and community concerns

A recent issue of the redesigned e-newsletter featured

- A commentary on current economic challenges in southwest Florida by a Bank of America vice president who is also the new head of the local Economic Development Council
- An article on leadership by a former city executive who is currently a professor at Florida State University
- A public policy update from a senior business executive who is on the chamber's board of directors
- Articles on Collier County leadership programs
- Links to a variety of business and community resources

Again, the chamber is reaching out to the Naples community with content that is relevant to the most pressing issues of the day. It reinforces the chamber's leadership role in the community—and reminds its members how much value they are receiving from their membership. Finally, it performs the practical role of linking readers back to the NaplesChamber.org Web site so that they're reminded each month of how much relevant business content the chamber is delivering.

The chamber's content marketing efforts help both the chamber and its members succeed. Although the chamber cannot specifically attribute membership strength to its much-improved content, its membership continues to grow, despite a weak local and national economy.

Content Marketing Takeaways

Although the chamber has nearly 2,000 members, it is a small organization with limited resources. But it has learned that by providing a rich variety of meaningful content to its members and to the broader community, it can extend its reach and its impact dramatically. What it cannot do in person, it can achieve in print and online via *Business Currents*, NaplesChamber.org, and *Leadership Link*.

Through its content marketing efforts, the chamber goes a long way toward making the intangible benefits of membership much more tangible. Thus, when busy entrepreneurs take the time to read the chamber's materials, the value of their membership becomes very clear indeed.

The chamber's core print and online publications deliver a level of revenue that significantly exceeds that of the older-generation information products. The ability to generate revenue is derived directly from the improved product quality.

CHAPTER 16

At Best Buy, It's All about Strengthening Customer Relationships

B est Buy is reinventing its entire company around the concept of customer-centricity. It has learned that a deep understanding of its ideal customers results in a host of trusted relationships, which, in turn, drive sales and profits.

Type of organization: Multibillion-dollar electronics and appliance retailer.

Major marketing objective: To find a way to build strong, lasting relationships with its very best customers.

Content types:

- Print magazine
- Electronic magazine version

Unique element: The content discusses products, services, and activities that relate to lifestyle, not to Best Buy.

Results: Trusted relationships with biggest spenders are strengthened via an enthusiastic publication that provides no apparent benefit to Best Buy.

While Circuit City was cutting, Best Buy was adding. Why? Because, at its heart, customer-centricity is all about providing excellent customer service. But customer-centricity is much more than that. It involves determining who your best customers are and how best to serve them. Here is how *Fortune* magazine described Best Buy's vision of customer-centricity in its March 29, 2006, issue:

> *Figure out which customers make you the most money, segment them carefully, then realign your stores and empower employees to target those favored shoppers with products and services that will encourage them to spend more and come back often.*

Best Buy has gone so far as to create elaborately described personas for its most important customers. One would be Jill, a busy suburban mom. Another would be Barry, an affluent tech enthusiast. An enormous amount of work is involved in preparing individual stores to cater to particular personas. Thus, a "Jill store" would be specially configured to match up with Jill's shopping habits and product interests. It would also have personal shopping assistants who would help her pick out just the right gadgets for her family and show her how to use them.

Best Buy has expanded its service focus dramatically over the last five years. The Geek Squad, which it acquired from a start-up in 2005, now numbers more than 17,000 technical support professionals. The ubiquitous geeks represent Best Buy's understanding of the need for high-touch customer care.

In fact, customer-centricity equates to enlightened self-interest that benefits both the customer and Best Buy.

Best Buy's continued focus on an ever-improving customer experience closely tracks its significantly increased U.S. market share. In a recent presentation to Morgan Stanley, Best Buy showed that as its computer return and exchange rate had dropped significantly between 2001 and 2006, its market share continued to expand—from roughly 14 percent in 2001 (pre-Geek Squad) to slightly more than 20 percent in 2006 (see Figure 16.1). Here is how the company described it in the Morgan Stanley presentation:

> *You can trust Best Buy and Geek Squad to make your computer and everything you connect to it always work seamlessly so that you can enjoy your passions. This is why we come to work.*

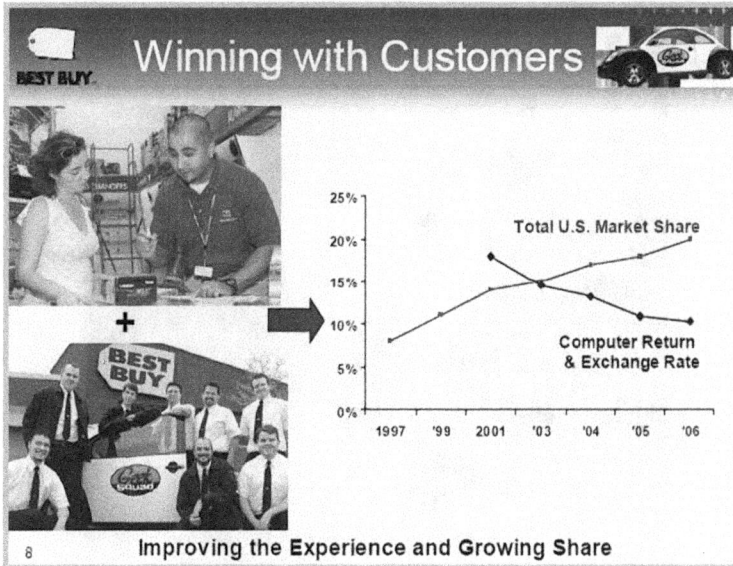

Figure 16.1 Market share is built on continuously improving the customer experience

Best Magazine Exemplifies Content Built on Customer-Centricity

Best magazine doesn't go to just anybody. Only Best Buy's very best customers receive it. This careful targeting is derived from the customer-centricity concept of treating your most profitable customers in a very special way (see Figure 16.2).

Chief Marketing Officer Barry Judge explains that *Best* magazine is designed to "share our passion about how technology can enhance their lives."

As Best Buy's top marketing executive, Judge guides its brand strategy; he drives the development of new marketing capabilities and empowers marketing innovation as the company transforms to put the customer at the center of its business model.

Judge believes that it is essential "to build credibility from a trusted perspective by making it clear that there is no obvious way that Best Buy will benefit" from the creation and distribution of *Best* magazine.

Figure 16.2 *Best* magazine goes only to the very best customers

He adds that the publication has generated a "pleasantly happy customer reaction," and concludes that *Best* magazine provides value "precisely because it doesn't appear to sell Best Buy" (see Figure 16.3).

Best Buy has learned that a deep understanding of its ideal customers results in a host of trusted relationships, which, in turn, drives sales and profits. Building on that understanding, the retailing giant continues to add value to the customer experience because it has learned, as Judge says, "When we invest in our customers, they will invest more heavily with us."

Best magazine contains absolutely no promotion for Best Buy. Except for a welcoming icon on the cover, the company takes a backseat to the magazine's content.

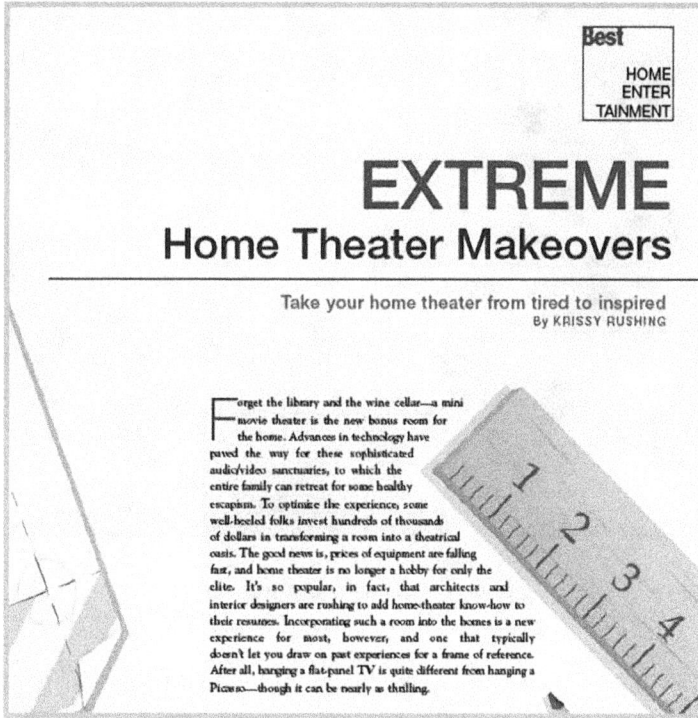

Figure 16.3 The content is designed to enhance already trusted relationships

The magazine itself is an enthusiast's paradise. Loaded with product information about everything from iPods to sports cars, the colorful, 76-page periodical tells readers all about what's "best" and how to get maximum enjoyment from the huge range of products it covers.

In a recent issue, *Best* magazine profiled an eclectic assortment of sport coupes (see Figure 16.4):

> But instead of arguing semantics, we preferred to play free association with driving enthusiasts. Given the stimulus of the word "coupe," this passionate demographic responded with "fast," "exhilarating," "sport," and—last but not least—"two-door hard-top" . . . we simply want to demonstrate that, when you're talking two-door sport coupes, grins come in all sizes and prices.

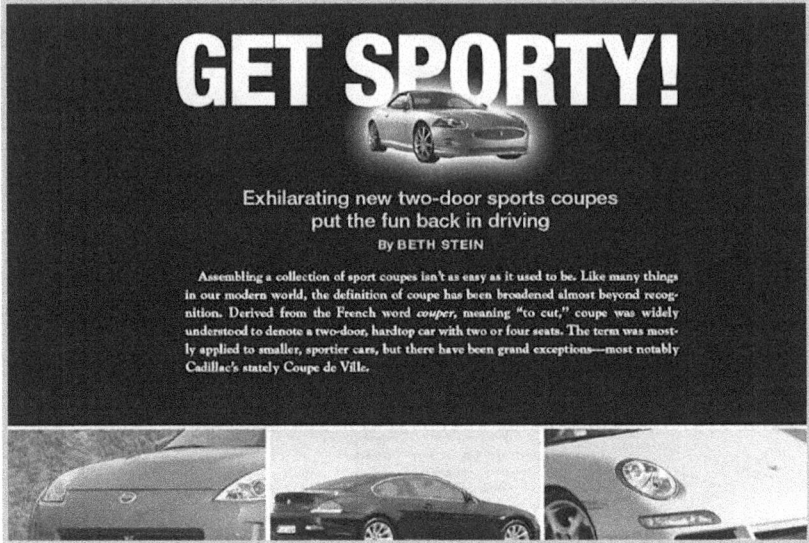

GET SPORTY!

Exhilarating new two-door sports coupes
put the fun back in driving
By BETH STEIN

Assembling a collection of sport coupes isn't as easy as it used to be. Like many things in our modern world, the definition of coupe has been broadened almost beyond recognition. Derived from the French word *couper*, meaning "to cut," coupe was widely understood to denote a two-door, hardtop car with two or four seats. The term was mostly applied to smaller, sportier cars, but there have been grand exceptions—most notably Cadillac's stately Coupe de Ville.

Figure 16.4 *Best* magazine is an enthusiast's paradise

Another article, aimed at sports fans who want to emulate professional sports photographers, explains how to get that perfect action shot. Here's the kind of immediately useful advice you get from the author, sports photographer extraordinaire Peter Read Miller:

> *In all my years shooting sports for* Sports Illustrated, *I've found no substitute for preparation when on an assignment. If you want to get that perfect shot, you can plan ahead, too. . . . There used to be a great spot at the old Mile High Stadium, in Denver, where there was a gap in the stands. As the sun went down, beautiful golden light would stream through the open space. When players hit the right spot, it created an amazing effect: They would be bathed in light, but the background would be in shadow.*

Best magazine is a genuine enthusiast publication in the finest tradition of *Sports Illustrated, Car and Driver, Flying*, and *Audiophile*. Although it covers lots of technical gadgets and electronic paraphernalia, its editorial content ranges far beyond that. Of course, the publication is aimed squarely at Best Buy's frequent big-ticket buyers who love to acquire the latest and greatest—and to learn how to put those products to work for maximum enjoyment and satisfaction. And that's exactly what *Best* magazine teaches them to do.

Online, Best Magazine Gets Even Cooler

The publication adds another layer of cool in its electronic version. It is clearly designed to be read online, with scrolling text that makes room for very large and high-impact graphical elements. Rather than the hodgepodge of banner ads that typically confronts Web site visitors, the online magazine ads have all the colorful impact of those in the print version. Even better, many of its ads go from static to interactive. Figure 16.5 is a live video ad from Sony showing off its high-definition DVD player. All in all, the online version of *Best* magazine delivers a superior experience.

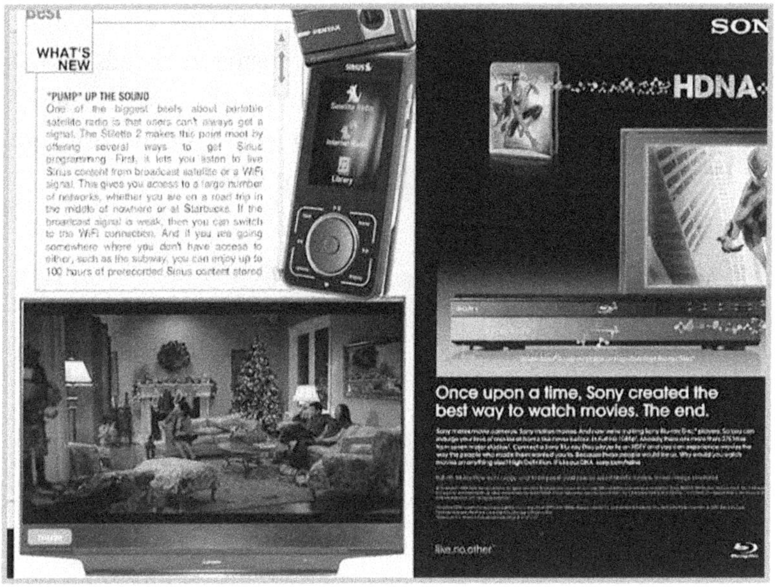

Figure 16.5 The online magazine is even cooler, with interactive content and advertising

Content Marketing Takeaways

When you really understand your customers and what they need, you're perfectly positioned to provide content that positions you as a trusted provider—first of information, and then of products and services. Best Buy has learned that you must take excellent care of your very best customers. It does this in a number of ways, of which *Best* magazine is the perfect content example.

Best Buy is reinventing itself around the concept of customer-centricity. This takes customer understanding to a new depth. It means that you must identify both your very best customers and your very worst customers. You need to cherish the very best and perhaps dump the very worst. For those ideal customers, carefully crafting a precisely targeted information product such as *Best* magazine will enable you to strengthen those all-important customer relationships.

Although Best Buy has a huge marketing budget and can afford to create a 76-page, four-color print magazine, you can accomplish a similar objective less expensively. You can create a more highly focused publication that targets the vital information needs of those customers with whom you want to forge long-term partnerships. As they begin to count on you as a reliable source of vital information, you will take a special place in the ranks of their suppliers.

Using Content Marketing to Accelerate the Acceptance of a Concept and a Product

M indjet® uses content marketing extensively to grow its sales because word of mouth is the single most important factor in the success of its products.

> *Type of organization:* Privately held software company that sells mind-mapping software worldwide to more than 1 million users.
>
> *Major marketing objective:* To use online content to extend the understanding and use of its mind-mapping software.
>
> *Content types:*
> Web site
>
> - E-newsletter
> - Blog
> - Webcasts
>
> *Unique element:* The Mindjet team created a personalized mind map for a new product launch aimed at reporters and analysts. By giving the reporters and analysts an actual tool that they could use in their work and personal lives, the Mindjet team demonstrated why mind mapping (and the product MindManager®) is so valuable.

Results: Mindjet has been able to replace all its traditional marketing methods with online content strategy, culminating in its most successful product launch in 2007.

San Francisco–based software company Mindjet has been developing mind-mapping software since 1993. Since 2004, it has grown dramatically from three dozen employees to almost 165—and more than 1 million users.

Mind mapping is a different way of thinking from the traditional vertical outline that we all learned in school. It involves a radial model with a core concept at the center and branches and subbranches extending from that core.

Although it does take a bit of explaining, former Mindjet marketing executive Katy Colletto likens the incredible productivity improvement she experienced when she started using MindManager to the difference between schlepping an old-fashioned suitcase and the ease of strolling along with a suitcase on wheels. As she puts it: "Today I can't imagine how I ever got along without MindManager."

Mind mapping is a wonderful way to improve your thinking, get yourself organized, and enhance your creativity. If you know about mind mapping, you know exactly what I'm talking about. If you don't know about mind mapping, we need to do some explaining.

Although most of us learn to organize our thoughts in linear outlines, mind-mapping theory suggests that our minds don't really work that way.

Wikipedia defines a mind map as

An image-centered diagram that represents semantic or other connections between portions of information. By presenting these connections in a radial, non-linear graphical manner, it encourages a brainstorming approach to any given organizational task, eliminating the hurdle of initially establishing an intrinsically appropriate or relevant conceptual framework to work within. . . . The elements are arranged intuitively according to the importance of the concepts and they are organized into groupings, branches, or areas.

The best way to understand mind mapping is to grab a large piece of paper and some colored pencils and pens and just begin putting down your thoughts, beginning with the central point, as in Figure 17.1.

Use single words or very short phrases for each category and related subcategory. Make your map as colorful and as creative as you can. If you're writing down a list of current projects, you'll want to include all the most important elements for each project. If you're

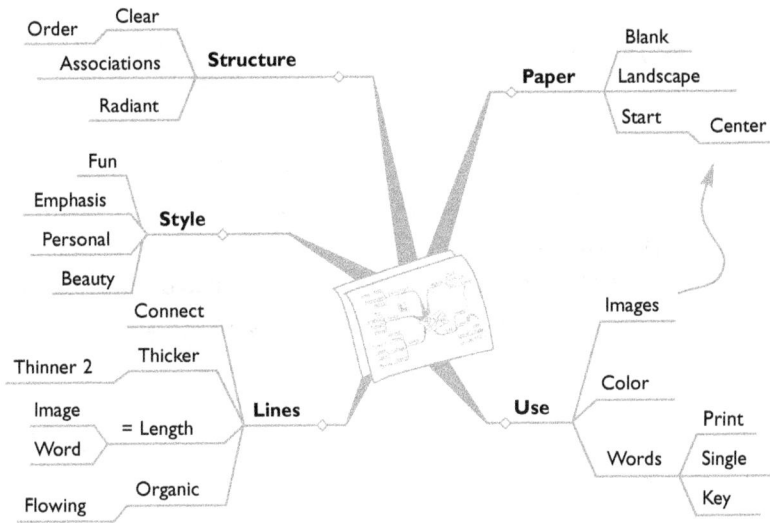

Clear
Order
Blank
Associations   **Structure**
Paper   Landscape
Radiant
Start   Center

Fun
Emphasis
Style
Personal
Beauty

Connect   Images
Thinner 2   Thicker
Image   Color
= Length   **Lines**   **Use**   Print
Word   Words   Single
Organic
Flowing   Key

Figure 17.1 Mind maps put the central point in the middle, with connections radiating outward

even the least bit visual, you will find that even a rudimentary mind map elicits creative thoughts and ideas that will surprise you. And if you're a process person, mind mapping will add structure, efficiency, and creativity to your days.

Recently, the *Wall Street Journal* mentioned MindManager as an effective organizational tool:

> *Fans say mindmapping software can give them a single view of all the aspects of a project. It gives an "air-traffic controller view of what you're doing," says William R. Miller, a controller for the information-technology group at a unit of Nationwide Financial Services Inc.[1]*

Mindjet's growth parallels the increasing acceptance of the concept of mind mapping. But, in spite of Mindjet's success, it faces a significant marketing challenge: unless you know what mind mapping is, it is difficult to explain.

That makes traditional advertising relatively ineffective. Even print advertorials did not do the trick for Mindjet. To overcome the disappointing results that it got from print advertising, Mindjet began to pursue a creative online content marketing strategy.

Putting Word of Mouth to Work on the Web

Fortunately for Mindjet, it has incredible word of mouth; in fact, 60 to 80 percent of its sales are driven by viral marketing. Even better, 85 percent of its users consider themselves "evangelists."

Therefore, Mindjet's primary efforts involve extending the reach and impact of these evangelists. The company has determined that most MindManager users tend to focus on a single application for mind mapping. Mindjet is convinced that by educating these enthusiasts on all the ways in which MindManager can improve productivity, process, and creativity, it will grow both the users and the uses of the product.

A Web Site That Really Works

When you land at Mindjet.com, the first thing you'll probably notice is a headline that explains exactly what Mindjet is all about: "Work smarter, think creatively, save time . . . every day Mindjet helps people visualize and use information."

The Mindjet Web site presents a wealth of compelling content that revolves around the visual metaphor of a mind map (see Figure 17.2). Mindjet.com is very much a get-to-the-point Web site that takes you exactly where you want to go. Whether you want to learn about business productivity, examine a powerful case study, review some very cool mind-mapping templates built with Mind-Manager, or contact support, you can find everything easily.

For example, you can link directly to the business productivity page, where the major feature is a large mind map with live links to

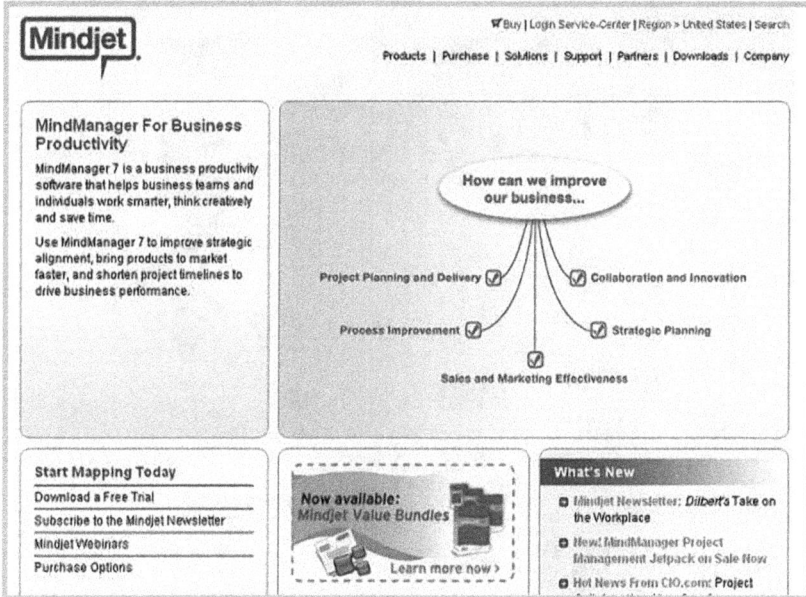

Figure 17.2 Mindjet's get-to-the-point Web site uses the visual mind map metaphor

in-depth business productivity examples. Thus, if you click on a strategic planning link, you go directly to a page that explains simply how MindManager enables strategic planning. There you will find even more links to sample maps, case studies, recorded Webinars, and white papers.

Mindjet's Web site is packed full of content that offers intrinsic value whether or not you ever decide to buy the company's software. Of course, much of that content is so compelling that you are pretty darn likely to become a new customer after you've read through it. Appropriately, when you're ready to buy the product, the Web site makes it incredibly easy for you to do so.

And Then There's a Really Useful Monthly E-newsletter

Mindjet's e-newsletter, shown in Figure 17.3, focuses almost entirely on how to achieve more by using MindManager. Newly improved in 2008, the current e-newsletter is more colorful and

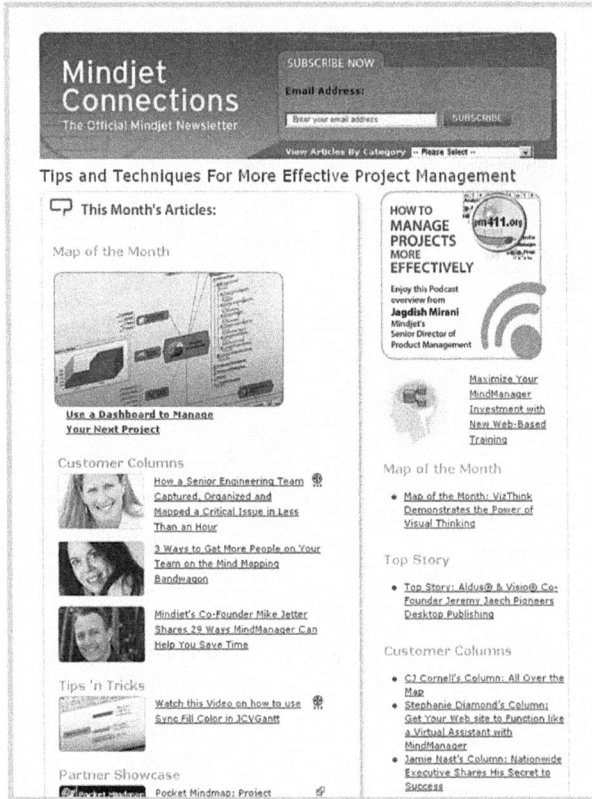

Figure 17.3 Mindjet's e-newsletter concentrates on making its readers more productive, with lots of advice from subject matter experts

compelling than the previous version. At the same time, it contains just as much useful content designed to make existing customers smarter users and to attract new users into the MindManager fold.

The e-newsletter makes excellent use of carefully chosen images that represent the concept, topic, or mind map featured in each article. Each article has a succinct and descriptive headline and just enough text to lure you into reading the entire article, downloading a mind map, or watching a video. For example, there is a video that shows how to link and attach documents. When you head off to watch the video, you have the opportunity to look at even more videos designed to help you become more productive when using MindManager software.

In addition, there are Customer Columns, which feature content provided by subject matter experts whose compelling use of Mind-Manager reinforces its broad range of uses. A recent issue presented ideas for strategic brainstorming and finding the perfect customer, and offered creativity methods that can be easily structured and reproduced. Each, of course, is presented with a mind map.

Although the content is 100 percent customer-centric, the e-newsletter offers you multiple opportunities to upgrade to the latest version of MindManager.

This e-newsletter illustrates the power of integrating relevant content with thoughtful visual design. The combination of images and text makes it much more likely that you will take action to go from the e-newsletter to the Web site. Each time you do so, Mindjet becomes essential in your eyes as a current or future supplier of productivity-enhancing tools.

Content Marketing Creates a Blockbuster Product Launch

When Mindjet was ready to launch version 7.0 of MindManager, the biggest challenge was that relatively few analysts or media professionals are familiar with the concept of mind mapping, let alone with the product, MindManager.

The marketing team decided to create a precisely targeted mind map that would be truly relevant to reporters and analysts. Rather than producing a PowerPoint presentation with a billion bullet points, they developed a mind map that was all about how to write an article in the world of Web 2.0 (see Figure 17.4).

For example, the map showed how to use an RSS feed to stay current on topics related to mind mapping. In fact, the map contained two live links to RSS feed tools on the Web. The mind map was full of put-it-to-work-now tips, resources, and how-tos.

The genius of this strategy was that it made mind mapping not just understandable, but truly relevant to jaded and skeptical reporters and analysts, most of whom have suffered through thousands of never-ending PowerPoint presentations. Although the targeted mind

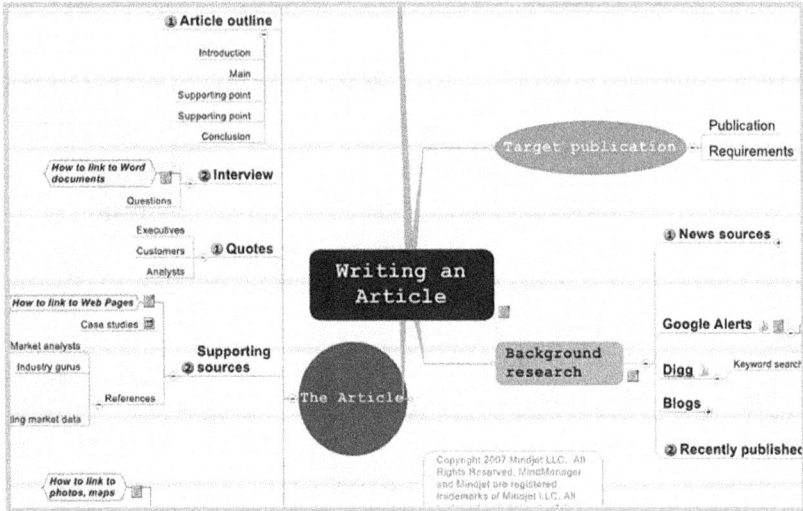

Figure 17.4 New product launch went beyond press releases and leveraged a rich mind map to engage both journalists and analysts

map was used for in-person presentations, it is also available for reporters over the Internet.

Did it work? Absolutely. Mindjet received more than 4,000 blog links and 232 media mentions. Perhaps most importantly, there are now hundreds of reporters around the world who understand what mind mapping is all about—and why MindManager is such a powerful product. Almost certainly, Mindjet won some converts among reporters, who are actually leveraging MindManager to improve their productivity.

Content Marketing Takeaways

Word-of-mouth marketing has always been important. Today, it's more important than ever because of the power of the Internet. Mindjet employs a content marketing strategy designed to maximize word of mouth.

Mindjet understands that its customers love the MindManager product—and that they will use it more extensively and promote it more actively if they are regularly exposed to all of its capabilities.

Thus, Mindjet uses its e-newsletter and its Webcasts to demonstrate the myriad ways in which MindManager can be used to improve professional and personal productivity.

Mindjet content creations are easy to pass along from one user to another. This gives real substance to word of mouth.

Mindjet used highly targeted and relevant content in its product launch so that reporters and analysts would intuitively understand how MindManager works and why it can be so powerful. Rather than issuing a standard press release that would be widely ignored, Mindjet put in a substantial amount of effort to create an elaborate mind map that actually showed how to write an article.

CHAPTER 18

Preserving the Value of Content

C ontent marketing provides 90 percent of the value of the Webkinz product, but will Ganz be risking it by placing ads at Webkinz.com?

Type of organization: Privately held Canadian toy manufacturer selling more than $100 million of Webkinz toy animals.

Major marketing objective: To create an interactive online community, Webkinz World, that supports the ongoing and increasing sales of its Webkinz stuffed animals.

Content type:

- Web site

Unique element: Although the physical products are toy animals, almost all the value comes from the existence of the highly interactive online Web site that kids love and parents trust.

Results: The perceived value of the company's relatively expensive toys is created by superb kid-friendly online content marketing. Parents are paying up because of the quality of the online content.

For those of you who are not familiar with Webkinz, they are very similar to what Cabbage Patch dolls were in the 1980s except that they are integrated with the Internet. Webkinz, owned by Toronto-based Ganz, are small stuffed dogs, pandas, cats, ducks, and other animals. Once the owner "adopts" a pet, she can go to the Webkinz Web site to register the pet, create a name, and bring her pet to life online (see Figure 18.1).

Figure 18.1 The Webkinz Web site: world-class content marketing for parents and kids

The Webkinz concept is so simple that it boggles the mind that no one had thought of it earlier. To experience its power, just watch a four-year-old navigate his way through the site. You have to see it to believe it.

- Here are a couple of points specific to the Webkinz Web site and content marketing:
- The Webkinz site may be one of the greatest examples of a successful content marketing Web site in the world.
- Because the role of content marketing is so critical to Webkinz's success, Ganz risks disaster if it impairs the purity of the content with obtrusive advertising.

The Webkinz Business Model

According to a *BusinessWeek* article entitled "Toys with a Second Life,"[1] Webkinz's annual sales are north of $100 million. The revenues come strictly from the sale of its stuffed toys and accessories such as charms and clothes. Frankly, the stuffed animals are no different from those you'd find at any toy shop in the world. The difference is the Webkinz World online community (see Figure 18.2).

The site is wonderfully constructed for both parents and kids.

It answers all the questions that parents might have about safety, managing a child's time on the site, how it serves as an educational tool, and even what to do if a Webkinz pet gets sick.

Kids who are new to the site get a lively tour that explains how to register their pet and how to keep it happy, healthy, and busy in Webkinz World.

The image shown in Figure 18.3 is a real-world example of the Webkinz experience. Here you see Joe's six-year-old son Joshua's Webkinz, a polar bear named (fittingly) Polar. Joshua (and his

Figure 18.2 The Web site creates a lively community built around otherwise ordinary stuffed animals

Figure 18.3 Kids who are new to Webkinz World get a fun tour teaching them how to keep their pets happy, healthy, and busy

younger brother Adam) has spent a good chunk of time on the Webkinz site, fitting his animals with clothes, toys, carpet and wallpaper for the bedroom, and more. Joshua takes Polar to the doctor, to the exercise room, and to other "social" rooms where Polar can play with other Webkinz pets. Joshua needs to go to the store to buy food for Polar that will keep him healthy, and he also has to play Webkinz games as a "job" in order to make money to buy more food, clothes, and toys for Polar.

As veteran marketer and mom Marie Kroesen Connell says:

From a parental perspective, it's an excellent way to extend what they learn in school without it being a "lesson." My kids are constantly telling me what they are doing on the site, because they are so excited about what they buy or which friends they can interact with.

It truly is a wonderfully educational and "sticky" site, and perhaps the best example of online content marketing that we can think of. Webkinz World is *not* the product; it's the retention and growth mechanism. But it ultimately is the reason that the brand is what it is today. The online component includes *free* content that educates its customer base and motivates buyers to buy more Webkinz products. Having more pets means that your pets can play with one another, and also opens up exclusive items for multiple pet owners.

Webkinz has done what every business in the world seeks to do with its online content, yet it has so integrated the product and the content that they seem indistinguishable. *What actually is the product? The toys or the online experience?* That is where Webkinz has perfected the art of content marketing.

When the content you produce for your customers becomes crucial to the success of the product itself, you have achieved perfect content marketing integration.

Could They Kill the Golden Webkinz?

Webkinz recently received a slew of hate mail from parents around the world when Ganz decided to open up a small amount of advertising on the site. This created a serious public relations problem for Ganz. Although it has taken the advertising down (such as ads for Jerry Seinfeld's *Bee Movie*), the company is still considering permitting advertising of "kid-friendly" products on the site.

We can see the storm coming now.

Judging by statements made in the *BusinessWeek* article mentioned earlier, it seems that Ganz's managers—as well as financial experts—just do not "get" the true nature of the Webkinz World site:

> *Ganz, which doesn't disclose its financials, must now strike a delicate balance: maximizing profit from the fad without alienating parents and kids. Visitors to Webkinz.com spent more than a million hours there in November, but the site is free. As a result, "they haven't made anywhere near as much money as you'd think," says Sean McGowan, an analyst at Needham, who guesses Webkinz sales are north of $100 million. He adds that none of the nascent competitors have figured out how to capitalize on kids' web time, either.*

The sales are north of $100 million because Ganz created a safe and educational Web site that parents can leave their kids on without having to worry.

As Marie Kroesen Connell notes:

I think the executives at Webkinz are trying to see what other avenues of income they can derive by modifying their business model. With traffic to its web site increasing exponentially, it is tempting for Webkinz to find a way to capitalize on it financially. I can't blame them. But it would seem to me, that it is important not to alienate their loyal customers who go there for the Webkinz content, not ads for other companies.

In other words, it's all about the content.

Webkinz has grown because it is delivering high-quality, *free* content, with the expectation that the Web site will drive more Webkinz sales, not that the Web site itself will produce revenue.

Opening up the site to advertising, no matter how kid-friendly, threatens the brand and diminishes the value of the site. Playhouse Disney opened its Web site to advertising a few years ago. When that happened, Joe stopped allowing his kids to go to that site. Joe's kids clicked on those ads like crazy and ended up heaven knows where. Disney forgot that the Web site was there not to make money, but to deepen the brand relationship—i.e., to get customers to watch more Playhouse Disney and buy more Disney toys.

If the management team at Ganz asked us (and they haven't), we would strongly advise them that Webkinz needs to keep its site advertising-free—or it will destroy the safe environment that it has created for children. As we go to press, Ganz is offering only "house" ads related to Webkinz products and not outside advertising.

Content Marketing Takeaways

All businesses need to create their own content channels, as Webkinz has done. Most businesses don't realize that they can create their own online resource centers for customers that will ultimately drive loyalty and sales. Miller Electric has done it with MillerWelds.com (see Chapter 8). Consumer or business-to-business—it doesn't matter. Just create content that meets the informational needs of your buyer, treat it for what it is, and watch what it can do.

When content marketing products, such as online content Web sites or custom publishing print magazines, succeed, brands almost instinctively want to open up those channels to advertising. This is almost always a bad idea. Opening up to other messages dilutes what you are trying to communicate to your customer. You also lose more control, as Playhouse Disney did when its customers clicked on other Web sites, alienating parents in the process.

The best content marketing doesn't have to be online. In the Webkinz case, it clearly is. In other cases, it might be in print or in person. It's most likely a combination of the three. Successful content programs meet the customers where they are. If you can do all three, it makes the content come alive that much more.

CHAPTER 19

ThomasNet—A Content Marketer's Content Marketer

Making the online leap, ThomasNet bet everything on the Internet. But its customers' Web sites weren't ready for the new buying paradigm. Now, ThomasNet uses online and in-person content marketing to help thousands of customers succeed with the new breed of industrial buyer.

Type of organization: Online division of large, 110-year-old private publishing company.

Major marketing objective: To grow its online revenues by using targeted, relevant, and valuable content to help its readers and customers succeed.

Content types:

- Web site
- Microsite
- In-person workshops
- Online directory
- Online product news site
- E-newsletter

Unique element: ThomasNet had to find a way to teach its small to medium-sized clients how to use content effectively in order to sell successfully online. Its clients' success was essential to its success.

Results: ThomasNet has helped hundreds of clients succeed. This, in turn, has made its 100 percent online content strategy succeed.

If you're not immersed in the world of manufacturing, you may not have noticed the disappearance of the venerable *Thomas Register*. This green-covered, shelf-filling printed directory is now 100 percent online.

Thomas Publishing Company, creator of the *Thomas Register*, is 110 years old. It was a pioneer at the end of the nineteenth century—and it's still a pioneer today.

The original concept was to provide comprehensive and current product information for manufacturers as the United States made the transition from an agricultural to an industrial economy.

Created in 1898 by Henry Mark Thomas, the *Thomas Register* grew to include product information on 650,000 distributors and manufacturers in more than 67,000 industrial categories. If you have ever called on an industrial purchasing agent, you have almost certainly seen bookshelves full of the distinctive green directories behind the desk.

Actually, Thomas Publishing was a twentieth-century pioneer in several other important areas. The company invented the first product news tabloid magazine and the reader service card. Both of these innovations kept buyers current on products and provided them with an efficient way to request product and service information.

In the old days—say the early 1990s—the buying process was still pretty much the way it had been for a hundred years. The *Thomas Register*, product news tabloids, and reader service cards worked just as they always had.

While projects were in the planning stages, buyers would request information about products that they had seen in magazines or had rooted out in the *Thomas Register*. They called vendors to determine whether they had appropriate products. Vendors would then send out product literature, which might have been outdated the day it was printed. Finally, a sales rep would probably call to see if the purchaser was ready to make a buying decision. A substantial percentage of this prepurchase research was done by contacting the vendor directly.

This was a comfortable and familiar process for the small to medium-sized manufacturers that make up the bulk of industrial companies in the United States.

By the early 2000s, however, the ubiquity and functionality of the Internet had changed the product research landscape. Buyers began to operate differently. Increasingly, they were conducting their research exclusively online. They were able to gather most of the information they needed before they ever contacted the manufacturer directly.

The creation of ThomasNet (ThomasNet.com) was enabled by the Internet to provide truly current and comprehensive product information for manufacturers in an online version. Even better, ThomasNet could provide additional online services that would help its customers sell more products more efficiently.

Ever the pioneer, the Thomas Industrial Network, a Thomas Publishing business unit, killed off the venerable *Register* in 2006. It gambled that by putting all of its efforts behind a powerful online directory, ThomasNet.com (see Figure 19.1), it not only would replace lost print revenues, but would find new revenue opportunities.

The online version offers incredible functionality that far surpasses that of its late print predecessor. ThomasNet considers itself a "destination site" where buyers come for the explicit purpose of finding the products they need and the vendors that can supply them.

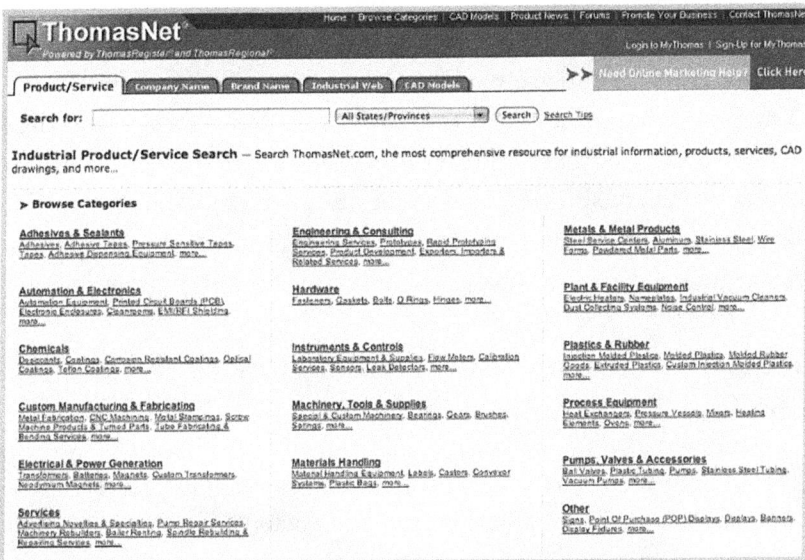

Figure 19.1 In 2006, the comprehensive Web site ThomasNet replaced the venerable print directory the *Thomas Register*

In fact, ThomasNet is the most logical place on the Web to look for products and services related to manufacturing. Even though you could probably search for the same thing on Google, it would be highly inefficient—and ultimately yield lots of useless results. Why go elsewhere? After all, according to the company:

> *ThomasNet.com is the one-stop destination that enables users to find the exact product, service, or supplier they need, at the exact time they need it. Through ThomasNet.com, buyers also have instant access to the detailed information they need to make a purchasing or specifying decision, including line-item product details, supplier product catalogs, CAD drawings, and more.*

So far, so good.

After its first year online, however, ThomasNet faced an unexpected problem: although it drove lots of traffic to its customers' Web sites, hundreds of customers were canceling their advertising.

Here's what the company found.

Although ThomasNet was sending thousands of highly qualified visitors to clients, that was all these prospects were doing—visiting. They weren't buying. Why?

The answer was deceptively simple. The majority of its clients' Web sites were not designed to make it easy for visitors to become buyers. Because most of ThomasNet's clients were small to medium-sized businesses, they typically were not Web-savvy. Nor did they have huge online budgets. Moreover, there was no proven model for success. The changed buying process was just too new.

ThomasNet Teaches Advertisers How to Build Web Sites That Make It Easy to Buy

As soon as ThomasNet understood the problem, it got to work creating a solution. The marketing team conducted research into online business-to-business buying patterns to determine what elements are critical to a successful site. It turned out that real content is essential. Without it, visitors will make a brief stop, get frustrated by a lack of substance, and leave, and they probably won't return.

Alienating prospective buyers is potentially disastrous. Why? Because Web sites provide the overwhelming majority of information about potential suppliers and their products.

Buyers don't have time to gab with salespeople anymore. They have very little leisure time at all. They are under the gun to deliver results now. So, your Web site needs to make their job easy. They have to know that you have what they need and that you are a company that they would like to buy from.

For ThomasNet, everything boiled down to a single question: "Does your Web site persuade visitors to become customers?" If not, you lose. If so, you have an excellent chance of succeeding.

Here is how Linda Rigano, director of strategic alliances at Thomas Industrial Network, explains it:

> *Your website needs to serve as your 24/7 salesperson. It needs to inform and persuade a visitor to become a customer. If it doesn't, your visitors will make a brief stop, hit the back button, and never return. You may never know. We learned that driving traffic to ThomasNet.com and to our advertisers' websites wasn't enough. We had to help our clients develop meaningful content and tools that can be implemented easily and economically. ThomasNet's business model has been instrumental in helping our clients succeed. In the end, it's all about providing content that makes it easy for customers to buy.*

Fortunately for its advertisers, ThomasNet was able to develop a formula to guide the creation of Web sites that make it easy to buy. The firm calls it V.S.E.T.:

- *Verify* that you offer the products that customers need. Does your Web site make it easy for potential customers to immediately determine whether you have what they are looking for?

- *Search* for specific products. Can buyers search your Web site in multiple ways (e.g., by part number, keyword, or product specifications)?
- *Evaluate* your product offerings. Do you provide buyers with enough detailed information to enable them to make a buying decision? Can they compare products side by side? Or do you offer CAD drawings for them to download, if applicable?
- *Take action.* Do you offer multiple ways for buyers to request more information from you or to buy from you, including contact information, RFQ links, your phone number on every page, or even e-commerce?

ThomasNet and its clients have been able to apply the V.S.E.T. methodology across a broad range of products and services. It offers simplicity and structure to what would otherwise be a very challenging effort to create Web sites that generate measurable ROI. ThomasNet then adds even more value for its customers by offering a rich microsite that takes current and prospective customers step by step through the creation of customer-centric content.

Microsite Provides a Deep Reservoir of Content That Teaches Content Marketing

ThomasNet provides a very useful microsite, PromoteYourBusiness.ThomasNet.com (see Figure 19.2). You don't have to be a customer to use the microsite—and you don't have to use ThomasNet's marketing services to benefit from the knowledge you gain from exploring it. This is an excellent example of content marketing at work.

The primary objective of the microsite is to make ThomasNet's customers smarter about how to manage their own content marketing efforts. Visitors can also access practical white papers that give them a more in-depth understanding of how to create a content-rich Web site, how to drive traffic, and how to integrate content marketing with a business plan. Of course, ThomasNet makes it easy for visitors to contact the company to pursue the purchase of products and services. Yet none of this takes away from the intrinsic value of the information that ThomasNet provides.

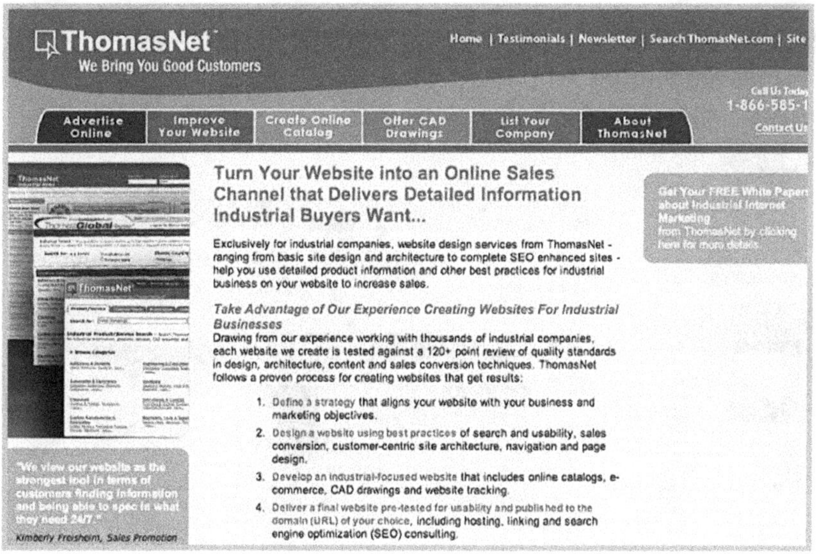

Figure 19.2 ThomasNet has created a microsite that teaches its customers how to create online content that generates sales

Advertisers who have built or rebuilt Web sites that follow the V.S.E.T. methodology have achieved dramatic increases in Web-based sales. For example, Flex Products, a small plastics packaging company with over $8 million in 2005 sales, had relied on the former *Thomas Register* print directories, along with trade shows, to reach prospects. As an increasing number of these prospects began turning to the Web, the company put up a very basic Web site, but it was hard to find online, and it lacked the detail to engage prospects and persuade them to call and place orders. The company turned to ThomasNet to enhance its site with a robust online catalog filled with a great deal of product detail. This replaced the print investment.

The results were spectacular. Sales jumped 20 percent to more than $10 million, and Flex began attracting overseas buyers at the same time. A substantial portion of the increase came from the company's new site (see Figure 19.3). For Flex Products, it boiled down to having really useful and relevant content online. The company was able to show not only what it stocked, but also the kinds of custom products that it could produce.

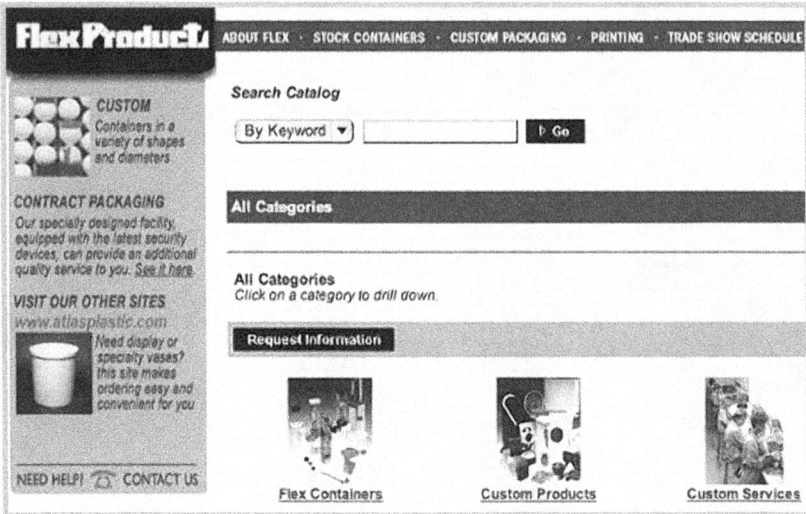

Figure 19.3 Flex Products' revenues grew 20 percent thanks to the online catalog that ThomasNet helped add to its site

ThomasNet Puts In-Person Content Marketing to Work

Although it might seem counterintuitive, Rigano and her team spend much of their time on the road conducting workshops with veteran manufacturing executives. Their objective is to teach these grizzled manufacturing veterans exactly how to put V.S.E.T. methodology to work (see Figure 19.4).

In fact, these workshops are another very important form of content marketing. The ThomasNet team has come to understand that for many of its customers, the Web learning curve is pretty darned steep. These clients rarely have an intuitive understanding of the magnitude of the changes in buying behavior—and how essential it is that they transform their Web presence. The industrial buying process has changed so dramatically that ThomasNet's customers and their companies have to relearn how to connect with their own customers around the world.

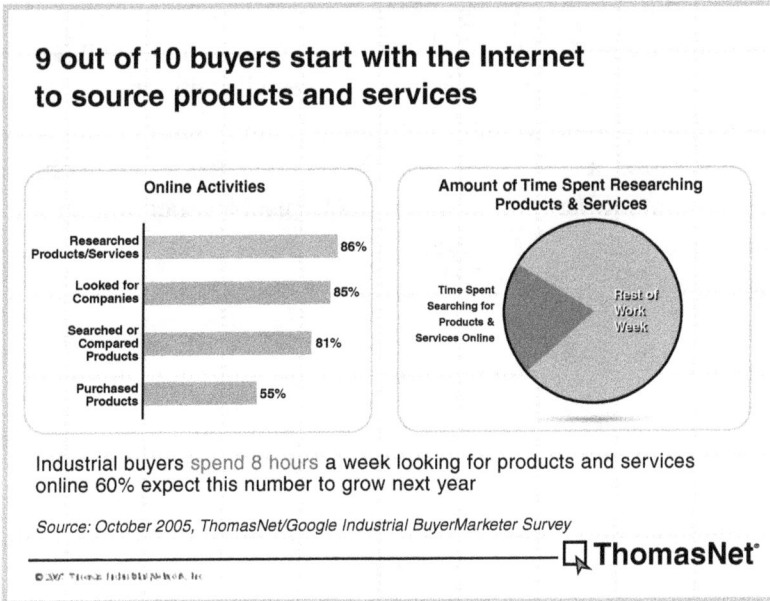

9 out of 10 buyers start with the Internet to source products and services

Online Activities

Researched Products/Services	86%
Looked for Companies	85%
Searched or Compared Products	81%
Purchased Products	55%

Amount of Time Spent Researching Products & Services

Time Spent Searching for Products & Services Online / Rest of Work Week

Industrial buyers spend 8 hours a week looking for products and services online 60% expect this number to grow next year

Source: October 2005, ThomasNet/Google Industrial BuyerMarketer Survey

ThomasNet

Figure 19.4 ThomasNet uses in-person content marketing to teach its customers how to market online

Content Marketing Takeaways

The fundamental changes in buyer behavior that we have discussed elsewhere in this book have had an earth-shattering impact in the industrial marketplace.

Engineers and purchasing executives today rely on the Internet for more than 90 percent of the product research they conduct prior to purchase. Therefore, vendors must utilize content marketing effectively so that they are under consideration during the 24/7 online research process.

In this marketplace, content does not need to be fancy, but it does need to be comprehensive, easy to find, and easy to use. The Flex Products catalog site is a perfect example. It's not elegant, but it is extremely easy to use and has resulted in a dramatic increase in the company's product sales.

Flex Products is simply one of hundreds of ThomasNet clients that have benefited from successful content marketing implementations.

Since 1898, Thomas Publishing has been all about providing current and comprehensive content. Today, it has taken the next step and is teaching its customers how to provide current and comprehensive content. In that way, when ThomasNet succeeds, its customers succeed.

CHAPTER 20

E-mail Software Provider Teaches Customers to Market Effectively

C onstant Contact really walks the walk when it comes to content marketing.

- *Type of organization:* Leading provider of e-mail marketing and online research services.
- *Major marketing objective:* To grow the usage of its services by helping its customers succeed with effective e-mail marketing.
- *Content types:*

  - Web site
  - E-newsletter
  - Webcasts
  - In-person workshops

- *Unique element:* Constant Contact's success is directly tied to the success of its customers; it must provide relevant and valuable content in order to help them succeed.
- *Results:* The company is growing users, usage, and revenues dramatically. Content marketing is at the heart of that growth.

As a fast-growing company, Constant Contact probably doesn't attribute all of its recent growth acceleration to content marketing. But having observed the company over several years, as customers while working in different organizations, we have realized that it has significantly improved its content marketing skills. Our guess is that its dramatic growth can be attributed, at least in part, to its effective implementation of a comprehensive content marketing strategy.

Today, Constant Contact does an excellent job of content marketing on its Web site and, of course, via e-mail. But, interestingly, it also does a great job of in-person content marketing via its regional representatives.

The company targets small to medium-sized businesses and organizations that want to grow their revenues or improve their communication by marketing more effectively. These targeted companies need to leverage their limited resources with both affordable tools and best marketing practices. Constant Contact provides the tools and teaches best practices.

Constant Contact understands that its more than 250,000 customers need to communicate effectively in order to grow. It also knows that most of its customers are not sophisticated marketing experts—and almost certainly are not e-mail marketing experts. Therefore, Constant Contact provides very practical, nuts-and-bolts teaching that empowers its customers to be successful through the use of its tools and through best practices in e-mail marketing and e-mail-based research. Eric Groves, the company's senior vice president for worldwide strategy and market development, explains it this way:

> *No matter how a customer wants to learn, we strive to provide an educational experience that meets their needs. We recognize that everyone learns not only in different ways, but at different times. To help educate and support our customers' needs, we offer seminars, webinars, how-to guides, newsletters, and a blog. This is complemented by our free, live support via phone, e-mail, and text chat.*

Current Web Site Shows Intense Content Marketing Focus

A quick look at Constant Contact's circa 2004 Web site on the Internet Wayback machine (Archive.org) shows a dramatic shift to a comprehensive content marketing strategy on its newest iteration. The old Web site did a good job of explaining what the product did and how it worked. It even offered some solid case studies to prove that Constant Contact's e-mail software worked. But it did relatively little to turn neophyte e-mail marketers into experts.

The big difference between the old Web site and the new Web site (Figure 20.1) is the new site's obvious focus on making the firm's customers successful.

From the get-go, this company makes it absolutely clear how it can help you solve your marketing problems:

No matter what size your organization, you can rely on Constant Contact to help you create email campaigns and online surveys that build lasting relationships with your customers, members or clients.

Within a few seconds, you can determine exactly what Constant Contact does and how it can help you. It invites you to take a tour. It shows you how inexpensive the software is. And it offers you a free 60-day trial—no credit card required.

Also on the home page is a link to live Webinars that teach you how to be effective by mastering basic e-mail marketing best practices, such as

- Building better lists
- Subject line design
- Creating marketing e-mails
- E-newsletter makeover
- Planning a survey

It also provides lots of recorded video tutorials that teach even more core concepts.

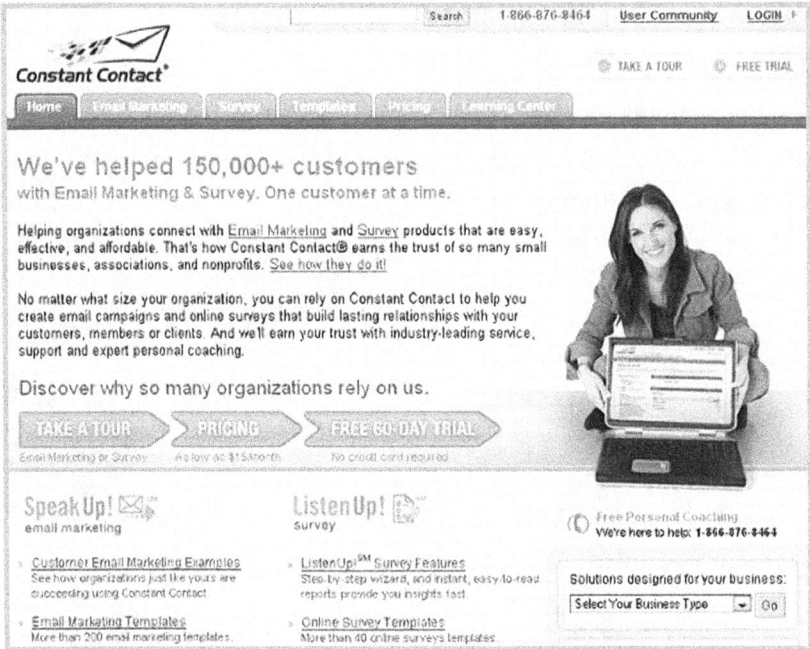

Figure 20.1 Constant Contact's current Web site is all about making its customers successful

Constant Contact offers a series of white papers that may be just what you need to convince management that it needs to get more serious about content marketing. These papers cover topics such as "Why You Need to Create an E-newsletter" and "How to Keep Your Customers with E-mail."

Of course, Constant Contact wouldn't be really walking the walk unless it also did a great job of creating its own compelling e-newsletters.

Great Customer-Centric E-newsletters

The strength of Constant Contact's e-newsletter comes from its content and its clean design—even though it probably has a marketing budget that most of us would die for. However, we can all afford to replicate the style and sophistication of this newsletter, even if we are small business executives with micro-budgets.

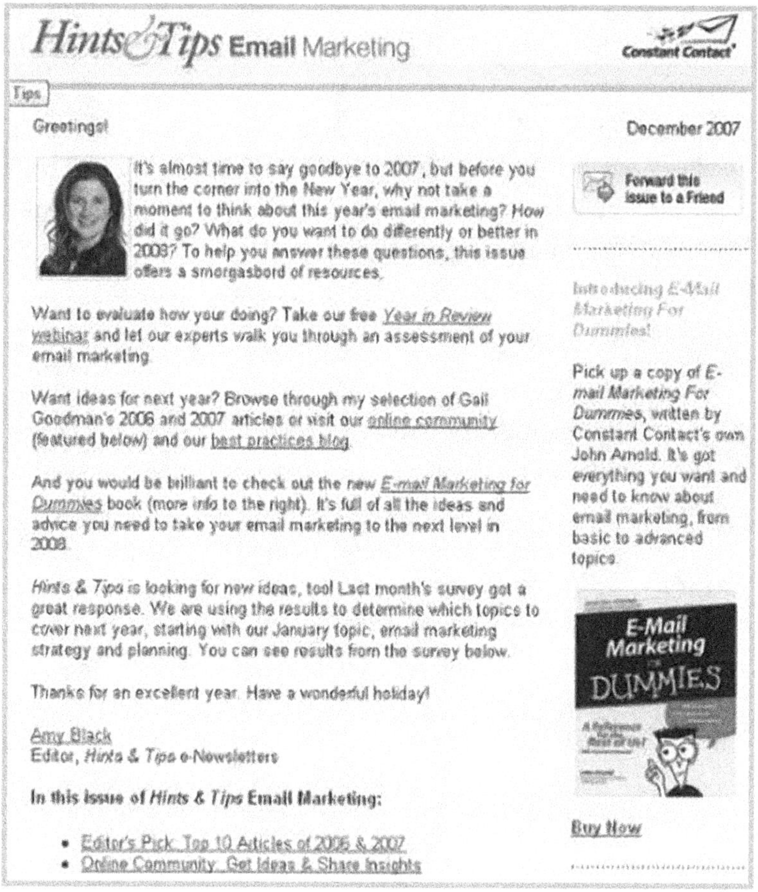

Figure 20.2

Constant Contact's software? Inexpensive. Its e-newsletter content? Invaluable. Figure 20.2 shows what you can learn from *Hints & Tips Email Marketing*.

Content-rich e-newsletters are one of the most effective marketing tools in the Internet age. But they won't work unless you carefully target the most pressing information needs of your prospective customers.

Constant Contact's e-newsletter is typically packed with information that is relevant to its target customers. Here are some samples from past issues:

- A focused "Year in Review Webinar" that helped subscribers evaluate the success of their e-mail marketing programs. Of course, it was free to subscribers.
- Links to live Webinars, the company's blog, and a place where readers can buy the book *E-Mail Marketing for Dummies*, written by marketing trainer John Arnold, the company's regional development director.
- An editor's choice of Top 10 articles from the past year, including

  - Why Am I Getting This? Making E-mail Communication Relevant to the Receiver
  - Ask and You Shall Succeed. Using Online Surveys to Improve Your E-mail Communications
  - Five Steps to Creating Better E-mail Campaigns
  - Getting the Subject Line Right

- A connection to Constant Contact's online community, ConnectUp!
- 2007 reader survey results.

Constant Contact's e-newsletter is very simple, with relatively few graphics. It gets right to the point and provides relevant links to a broad range of information resources. While scrolling, you just keep getting more and more information. When you go to the editor's Top 10 article picks, you see a one-paragraph summary of each article with a link to click on if you want to read the entire article (see Figure 20.3). The paragraph gives you just enough information to decide whether or not you want to click on the link.

Extending In-Person Content Marketing All Over the World

Newt had the opportunity to participate in a marketing workshop with Lisa Sparks, Constant Contact's regional director for south

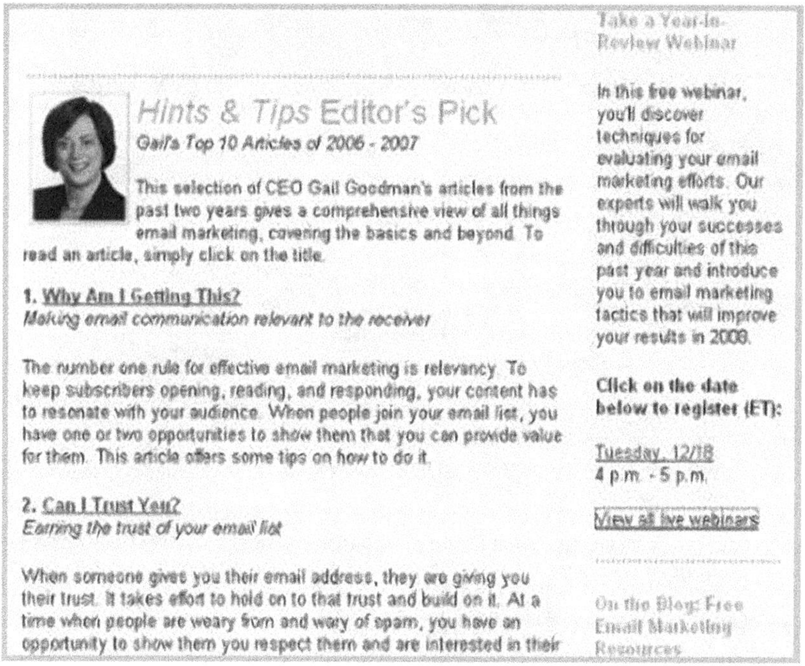
Take a Year-In-Review Webinar

In this free webinar, you'll discover techniques for evaluating your email marketing efforts. Our experts will walk you through your successes and difficulties of this past year and introduce you to email marketing tactics that will improve your results in 2008.

Click on the date below to register (ET):

Tuesday, 12/18
4 p.m. - 5 p.m.

View all live webinars

On the Blog: Free Email Marketing Resources

Hints & Tips Editor's Pick

Gail's Top 10 Articles of 2006 - 2007

This selection of CEO Gail Goodman's articles from the past two years gives a comprehensive view of all things email marketing, covering the basics and beyond. To read an article, simply click on the title.

1. Why Am I Getting This?
Making email communication relevant to the receiver

The number one rule for effective email marketing is relevancy. To keep subscribers opening, reading, and responding, your content has to resonate with your audience. When people join your email list, you have one or two opportunities to show them that you can provide value for them. This article offers some tips on how to do it.

2. Can I Trust You?
Earning the trust of your email list

When someone gives you their email address, they are giving you their trust. It takes effort to hold on to that trust and build on it. At a time when people are weary from and wary of spam, you have an opportunity to show them you respect them and are interested in their

Figure 20.3 A simple, easy-to-follow design draws the reader right into the e-newsletter

Florida, at the Greater Naples Chamber of Commerce. The attendees were precisely the type of small business owners and executives that Constant Contact targets. They were hungry for information about how to leverage the Internet and e-mail to market their organizations more effectively.

Lisa is an excellent speaker, knowledgeable about small business marketing topics and, of course, about e-mail marketing. She spends much of her time at events like this, where she can share her knowledge about the use of effective e-mail marketing to attract and retain customers. When asked how much of her business comes from this highly effective in-person content marketing strategy, she replied, "Eighty percent."

And, of course, she has her own monthly e-newsletter that provides practical advice about marketing more effectively (see Figure 20.4). It also provides links to great resources and free tools.

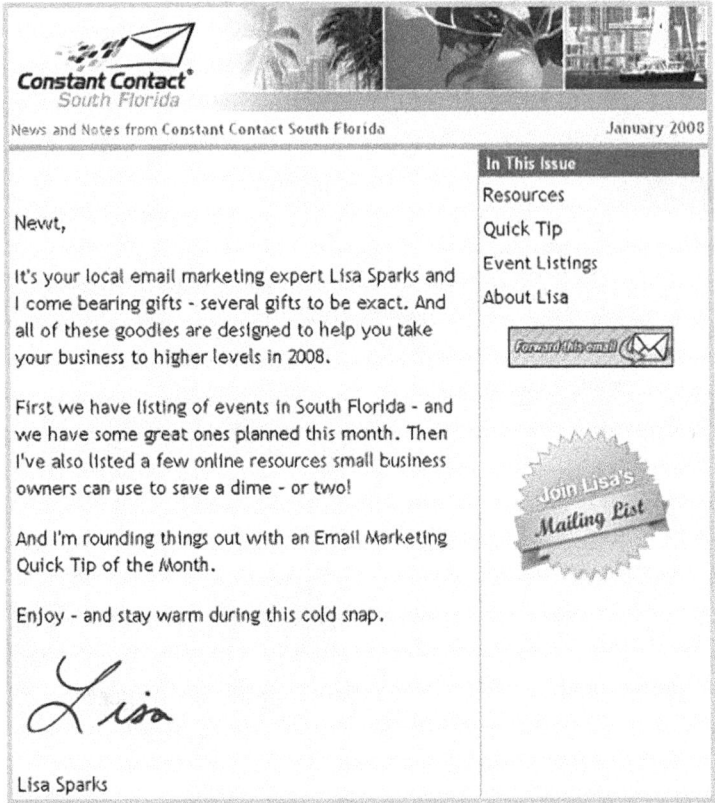

Figure 20.4 Regional Director Lisa Sparks publishes her own content-rich e-newsletter

This Company Actually Uses What It Sells!

Constant Contact eats its own dog food. These folks use the software they sell to demonstrate how to communicate effectively via e-mail and e-newsletters.

By making very good use of its own products, the company proves in the most obvious way that e-mail marketing works—and that its products work. No marketing strategy is more effective than proving that the products you sell enable you to sell more products.

Content Marketing Takeaways

When your success ultimately depends directly on your clients' success, content marketing that enables them to succeed not only is a great strategy, but may be the only strategy that makes sense.

Turning your customers into experts in the use of your products to grow their businesses will make them your best salespeople.

In-person content marketing works brilliantly when you provide information that solves your customers' problems—and secondarily involves the use of your products.

You can conduct sophisticated e-mail marketing campaigns without a significant dollar investment.

A Web site that is all about helping its customers succeed will pull in both new visitors and returning customers.

When you're selling a technology product, make it very, very easy for your customers to try it for free.

CHAPTER 21

U.K. Law Firm Uses Content Marketing to Build Powerful New Brand

Type of organization: 1,000-lawyer legal firm with headquarters in London.

Major marketing objectives:

To be the biggest legal brand on the Web

To replace traditional marketing with content marketing

To generate demonstrable return on marketing investment

Content types:

- Web site
- Weekly e-newsletter
- RSS feeds
- Semiannual print magazine
- Podcasts

Unique element: Created a dedicated content team in 2000 that drives a coherent, consistent complement of content, both in print and online.

Results: A multimillion-dollar return on a relatively small content marketing investment.

If you think all British law firms are stodgy and old-fashioned, you haven't yet encountered Pinsent Masons. The only thing that's old-fashioned about this firm is its name. In fact, it has been doing online and print content marketing for nearly a decade.

The firm's Web site, Out-Law.com, provides a wealth of timely and useful content for its current and prospective clients. In addition, the firm produces a semiannual print publication, also called *Out-Law*. Neither information product is the kind of very traditional marketing you would expect from a venerable global law firm. But that's because this team understood from the beginning that great content was fundamental to building a great brand.

Back in 2000, before the dot-com implosion, this law firm and many of its peers in the U.K. launched Web sites. Most of the others dropped by the wayside or contented themselves with brochure-style Web sites.

The common thread of the also-rans was that they failed to provide relevant content. Because they relied on overworked lawyers to provide the content, they lacked the single-minded focus required to drive a successful content marketing strategy. After all, when your responsibility is to generate billable hours, spending time writing articles for a Web site just doesn't make much sense.

Pinsent Masons took a quite different tack. From the beginning, it made a number of very smart decisions that have been executed effectively by its content marketing team:

- Although it has 1,000 lawyers, the firm realized that it had to form a dedicated content team if it wanted really high-quality content. So, in May 2000, it hired Struan Robertson, who is both a lawyer and an excellent writer. From the outset, his entire job responsibility has revolved around the firm's content marketing efforts.
- It chose a slightly edgy name, Out-Law.com, to brand its Web site. It was meant to evoke a slight feeling of the American Wild West and suggest outside-the-box thinking. The name is also easy to remember and easy to find through search engines.
- Its content is tightly focused on technology law. It is crystal clear on its positioning:
  - It seeks to provide everything about the law for technology firms.

- It seeks to provide everything about technology law for other firms.

- Soon after Struan was hired, the organization added a full-time professional journalist to ensure that the content would be client-centered.
- The writers always write like business journalists because they know that a high percentage of their current and future clients are business executives, not lawyers. They have also learned that even lawyers enjoy great journalism.
- They do real reporting, including interviews with high-level executives and technology experts. In early 2008, they scooped a number of publications by interviewing a European browser maker who was about to take on Microsoft in court.

Before 2000, the firm's marketing was conventional. As Struan puts it, "We were producing thousands of boring brochures that recipients tossed upon receipt." The firm was unable to attribute any significant return to this brochure investment. It was producing brochures because that was what it had always done.

Three team members—attorneys John Salmon and Jon Fell, joined by marketing manager Vincent Gray—decided that it was time for some significant marketing changes. They originated the idea of a Web site that would deliver valuable content that their current and future clients would actually want to read.

Web Site Reaches 120,000 Visitors per Month

Online, the firm's goal is simple and ambitious: "To be the biggest legal brand on the Web." After nearly a decade of continuous improvement, it may well have nailed that goal. In its first year on the Web, it averaged just 1,000 visitors per month; today, it attracts 1.4 million visitors over the course of the year. That's a 10,000 percent increase!

The Web site is very much news-driven, delivering three to five new stories every day (see Figure 21.1). Overall, the site contains more than 8,000 articles on technology law and on law for technology companies.

Figure 21.1 Out-Law.com delivers content from a law firm that clients actually want to read

The site is well organized, providing a wealth of logically structured information, including:

- Guides on specific topics
- Articles divided into more than two dozen categories
- Articles sorted by the ultimate application, such as start-ups, financial services, media and entertainment, and interactive media
- In-depth case studies that explore some of the most pressing technology law issues
- Information on the variety of services the firm provides
- Who the firm is and why you might want to do business with it
- Whom to contact when you're ready to do business

Almost all of the content on Out-Law.com is customer-centric. The Web site is carefully designed to make its readers more knowledgeable about legal issues within the firm's areas of expertise. It makes it very easy for you to find exactly what you're looking for.

The firm is now also making all of its content available for PDAs and other mobile devices. That way you can find exactly what you need even when you're on the run.

Weekly E-newsletter Directs 15,000 Subscribers Back to the Web Site

Also in 2000, the firm created a weekly e-newsletter that now reaches 15,000 subscribers (see Figure 21.2). It provides quick summaries of the top six stories of the week, with links back to the firm's Web site. In addition, you can click on a link that takes you back to last month's stories.

Other than its header, which focuses on the Out-Law.com sheriff's badge logo, the newsletter has no graphical elements at all. It's designed

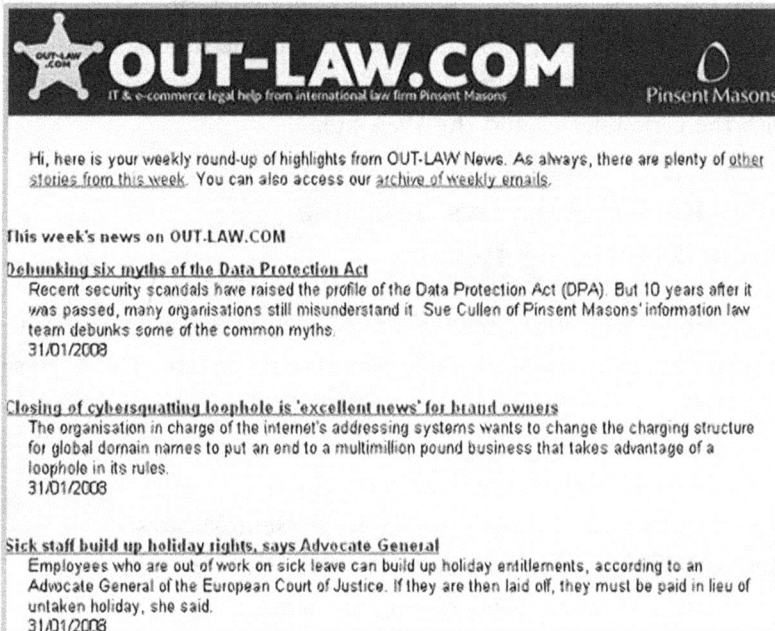

Figure 21.2 The weekly e-newsletter delivers quickly read content that is tightly linked to Out-Law.com

to be a very quick read that enables its recipients to decide whether they want to pursue a particular article or move on with their day.

The e-newsletter is archived on the Web site going back to the beginning of 2007. In addition, you can choose to receive it via RSS feed. It has a smart and client-centric twist to RSS: it makes 10 different RSS feeds available that focus on specific legal and technology topics.

Pinsent Masons Has Been Podcasting Since August 2006

Although business-related podcasting is relatively new, the firm was characteristically a pioneer in this area. Just as the team members have been careful to operate more as business journalists than as lawyers, they have approached podcasting in a similar way.

The weekly podcasts are treated like the commercial business radio broadcasts that you might expect from NPR, ABC, or CNN in the United States. The objective is to conduct interesting or relevant interviews with experts who can provide unique insights to podcast listeners. Of course, there are links to the podcasts from both the e-newsletter and the Web site.

Recent Research Shows Tangible Content Marketing Results

In a recent e-mail survey that generated an impressive 700 responses, Pinsent Masons made some important discoveries about its Web site visitors:

- About 38 percent are decision makers.
- A full 96 percent plan to contact Pinsent Masons.
- About 63 percent found the law firm via the Web.
- Only 14 percent were existing clients.

More importantly, the firm is confident that it can track millions of British pounds' worth of business to its online content marketing efforts.

Relevant Magazine Replaces Ineffective Brochures

When a law firm puts Homer Simpson on the cover of its magazine, *Out-Law*, you know it's doing something very different from its peers (see Figure 21.3). As Struan says, "We set out to design a magazine that you would want to pick up on the newsstand." With Homer on the cover, how could you *not* pick it up?

More than 10,500 targeted clients have requested copies. An additional 7,000 are handed out at industry events each year.

The firm strives to make the magazine as interesting and compelling as any high-quality business journal. The content is written for CEOs, CFOs, and COOs—not for lawyers.

Pinsent Masons does an excellent job of integrating the magazine's content with high-impact graphics that enhance the readability of the

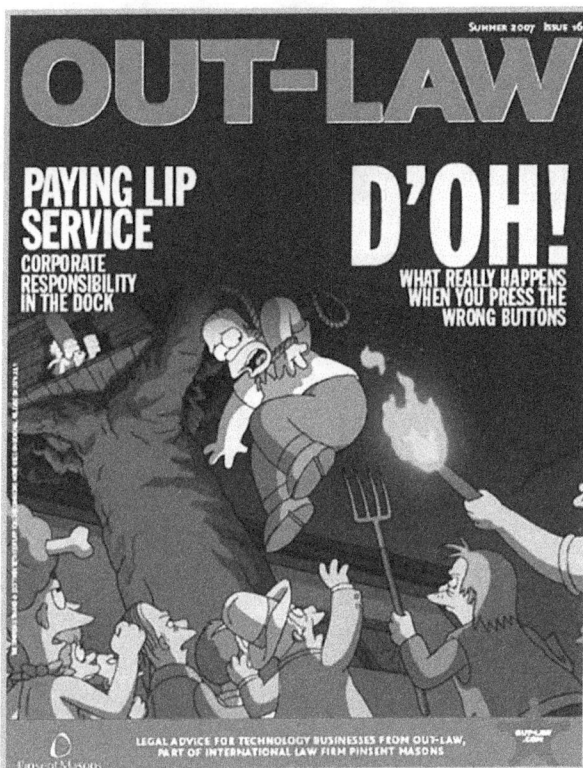

Figure 21.3 *Out-Law* magazine is readable, relevant, amusing, and graphically unique

feature articles. This is not a law journal—it's an enjoyable business publication that just happens to cover topics in technology law.

The content team has been very clever with its use of high-profile entertainment images (e.g., pictures of Homer Simpson and actor Matt Damon, Figure 21.4), approaching studios that are in the process of releasing films. Not only doesn't the firm have to pay high prices for great artwork, but it gets the artwork for *free* from studios that are only too happy to receive the extra promotion. Brilliant.

A recent issue of *OutLaw.com* magazine covered the following topics:

- The potential assault on personal privacy by mega-technology companies

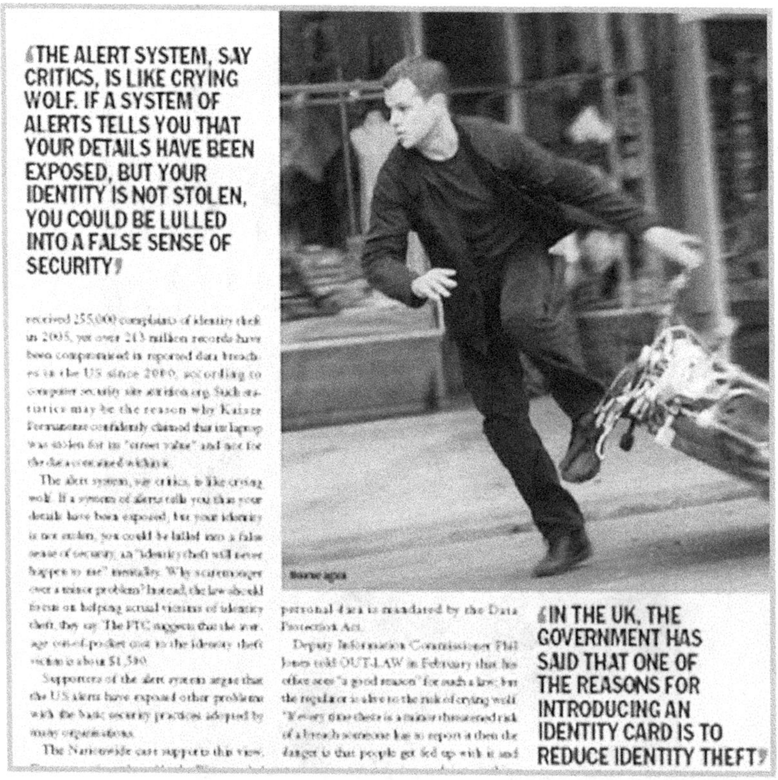

"THE ALERT SYSTEM, SAY CRITICS, IS LIKE CRYING WOLF. IF A SYSTEM OF ALERTS TELLS YOU THAT YOUR DETAILS HAVE BEEN EXPOSED, BUT YOUR IDENTITY IS NOT STOLEN, YOU COULD BE LULLED INTO A FALSE SENSE OF SECURITY"

"IN THE UK, THE GOVERNMENT HAS SAID THAT ONE OF THE REASONS FOR INTRODUCING AN IDENTITY CARD IS TO REDUCE IDENTITY THEFT"

Figure 21.4 The magazine uses timely, memorable, and free images that are usually tied to new movie releases

- The unfortunate import of class-action litigation from the United States to Europe
- The danger of trampling on basic consumer expectations in a Web 2.0 world
- The risks posed by "typo infringement" of your Web address by cybersquatters
- A company's legal responsibility in the face of a security breach

The magazine also has a lively mailbag section with spirited responses from readers to the magazine's content.

Each of these topics could have been treated in a boring fashion and written in pedantic legalese. Instead, the editors write in a comfortable, colloquial style that reminds us of how wittily articulate our British cousins can be. Here's a snippet from the article about personal privacy:

These are companies with so much personal information about us that they see into the darkest reaches of our souls more clearly than Sigmund Freud channeled by Mystic Meg. They are peopled by zealous superbrains who doodle weather system algorithms while chatting to granny on the phone, yet even they can't decide on the right way to handle our personal data.

Out-Law magazine is an unexpected pleasure, full of well-written articles enhanced by professional design and compelling graphics.

Great Content Marketing Has Replaced Old-Fashioned Ways of Communicating with Clients

Because of its single-minded focus on delivering great content, Pinsent Masons has avoided spending money on the sort of unproductive marketing efforts that most of its competitors are still pouring large sums of money into. This has proved to be both a smart and a cost-effective approach.

Apart from staffing, the firm's costs are minimal. Because it has a sophisticated content management system, it can manage all of its online efforts in-house. The most expensive components of its approach are printing and mailing the twice-yearly magazine. The art budget is just $600 per year.

Pinsent Masons does no other advertising beyond its Web site, e-newsletter, podcasts, and magazine. In fact, it is able to "trade" promotion in its online or print vehicles for trade show booths and other event sponsorships.

Today, the Out-Law.com brand stands for technology law leadership. It is recognized by thousands and thousands of Web visitors, e-newsletter readers, and magazine subscribers. This unique and powerful brand enables Pinsent Masons to stand out from the hundreds of other firms whose names are still those of long-dead partners.

As indicated earlier, this firm has been able to track millions of pounds' worth of business to its integrated content marketing efforts. Moreover, because it does no other advertising or direct marketing, it knows that its content marketing strategy is its most important growth driver.

Content Marketing Takeaways

Even a small dedicated content creation team can make all the difference when it comes to providing relevant and valuable information. Because it has a single-minded focus, Pinsent Masons's team of talented and motivated professionals has been able to outperform the armies of lawyers in other firms who have been drafted to create articles. These legal conscripts lack either the time, the inclination, or the talent—or all three—to provide timely and consistent content.

A business organization can build a brand with a carefully chosen name that comes to symbolize a wealth of valuable content that, in turn, reinforces the quality of its people, products, and services.

In the business-to-business arena, it is possible to completely abandon traditional marketing in favor of a well-planned and well-executed content marketing strategy.

A small investment in content marketing by a company of any size can deliver returns that are disproportionate to the level of investment. Once a basic content marketing infrastructure has been created, delivering that content can be both less expensive and more effective than paying for an advertising presence in traditional media outlets.

CHAPTER 22

Rockwell Automation Uses Content Marketing to Be Global, Local, and Cost-Effective

This global manufacturing company goes way beyond promoting the features of its products and services by clearly explaining how it provides solutions for its customers.

Type of organization: A $5 billion multinational corporation with headquarters in Milwaukee, Wisconsin.

Major marketing objective: To strengthen its ties to Australian customers with an integrated print/online content marketing program that bridges cultures and languages.

Content types:

- Print magazine
- E-zines
- E-newsletters
- Comprehensive online product and service library

Unique element: The Asia Pacific marketing group creates a core publication in English that is customized by language and content to match local needs.

Results: Content-rich publications build trusted relationships with a diverse customer base by helping to solve problems and teach best practices.

You just know that a company whose service mark is "Listen. Think. Solve." will have a pretty good handle on content marketing. This global manufacturing company uses both print and online content marketing effectively to connect with its technically savvy buyers around the world.

Even with a limited budget, the Rockwell Automation Asia Pacific division is able to reach out to customers and prospects in multiple languages and multiple ways. Traditional trade publication advertising has become less effective over the years. In addition, trade shows, which are big in North America and Europe, are relatively rare in the Asia Pacific region. This limits the ways in which this manufacturing giant can communicate effectively and regularly with its audience.

Because of these limitations, Rockwell has chosen to create its own high-quality content that reflects the high quality of its products and services.

Custom Magazine Targeted to Specific Countries

Rockwell's Asia Pacific magazine *Automation Today* (see Figure 22.1) is an excellent example of how to provide relevant content that is both broadly applicable to customers and customized to individual countries.

Gail Anderson, manager of Asia Pacific marketing communications, notes that Rockwell's current approach is quite different from the way it used to handle customer communications:

> *We used to be very feature-oriented and internally focused. But we have learned that our customers are looking for solutions. We now take a customer-centric selling approach to determine what our customers need to solve their problems.*

Gail's comments about being customer-centric ring true on the Web. Here's how the company describes what it does at the very top of its Web site's home page:

> *When it comes to automation, your requirements are unique. So are our solutions. We listen to you, then apply our resources to build*

cost-effective, results-based solutions. It could be a single, powerful component. An information or asset management solution. Or an enterprise-wide, integrated system. Whatever your automation requirement, you'll find the answer by partnering with us.

Rockwell Automation is a $5 billion global company with 20,000 employees worldwide, serving customers in 80 countries. It provides solutions both to manufacturing end users and to OEMs. According to the company, these solutions are "designed to give our customers a competitive edge."

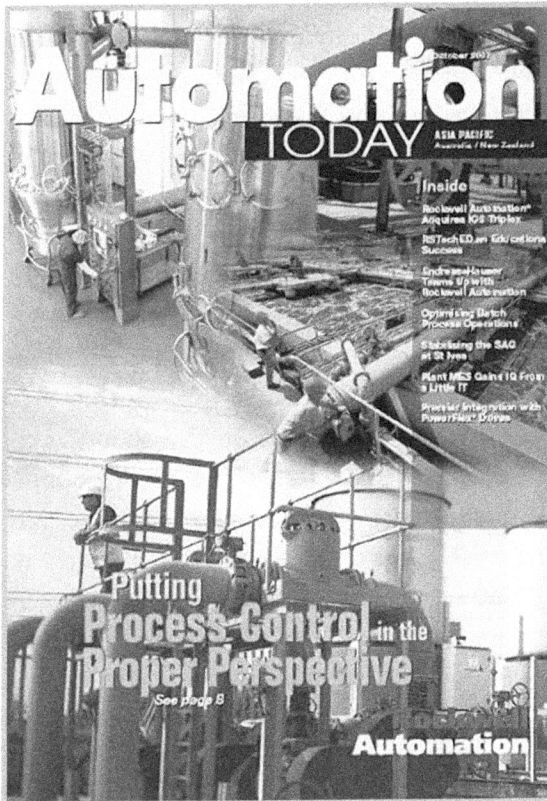

Figure 22.1 *Automation Today* reflects Rockwell's "Listen. Think. Solve." approach to its customers and to content marketing

In fact, Rockwell Automation is a veteran content marketer; in North America, it has long published a monthly magazine called *The Journal*. This magazine is very much customer- and solution-focused. Although *The Journal* is a custom publication, it could certainly stand on its own as a solid monthly manufacturing magazine.

Automation Today stands on the shoulders of its North American sister publication. Gail and her team launched the new magazine in 1999 to provide relevant and meaningful content to a diverse audience of customers in the Asia Pacific region. Previously, the firm had simply mailed copies of *The Journal* from the United States This was less than optimal because it was expensive and because the magazine contained a great deal of North American advertising that had relatively little relevance to the Asia Pacific market.

Although *Automation Today* can pick up stories from its sister magazine, its content tends to be unique and specific to its own markets. To be certain that the publication is relevant to its readers, the team has conducted research asking its customer readers whether the magazine gives them what they need, whether the articles are the right length, whether the frequency is right, and whether the magazine is written to the right technical level. The team has also determined exactly who is reading the magazine and whether it's being shared with colleagues.

The magazine is prepared in electronic format with 18 fixed pages and 2 blank pages that can be filled with local content. Some country teams actually add extra pages to the publication. It is printed in five languages: two versions of Chinese, plus Japanese, Korean, and British English. Each country manages its own final production, printing, and circulation.

Typical feature articles are fairly horizontal so that it is clear to readers in different disciplines how they can benefit from the solution described. Although many of the articles do feature Rockwell products and services, they are always written from the perspective of solving customer problems.

For example, a typically practical article described a three-step migration program that enables manufacturers to make the transition from aging distributed control systems ($65 billion worth of existing control systems are estimated to be near the end of their life cycle). The process described is designed to eliminate most of the pain from a complex transition. Even though the process is illustrated with Rockwell Automation equipment, it would apply no matter what kind of automation equipment was involved.

Detailed and useful graphics accompany the more complex feature articles. Thus, an article about process control automation included a very detailed graphical diagram of the system and process described (see Figure 22.2). It's obvious that a great deal of care has gone into each element of the magazine.

Each issue also features a number of customer success stories. A recent issue described an incredibly complex Rockwell Automation application in an Australian gold mine (see Figure 22.3). It involved the implementation of an "expert control" system in a very challenging process control situation. The discussion of the implementation is sophisticated, high-level, and well written.

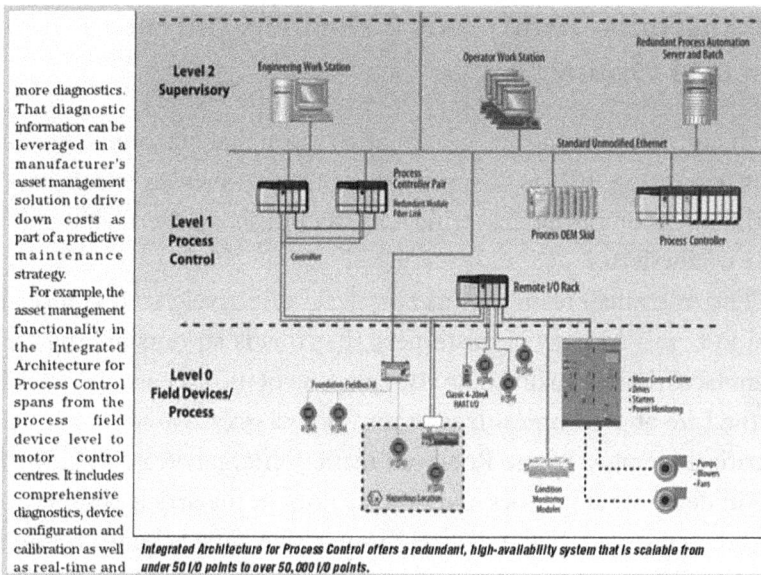

Figure 22.2 Detailed and useful graphics accompany more complex feature articles

APPLICATION STORY

The Lefroy mill's centrepiece is the 11 m-diameter SAG mill, which utilises an advanced multi-variable control system founded on ControlLogix.

Manta Controls has taken advantage of the unique advanced process control functionality of the mill's existing ControlLogix platform, coupled with the open nature of the ControlLogix development environment.

Closed-Loop SAG

Located at Kambalda, 80 km south of Kalgoorlie, the Lefroy mill comprises four main process circuits: comminution, gravity separation, leach/adsorption and carbon handling/electrowinning. The comminution circuit largely comprises primary crushing, coarse-ore storage and feeding, a bank of 10 hydrocyclone classifiers, and the SAG mill – an enormous tumbling mill mounted on load-cells and powered by a 13MW wrap-around drive.

Stabilising the SAG at St Ives

Figure 22.3 Success stories make customers look great

The Australia Team Adds Valuable Content in Print and Online

Each country within the Asia Pacific region can customize its content marketing efforts. The Australian team does an excellent job with its version of the magazine. It also publishes a useful and enjoyable e-newsletter.

The Australian team uses its two pages effectively, so that it seems to the firm's Australian customers that this is an outstanding local manufacturing magazine. For example, one of its brief articles, "A Day in the Life of a Technical Instructor," does a great job of humanizing a critical member of the Rockwell team, John Sciberras. By describing in detail what he does and how he does it, the article shows readers how a talented Rockwell veteran spends his time helping customers just like them to keep their technical knowledge and skills current.

The Aussie team does a great job of content marketing online as well. Its e-newsletter is delivered bimonthly and is promoted as being "packed with the most up-to-the-minute news . . . this eNewsletter will enable you to be among the first to find out about new products, training, services, events, workshops, and any special offers from Rockwell Automation Australia."

Another recent issue included 10 articles on a wide variety of topics. Readers could find everything from how to protect their automation investment, to asset management, to how to complete their annual training schedule.

The lead story highlighted a group of Adelaide University students who have created an automated version of foosball that can blow away the human opposition (see Figure 22.4). Several stories in the newsletter, including this one, feature local partners. In this way, the newsletter provides useful and interesting content to its end users—and helps to promote the services of its trusted local partners.

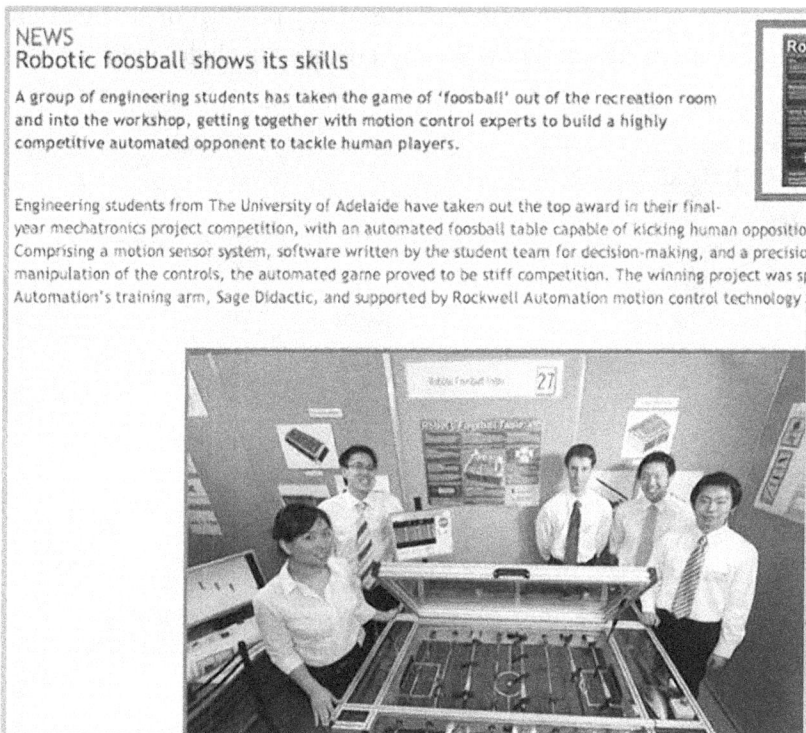

NEWS
Robotic foosball shows its skills

A group of engineering students has taken the game of 'foosball' out of the recreation room and into the workshop, getting together with motion control experts to build a highly competitive automated opponent to tackle human players.

Engineering students from The University of Adelaide have taken out the top award in their final-year mechatronics project competition, with an automated foosball table capable of kicking human oppositio Comprising a motion sensor system, software written by the student team for decision-making, and a precisio manipulation of the controls, the automated game proved to be stiff competition. The winning project was s Automation's training arm, Sage Didactic, and supported by Rockwell Automation motion control technology

Figure 22.4 The Australian e-newsletter includes custom content that resonates with local customers

Vital Global Customer Resource: The Corporate Online Literature Library

The Asia Pacific team benefits from a well-structured corporate site that includes a wealth of product-related content to make it easier for customers to buy.

The Literature Library is a perfect example. It is clearly organized by

- Products
- Industries and applications (see Figure 22.5)
- Services and support
- Solutions

Current and prospective customers can drill down to find an incredible amount of information about any product or service they are likely to need—and how it would be used in their application or

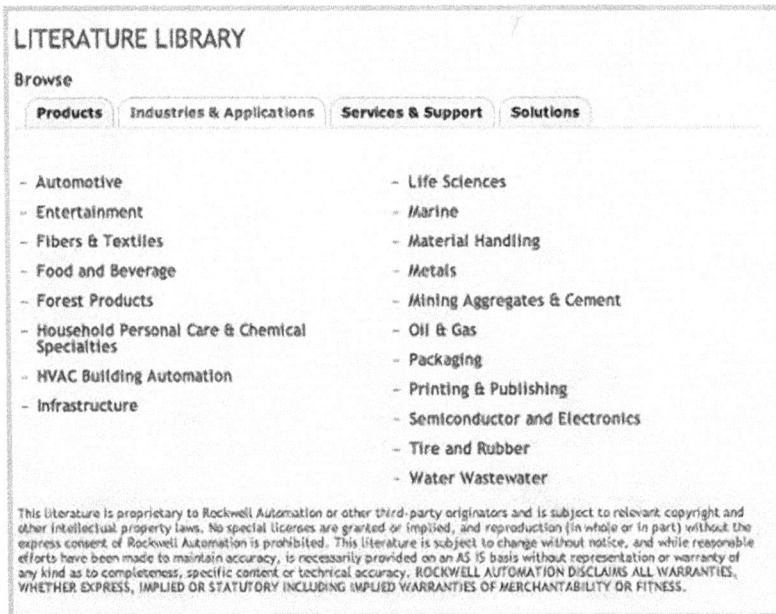

Figure 22.5 The corporate literature library is an invaluable resource for Asia Pacific customers

industry. Thus, in a few minutes, buyers can access what would have taken many phone calls, lots of postage, and lots of time just 5 or 10 years ago. Rockwell Automation provides instant information gratification for its Web visitors.

Content Marketing Takeaways

The Asia Pacific division of Rockwell Automation has a limited marketing budget. It has chosen to focus much of its effort on content marketing because this accurately reflects the company's customer-centric focus.

When the folks at Rockwell talk about listening, thinking, and solving, they are dead serious. The quality of their print and online publications makes it clear to their customers that Rockwell means what it says.

Rockwell's products and services provide solutions to thorny manufacturing problems. Its content marketing efforts focus on providing relevant information that describes how to solve those problems. Although the articles in its magazines typically talk about Rockwell products and services, they have intrinsic value based on the thoroughness and clarity of their discussion of technical, process, and automation issues.

Rockwell Automation proves that just because you're a technology company doesn't mean that you have to live in a feature-oriented universe. In fact, customer-centric content marketing is probably even more important if this is the world in which you operate. If you can describe to your potential customers how they can stay at the top of their game technologically and how they can solve very difficult manufacturing problems, you will begin to earn their trust and show them that you and your organization are the competent and caring partners that they need.

PART FOUR

Putting the Lessons into Action

CHAPTER 23

Top 10 Content Marketing Lessons Learned from Successful Practitioners

1. Only content that is intrinsically valuable to your customers will work as a core component of your content marketing strategy.

2. You must have a thorough understanding of your customers and what is most important to them. If you do not understand the problems and challenges that they face, you cannot hope to create content that is truly relevant to them. Without understanding their problems, you cannot provide solutions.

3. A comprehensive content marketing strategy may completely or partially replace traditional advertising and marketing. Such a strategy can be both more effective and less expensive than doing things the old-fashioned way.

4. Print magazines can be a powerful weapon in your content marketing arsenal. They enable you to reach out to your customers with precision, offering carefully targeted messages that are totally under your control.

5. Great design adds significant value to content marketing by making it more accessible, more appealing, and more actionable for your customers.

6. Your best content marketing investment may be in the creation of a dedicated internal or external team that understands

how to produce great content and that lives and dies by the success of your content marketing program.

7. Drink your own Kool-Aid. Whenever possible, use your own company's products or services to prove their worth to your customers.

8. Get your customers to participate actively with the content that you create in print and online. Begin a conversation and keep it going in order to earn your customers' loyalty and trust.

9. Relevant and valuable content is just the first step in turning prospects or visitors into customers. You must then make it easy for them to buy.

10. Most of the best practices from the larger companies we profiled can be emulated in whole or in part even by very small organizations. It's not the money. It's the content marketing mindset that counts. Big ideas can trump big bucks.

CHAPTER 24

An In-Depth Case Study— Developing a Content Marketing Strategy from Start to Finish

The following is a fictitious case study based on real-life situations. MODEL, Inc., creates software specifically for engineers who design manufactured products such as paint cans, plastic spray bottles, and even eyeglass frames. MODEL's software integrates with the larger design engineering software programs such as those by Autodesk (Inventor) and SolidWorks (two very large, multinational software companies), so MODEL's software is often bundled by these "affiliate" companies, with MODEL taking a cut.

MODEL's software focuses on three-dimensional (3D) analysis. For years, MODEL has been fighting it out with two major competitors for the same customer base and has been able to scrape together a small market share without having any direct sales representatives. It has a great product that has been sold and distributed by two of the leading design software companies, Autodesk and SolidWorks, which have generated the majority of its business for the last five years.

Recently, MODEL has seen more competitors come into the market, taking away market share. In addition, MODEL has been hearing rumors that both Autodesk and SolidWorks, as well as other design engineering software companies, are planning on creating their own analysis software that would compete directly with MODEL's.

Positioning MODEL as a Leader in Analysis Software

MODEL, a small 30-person firm with about $10 million in revenues, has an excellent core group of engineers and has been run by the same executive team since its launch in 1997. Unfortunately, MODEL has very low brand awareness in the industry, since it has never had to market aggressively in the past. Many of its customers actually think that the software it creates comes from Autodesk and SolidWorks, both of which sell MODEL's software as an add-on product.

MODEL's executive team is freaking out. It has begun to invest in a sales force and customer service, but it is concerned about what it can spend on marketing and, ultimately, how it should communicate with its customers and prospects. What should this company do?

Step 1: Define the Organizational Goals

The CEO called an off-site meeting to discuss the current situation. During that day, the team developed a renewed business plan that included some specific marketing goals. Among those were

- *Build a robust Web site.* This specifically means acquiring 2,000 qualified names through its Web site efforts during the next year. MODEL believes that it needs to close 5 percent of these corporate clients (100) in the next year (without the help of its design partners) to make an impact on the company's strategic goals.
- *Be the name in analysis.* Company executives believe that MODEL has the engineering excellence to be the "Intel Inside" of design analysis software. The measurement of this would be the firm's becoming "the preferred brand name"

when it came to analysis software within the next 12 months. MODEL is beginning the process with a benchmark study so that it can clearly measure its increased awareness.

- *Sell direct to customers* at least 50 percent of the time within 18 months. Currently, this number is 10 percent.
- *Keep the core base of users.* Customer loyalty is key, so MODEL set customer renewal at 95 percent for the next year.
- *Double revenues over the next five years.* This is an aggressive goal that MODEL will meet through organic growth and possibly one key acquisition.

Step 2: Determine the Informational Needs of the Buyers

Before doing anything, MODEL decided to talk to its core customers. It did this in two ways. First, the CEO and COO went out to see 20 customers and prospects (some big, some small) face to face. In addition, MODEL conducted an online research study through Zoomerang that focused on not only what its customers and prospects thought, but what their informational needs were. In other words, what were the problems that kept its customers (design engineers) up at night?

The results of the research amazed the executive team. Here is what they found:

- MODEL customers are very loyal. They love the software and often request it when they move to a new company or are working with outside partners.
- Newer MODEL customers did indeed think that MODEL software came from another company.
- Outside of MODEL customers, most design engineers had little awareness of MODEL or its software.
- Decisions about purchasing MODEL software were often made not by the design engineer, but by the owner of the company or the vice president of engineering.

- A top-three challenge among prospects was analysis concerns. These prospects usually reached out to the larger software firms, not to MODEL, with questions on analysis.
- Many design engineers were uneducated about analysis software and weren't sure how to learn more about how it could help them in their jobs.
- Customers and prospects named MODEL as their preferred analysis brand only 7 percent of the time. There were seven other companies ahead of it, two of which did not create analysis software.

Step 3: Determine What You Want the Customer to Do and Why This Helps the Business

Once MODEL executives had completed Steps 1 and 2, Step 3 seemed pretty easy to do. Here are some of the notes that the marketing team put together:

- "We need some downloadable information so that we can provide qualified design engineers with information and communicate with them on an ongoing basis."
- "We need to create targeted marketing information for two groups: design engineers and C-level executives. Design engineers are both influencers and decision makers, depending on the size of the company. C-level executives are decision makers only and care about product quality, cost, and time to market. When either of these populations thinks about analysis, MODEL needs to be at the top of the list."
- "We need to get engineers to try the product in some way . . . possibly offer a free trial of the software." (MODEL does not offer a free trial at this time).

Step 4: Determine the Product and Content Mix

Armed with all of this information, MODEL executives sat in a half-day brainstorming meeting and created the following plan. They hired a facilitator to run the meeting, and they also invited two key customers and an industry expert to participate (all three signed nondisclosure agreements). Here is the plan they came up with.

Print Newsletter

The core of the content marketing initiative would be a 16-page print newsletter called *Design Analysis*. In order to differentiate this direct-mail initiative from other mail programs, MODEL decided to go with a digest-style, four-color format. *Design Analysis* would be mailed quarterly to 10,000 customers and prospects who were already in the company's database (the same target as the research study), as well as an additional list of 15,000 design engineers rented from an industry publication. MODEL also decided to hold 2,000 customers/prospects out of the distribution to serve as a control group for measurement purposes. MODEL would integrate an opt-in strategy over the first nine months to enable customers and prospects to request the newsletter.

The marketing team worked with an audience development company to produce the final list size and target, determining that the final distribution would target 90 percent of MODEL's "model" company target. In companies with more than 100 employees, *Design Analysis* would be sent to at least three decision makers within the organization, including an engineering manager.

The content plan for the newsletter was simple: no selling, only educating. MODEL contracted with a leading freelance journalist to create the content plan for the newsletter, and with other freelancers from the industry to deliver the content. The ultimate goal was to position MODEL as *the* thought leader on analysis software. The publication was clearly marked as coming from MODEL, provided one customer success story in each issue, and included a small ad on the mailing page of the issue.

Each article in the newsletter had multiple links to additional information on the MODEL Web site or other relevant Web sites. MODEL also made it easy for design engineers to sign up for the e-newsletter, including a clear subscription form on the MODEL home page and all content pages, a "forward to a friend" viral component, and a "widget" that customers and other engineers could use to feed in MODEL content on a daily basis.

E-book

The MODEL content team (made up of the MODEL marketing team and a freelance editorial team) created *The Ultimate Survival Guide to Design Analysis*, a five-chapter e-book (about 60 pages) that would be promoted in every issue of the newsletter. Downloading the e-book from the MODEL Web site would be free, as long as the buyer completed some profile information.

The e-book would also be promoted via pay-per-click (PPC) on Google and Yahoo!. One chapter of the e-book would be promoted via a news release to (1) help in search engine optimization efforts and (2) attract the attention of industry bloggers and other influencers.

MODEL also bought text ads in key industry online newsletters to promote the e-book.

White Paper Series

In conjunction with each quarterly print newsletter, MODEL released a white paper on analysis, targeted at senior-level engineers, VPs of engineering, and owners, regarding the key benefits of analysis, such as reduced time to market, product and process improvement, and cost savings during the manufacturing process.

A short abstract of each white paper was promoted in the print newsletter. Each white paper was also promoted via a news release (multiple releases) and delivered to MODEL's opt-in management distribution e-file. MODEL also partnered with an industry media source to co-brand the white papers and promote each one to management.

All white papers were available for free to anyone who answered two brief qualifying questions and provided his name, title, company, and e-mail address.

Finally, the white papers were promoted through a targeted PPC campaign and by contracting with a small search engine optimization company that worked on organic placement of the white paper landing page.

The MODEL Web Site and Blog

Previously, the MODEL Web site had been entirely product-oriented. Now, half of the home page was taken up with consistent and relevant content from the previous initiatives.

The biggest improvement was the launching of the *Design Analysis* blog, which was maintained by MODEL's engineering and technical support department. All six team members were given instructions to blog at least once per week, and were also responsible for five outside blogs and Web sites, where they would become active in those blog communities by commenting and linking back to the MODEL blog.

The blog was registered with all major blog directories and with Technorati, a blog search site. It focused on helpful analysis tips, shortcuts, and industry trends. A news release announcing the blog to the industry was sent out after three months of blog posts.

Customer Facebook Fan Page

MODEL partnered with its top customers to create a customer Facebook group, where customers could share tips, tricks, and expertise through the social networking site. MODEL appointed two customers as co-moderators, along with one of MODEL's engineers. They are currently looking into the feasibility of a LinkedIn group as well.

Article Marketing Program for Affiliates

In addition to its own content, MODEL created articles about the benefits of analysis for key affiliates in multiple industries. This was done for free, as long as the article cited MODEL as the source and linked back to the MODEL Web site. MODEL's team also worked with a small public relations firm to help place modified articles where relevant and promote the use of their content via Creative Commons Attribution 3.0 (http://creative commons.org/licenses/by/3.0/).

News Releases

In addition to the news releases mentioned previously, MODEL set up a news release calendar that included no fewer than two news releases per month. Eight out of ten news releases had to contain educational content, while the other two were to be company announcements of some sort.

Note: Before any Web launches, MODEL purchased 10 hours of an SEO expert's time to make sure that all Web content would be properly tagged and indexed for search engines. It also used a search engine marketing expert to assist with keyword choices for both the PPC e-book and the white paper program.

Listening Program

MODEL assigned a "chief conversation officer" to actively monitor what was being said on the Web about the MODEL brands and about key industry topics. Using free reputation management tools such as Google Alerts and Twitter, MODEL is able to keep the pulse on what is going on in the industry and target any customer service issues or opportunities.

Final Step: Measuring the Program

MODEL took a snapshot of where it was before any content initiatives were in place, then measured everything it could on a monthly basis. The following measurements were tracked.

Benchmark Study

At six months and one year from launch, MODEL repeated its initial benchmarking study against its control group. In the process, it also continued to get great ideas for its content through additional editorial questions.

Awareness levels and purchase intent, both among design engineers and among engineering management, were measured.

Web Statistics

MODEL tracked a number of Web statistics, including:

- Alexa.com rating
- Blog RSS subscribers

- Blog comments
- Blog Technorati ranking
- Print newsletter subscriptions
- Unique site visitors
- Unique site page views
- Percentage of new visitors
- Pages per visit
- Google page rank
- Top referrers
- Top exit pages
- White paper downloads
- E-book downloads
- Most popular pages
- Twitter customer conversations

Sales-Related Statistics

The marketing team measured conversions of e-book downloads to sales and pipeline, white paper conversions, and print subscription conversions. Also, measurements were analyzed for both those who just signed up for the free trial and those who signed up and also downloaded one or more additional content products.

Current customers who downloaded content products were compared against current customers who did not download any products. MODEL found that customers who downloaded or subscribed to a content product had a 20 percent better retention rate and purchased an average of 1.2 additional products.

In Summary

By looking at marketing through the lens of content marketing, MODEL, Inc., was able to outperform in a highly competitive environment. Previously, MODEL hadn't seen marketing as important because it hadn't had to market to survive and, truthfully, hadn't understood it. Today, MODEL's entire marketing plan is about making its customers smarter, which not only is more fun to implement, but works better than anything else the company could have executed.

CHAPTER 25

Marketing Survival

When you began reading this book, you were probably skeptical about the content marketing revolution. Frankly, not that long ago we were pretty much traditional marketers ourselves. Today, we are unapologetic content marketing evangelists.

That's why we have written *Get Content Get Customers*. We are compelled to share the lessons that we have learned as media executives, as observers of content marketing best practices, and, ultimately, as content marketing practitioners ourselves. Of course, as you have certainly realized by now, this book is part of our own content marketing strategy.

Although most organizations still rely primarily, if not exclusively, on traditional marketing tactics, a rapidly growing number of companies of all sizes is proving that content marketing is the one strategy that will pay dividends both for customers and for the companies themselves.

In fact, the accelerating shift to content marketing is occurring not because it's fashionable, but because it's effective.

Smart marketers around the globe are using the concepts from this book to create customer-focused, innovative organizations. Bottom-line-driven multinationals are moving megabucks from traditional media to content marketing initiatives because content marketing drives both sales and profitability.

Moreover, many practitioners have been able to eliminate traditional marketing strategies altogether. In fact, as we've written, even very traditional companies have successfully deployed content marketing strategies in print, online, and in person.

You now understand that the transformation from traditional strategies to content marketing often requires both a new mindset and a new skill set. Although it's easier to say than to do, we are convinced that you and your team must make that transformation.

You may be concerned about the risks of making dramatic changes in your approach to marketing within your organization. We urge you to concentrate instead on the risks inherent in failing to make the changes necessary to compete for the new breed of buyer. We all know that many otherwise-smart companies remain mired in prehistoric marketing methodologies. If you're hesitating, think once again about the fate of the dinosaurs.

We don't know what caused the dinosaurs' demise eons ago. But when it comes to the fate of marketing dinosaurs in the twenty-first century, we know for sure what will kill them off: the failure to develop and deploy successful content marketing strategies in the face of a game-changing metamorphosis in the business environment.

Don't be a marketing dinosaur. Start implementing your content marketing strategy today. As they say over at Nike, "Just do it."

Notes

Chapter 1

1. *New York Times*, October 14, 2007. http://www.nytimes.com/2007/10/14/business/media/14ad.html

Chapter 2

1. PaidContent.org, October 24, 2007.
2. Alexa.com, November 2008.
3. MediaLifeMagazine.com, October 17, 2007.

Chapter 9

1. *Gulfcoast Business Review*, September 13, 2007.

Chapter 17

1. Michael Totty, "Operation Overload," *Wall Street Journal*, December 11, 2007.

Chapter 18

1. "Toys with a Second Life," *BusinessWeek*, December 20, 2007.

Acknowledgments

There are countless people and organizations that made this book possible. Special thanks to our editor, Lisa Murton Beets, and to Mike Azzara and David Drickhamer, who showed us some tough editing love. These three individuals gave us the greatest gift we could have imagined: they told us when we were wrong. Thanks to each of you for your guidance and expertise.

Thanks to those people who opened the door to our many interviews and provided core information about the content marketing process, especially (in alphabetical order) Gail Anderson, Lisa Arthur, Mike Azzara, Bob Bloom, Judy Bricker, Mary Briggs, Chris Carson, Linda Cleary, Katie Coletto, Marie Kroesen Connell, Katie Danforth, Stephanie Diamond, Chris Elliott, Carlos Fernandes, Paul Gerbbino, Brett Gilbertson, Eric Groves, Eric Holter, Barry Judge, April Kettelle, Pam Kozelka, Jennifer LeClaire, Michael Linenberger, Gaelen O'Connell, Carol Orsborn, Ann Porter, Mike Reagan, Kamilla Reid, Vickie Reiner, Tonia Ries, Linda Rigano, Struan Robertson, Rebecca Rolfes, John Sprecher, David Strom, Melinda Venable, and Mitch York.

A final thanks to those who influenced us and this book along the way, including (in no particular order) Don Schultz, David Meerman Scott, Seth Godin, Stephanie Diamond, Paul Gillin, Rohit Barghava, Jim McDermott, Angela Vannucci, Simon Kelly, Ardath Albee, Peter Banks, Christian Coughlan, Kenneth Kessler, Ian Alexander, Hans de Keulenaer, Paul Conley, Chuck Francisco, Rex Hammock, Bob Rosenbaum, Michael Hurley, Aaron Kahlow, Greg Kiskadden, Benson Lee, Scott Owen, Glenn Sabin, Jim Meyers, Eric Schneider, Jeremy Morris, Glenn Nicholas, Jim O'Hare, Janet

Robbins, Tony Pulizzi, Lea Smith, Tom Corcoran, Jackie Ross, Antoinette DeJohn, and Patrick Schaber.

From Newt Barrett

My wonderful wife, Maxine, has been the perfect partner in work and in life. Through all my professional highs and lows, she has kept me centered and motivated to keep doing the work that I love. Her gifts of laughter and love bring joy to all around her. Thank you, Maxine, for everything.

My joyous gratitude also goes to my extended family, from my wonderful sisters, Dibbie and Susan, to an awesome clan of aunts, uncles, and cousins who collectively possess the planet's most wonderful sense of humor. They have made even the bad times seem like good times.

I've been very lucky in my life to have made friends and colleagues that I cherished even in jobs that I hated. I have been further blessed to experience a series of golden moments where great colleagues, great work, and great companies came together all at once. My thanks go to all those colleagues and friends who enabled me to achieve a level of success that I could never have imagined as a kid growing up in Cleveland, Ohio. Together, we accomplished a lot, laughing all the while. It just doesn't get any better than that.

Finally, to my coauthor, Joe Pulizzi, thank you for including me on this wonderful literary adventure. Let's do it again—just not too soon.

From Joe Pulizzi

To me, a book seems like the culmination of two things: the people I've met and known, and the books and blogs I've read. I could literally go on for pages about all the people who have positively affected me to this point in my life and my career. That said, this short list contains the people who, in their own way, have done something truly remarkable that I take with me each day. I wish I had room for more.

To my wife, Pam, my partner in all things. From you I learned how to be a better man, a better husband, and a better father, and what it really means to be successful. All my love.

To my son Joshua. From you I learned that a man is a success when he is loved by a child. Always remember that it is not the biggest or the strongest or the fastest who wins, but the one with the most heart.

To my son Adam. From you I learned that God comes in the form of a smile, a hug, or a laugh. Heed the words of Yoda, "Do or do not . . . there is no try."

To Tony and Terry, my parents. From you I learned faith, true love, and unselfishness. Thanks for always being there for me.

To the late F. Leo Groff, my grandfather. From you I learned that the smallest action can literally change the course of someone's future.

To James McDermott, my mentor. From you I learned that in the value of a process, execution is what counts, and that playing it safe can be the biggest risk of all.

To Newt Barrett, my coauthor. From you I learned dedication and the ability to execute, even with no available time. You are an inspiration.

Philippians 4:13.

Index

Absolut vodka print campaign, 15
Ace Mobile Mechanics, 138, 139
Aflac duck, 15
Akron Beacon Journal, 14
Amazon.com, 16, 120
Anderson, Gail, 222
Archived Webcasts, 40
Arnold, John, 206
Ask Ann weekly blog, 127–128
Author, self-published, 120–124
Autodesk, 47
Automation Today, 222–225

Baby boomers, 98
Barrett, Newt, 248
Baumann, Bill, 58
Best Buy, 16, 19, 165–172
   Best magazine, 19, 166
   Geek squad, 166
   lessons learned, 172
   Morgan Stanley presentation, 166
   online version of *Best* magazine, 171
   overview, 165
B.E.S.T. formula, 27–29
Best magazine, 19, 166
Best practice success stories:
   Best Buy, 165–172
   Bitemark, 133–140
   Constant Contact, 201–220

David Lawrence Center, 107–117
Fleishman-Hillard, 97–105
Ganz, 183–189
Greater Naples Chamber of Commerce, 151–163
MillerWelds.com, 79–88
Mindjet, 173–181
Northern Trust, 141–149
overview, 77–78
Rockwell Automation, 221–229
solopreneurs, 119–132
ThomasNet, 191–200
'Tween Waters Inn, 89–96
See also Case study; subentries
Bitemark, 133–140
   Ace Mobile Mechanics, 139
   Conversion Rate blog, 137
   Fort Knox Self Storage, 138–139
   home page, 136
   lessons learned, 140
   overview, 133
Blendtec, 4–5, 46, 68
Blog, 43–44
Blog impact, 59
Blogger, 130
Blogging, 66. *See also* Fleishman-Hillard
Bonita Bay, 34
BookSurge, 120

BOOM: Marketing to the Ultimate Power Consumer—The Baby Boomer Woman (Orsborn et al.), 100
Boomer Blog, 45
Boston Globe, 11
Business blogs, 43–44
Business Currents magazine, 155–158
Buzz Marketing for Technology, 46

CAN-SPAM law, 62
Case study, 235–243
    article marketing program for affiliates, 241
    benchmark study, 242
    buyers' informational needs, 237–238
    customer Facebook fan page, 241
    e-book, 240
    listening program, 242
    measuring the program, 242–243
    news releases, 241–242
    newsletter, 239
    organizational goals, 236–237
    product/content mix, 238–242
    sales-oriented statistics, 243
    Web site and blog, 241
    Web statistics, 242–243
    what you want customer to do, 238
    white paper series, 240
    See also Best practice success stories
Chamber of Commerce. *See* Greater Naples Chamber of Commerce
Christian Science Monitor, 13
ClickToClient.com, 43
CoffeesAndSmoothies.blogspot.com, 129
CoffeesAndSmoothies.com, 129
Colletto, Katy, 174
Comprehensive research, 52
Connell, Marie Kroesen, 186, 188
Constant Contact, 201–209
    e-newsletter, 204–206, 207, 208
    home page, 203–204

in-person content marketing, 206–208
lessons learned, 209
overview, 201
using its own products, 208
workshops, 206–208
Content marketing:
    alternative names, 6
    content types. *See* Content types
    examples, *See* Best practice success stories; Case study
    making content happen, 49–60. *See also* Making content happen
    marketing. *See* Marketing
    why important, 9–20
Content plan, 55
Content promotion, 62–63
Content schedule, 55
Content syndication, 69
Content types, 31–48
    in-person, 46–48
    online. *See* Online content types
    print, 31–35. *See also* Print publications
Content vs. promotion debate, 63
Content Web portals, 37–38
Conversions, 53
Corporate blog, 71
Custom magazines, 32–34
Custom publishing, 6

David Lawrence Center, 107–117
    home page, 109
    lessons learned, 116
    new Web site, 111–113
    newsletter, 114–115
    old site, 110–111
    overview, 107–108
    page views, 115
    Your Help page, 113
"A Day in the Life of a Technical Instructor" (Sciberras), 226

Dell, 68
Dentino, Catherine, 155
Diamond, Stephanie, 39
Dickson, Tom, 5
Digg.com, 18, 68, 69, 72, 73
Digital magazines, 41–42
Dunay, Paul, 46

E-books, 38–40
E-Mail Marketing for Dummies (Arnold),
    206
E-mail software provider. *See* Constant
    Contact
E-newsletters, 42–43
E-zines, 42–43
Editorial plan and schedule, 55
Edwards, Trevor, 3
Examples. *See* Best practice success
    stories; Case study
Executive roundtables, 48
Exploritech, 115

Facebook, 68, 72
Facebook fan page, 73
Feldkamp, Sue, 84
Fell, Jon, 213
Flash, 126
Fleishman-Hillard, 45, 97–105
    Boomer Blog, 98–99
    Chinese 101, 104
    Daily Digest, 100, 101
    daily updates, 101, 102
    lessons learned, 105
    NextGreatThing blog, 103–104
    overview, 97
Flex Products, 197, 198
Folio, 13
Fort Knox Self Storage, 37, 138–139

Ganz, 183–189
    advertising, 187–188

lessons learned, 188–189
    overview, 183
    Webkinz, 183–187
Geek squad, 166
GEICO cavemen, 15
General Motors, 3
GetContentGetCustomers.com, 31
Gilbertson, Brett, 134, 135, 137
Gillin, Paul, 15
Google, 10
Google AdWords, 68
Grant Thornton LLP, 41
Gray, Vincent, 213
Greater Naples Chamber of Commerce,
    151–163
    Business Currents magazine, 155–158
    e-newsletter, 161–162
    lessons learned, 162–163
    members' business needs, 154
    overview, 151
    small companies, 152
    Web site, 159–161
Groves, Eric, 202

Hints & Tips Email Marketing,
    204–206
HomeMadeSimple.com, 37, 38
HTML pages, 72
Hyder, Shama, 43

IBM, 37
Illinois Tool Works, 79
IMC, the Next Generation (Schultz), 61
In Good Company magazine, 34
In-person content marketing, 46–48
    executive roundtables, 48
    repurpose, 48
    road shows, 47
Industry bloggers, 72
Internet. *See* Online content types
Interruption marketing, 4

Interview, 71
"Is Social Media Killing the Campaign
    Microsite?" (Morrisey), 65
ISOOSI, 159, 160

John Deere, 6
Johnson & Johnson, 3
Journal, The, 224
Judge, Barry, 167, 168

Kawasaki, Guy, 17, 35
Keywords, 68
Kintz, Eric, 66
KitchAnn Style, 126
Kitchen designer, 124–129
KitchenStudioOfNaples.com, 125
Kodak, 68

Law firm. *See* Pinsent Masons
Leadership Link, 161–162
Lessons learned, 233–234
Levin, David, 10
Lincoln Electric, 82
Literature Library, 228–229
Los Angeles Times, 13

Magazines:
    digital, 42
    e-zines, 43
    print, 32–34
Making content happen, 49–60
    buyers' informational needs, 50–52
    measuring the program, 57–60
    organizational goals, 49–50
    product/content mix, 53–56
    project manager, 56–57
    what you want customer to do, 52–53
Marcus, Eileen, 98
Marketing, 61–73
    awkwardness, 64–65
    content promotion, 62–63

defined, 61
media promotion strategies,
    67–70
meet customers where they are,
    60–64
news releases, 70–71
putting ideas to use, 71–73
Maui Wowi blog, 130
McDermott, Jim, 56
Measuring engagement, 59
Media promotion strategies, 67–70
Meister, Trista, 115
Microsites, 37–38, 66
Microsoft, 16, 40, 41
Miller, Peter Read, 170
Miller Electric Mfg, 80
MillerWelds.com, 79–88
    article archive, 83–84
    blog, 85, 86
    competitor, 82
    content types, 79
    e-newsletter, 84, 85
    home page, 82
    in-depth vertical content, 83
    lessons learned, 88
    overview, 79
    product selection tools, 87
    ready to buy page, 85–87
Mind mapping, 174–176
Mindjet, 36, 43, 173–181
    e-newsletter, 177–179
    evangelists, 176
    lessons learned, 180–181
    mind mapping, 174–176
    overview, 173–174
    product launch, 179–180
    Web site, 176–177
    word of mouth, 176
MindManager, 175
MODEL. *See* Case study
Morgan Stanley presentation, 166